Truth
and
Religious
Belief

Truth
and
Religious Belief

*Conversations on
Philosophy of Religion*

Curtis L. Hancock and
Brendan Sweetman

M.E. Sharpe
Armonk, New York
London, England

Library of Congress Cataloging-in-Publication Data

Hancock, Curtis L., 1950–
Truth and religious belief : conversations on philosophy of religion /
Curtis L. Hancock and Brendan Sweetman.
p.   cm.
Includes bibliographical references and index.
ISBN 1–56324–852–2 (hardcover). — ISBN 1–56324–853–0 (pbk.)
1. Religion—Philosophy. I. Sweetman, Brendan. II. Title.
BL51.H3126 1997
210—dc21   97–23717
CIP

Printed in the United States of America

The paper used in this publication meets the minimum requirements of
American National Standard for Information Sciences—
Permanence of Paper for Printed Library Materials,
ANSI Z 39.48-1984.

EB (c)   10   9   8   7   6   5   4   3   2   1
EB (p)   10   9   8   7   6   5   4   3   2

To Jason and Lisa
Curtis L. Hancock

To My Mother and Father
Brendan Sweetman

Contents

Introduction

This book is intended as an introductory text for students taking courses in philosophy that deal, either in whole or in part, with topics in the philosophy of religion. Its aim is to introduce the reader, through a series of stimulating and probing dialogues, to some of the key questions frequently raised about religious belief: Is there a God? What is God like? Why does God allow evil? Are human beings immortal? Does one have to be religious in order to be moral? and so on. Our choice of the dialogue style, rather than the more traditional monologue style employed in most textbooks dealing with these issues, emerged naturally from our teaching of the subject matter of this book over several years. We have discovered that this mode of presentation is advantageous, not just because it allows us to present the material in a more appealing and engaging way for the student, but also because it allows one to capture more accurately the typical student's attitudes and questions concerning religious belief.

Thus, our format allows us to compare and contrast important themes throughout the dialogues (such as the relationship between religion and science, for example); to interject with observations, insights, questions, and objections; to introduce related, but tangential, points, instead of relegating them to another time; and to cross-reference with other topics, arguments, and insights. More generally, the use of dialogue allows us to produce a comprehensive synthesis of the main themes and prevents the material from becoming unwieldy or disjointed. This gives the dialogue form an advantage over the monologue style, which is undoubtedly one reason philosophical dialogues have become more popular in recent years.

Our method also has the distinct advantage of communicating in an interesting and realistic way a sense of the value and importance of philosophy itself. Throughout the dialogues one cannot fail to see the contribution that philosophical reflection—with its emphasis on ordinary experiences, rationality, consistency, and knowledge of the history of ideas—can bring to one's reflection on one's most cherished beliefs, whether religious or not. The dialogues illustrate that philosophy is not simply a scholarly endeavor, nor is it an abstract game; rather, it is a discipline that, in terms of its content and methodology, stimulates and cultivates intellectual thinking about important questions and problems in a systematic, thorough, rigorous, and historically informed way. In this way, we hope to illustrate that philosophical reflection is an activity of which *everyone* is capable, and that can make a contribution to everyone's understanding of the central questions of human experience.

The book contains eight chapters, each a self-contained dialogue on a key topic in the philosophy of religion. The first conversation discusses the question of the existence of God, with the cosmological and design arguments the main focus of discussion. The dialogue ends with a consideration of the relationships among religion, atheism, and science, and between religion and evolution. The second dialogue takes up the question of the nature of God. The traditional attributes of God, eternity, omnipotence, omniscience, and so on, are examined. Chapter 3 deals with the troubling question, How can an all-good and all-powerful God allow all the terrible evils in the world? Two different versions of this problem of evil are explored, and the conversation ends with a comparison of Augustinian theodicy and Ireanean theodicy. Chapter 4 examines the question of immortality. The topic is approached through an examination of issues pertaining to the philosophy of mind, especially the question of whether the mind is nonphysical and thus might exist after death.

Chapter 5, on religion and morality, examines three issues: the divine-command theory of ethics; the relationship between secular ethics and relativism; and the question of whether it is possible for religious believers and atheists to discuss and debate moral issues in a meaningful and productive way, given their radically different starting points. Chapter 6 is a discussion of influential twentieth century arguments, based on religious experience, for the existence of God. In this chapter, the participants in the dialogue take up the work of Alvin Plantinga, John Hick, and D.Z. Phillips. The timely issue of religious pluralism is the subject of Chapter 7, and the main focus is on the question of whether it is possible to judge which of the world religions is true, and if not, how we are to deal with the question of truth in religions. Finally, the book concludes with a chapter on the meaning of life; it explores further several of the issues mentioned in some of the earlier dialogues and probes matters relating to religion, secularism, and the meaning of life. All of the chapters are written at an introductory level, with the main positions, terms, and distinctions carefully explained; no background in philosophy is assumed. Each chapter is followed by a list of the key terms and distinctions used in the chapter, by a set of study questions, and by a short bibliography.

The book does not pretend to be an exhaustive study of issues in the philosophy of religion, nor does each dialogue claim to be an exhaustive treatment of its subject matter. However, we do believe that each dialogue presents a fairly thorough and balanced discussion and will provide a detailed, careful, and probing introduction to its subject matter for the reader. We believe also that the book is unique in its focus on the relationship between religion and science, especially as this relates to the issues of the dialogues, and also in its chapter on immortality, which takes naturalism at its word and subjects it to analysis and criticism. The book may be used in philosophy of religion courses, perhaps as a complement to an anthology of primary sources. At the end of each chapter there are brief bibliographies, which refer to the main sources cited in the chapter, including many of the standard primary sources in the philosophy of religion. The book would also fit very nicely as a text for general introductory courses in philosophy, since these courses normally deal with several of the topics raised in the dialogues.

We wish to record our thanks to several people who assisted us at various stages throughout the project. We would like to extend our gratitude to Rockhurst College for a Presidential Grant to support our work on portions of the book. Edward Furton and R. Douglas Geivett read various portions of the manuscript and offered valuable suggestions. We wish to thank all at M.E. Sharpe for their professionalism and support: Esther Clark, Eileen Maass, and especially Peter Coveney.

Finally, our biggest debt of gratitude goes to our families, especially our wives, Sandra Hancock and Margaret Sweetman, without whose support and encouragement this work would not have been possible. Brendan Sweetman, Jr., aged 17 months, also frequently demonstrated that not all problems are philosophical ones and that computer equipment can serve many purposes in addition to manuscript preparation!

Truth
and
Religious
Belief

The Setting and the Cast

The Setting

These conversations take place at a seminar at the Rocky Mountain Institute in Estes Park, Colorado, in the heart of the Rocky Mountains. The seminar is designed to allow people to get away from their regular activities for a couple of weeks for a period of reading and reflection. This year's topic is "Religion, Atheism and the Meaning of Life." Seminar activities involve a number of voluntary events including scholarly lectures, group discussions, movies, spiritual meetings, and religious services. There are also various outdoor activities spread over the two weeks, including touring local places of interest, sports, hiking, swimming, and backpacking.

The participants in our conversations are also using the seminar as an opportunity for a class reunion; they attended the same university and know each other well. They have all taken at least three philosophy courses in college. Several of the participants—especially Brian, Frank, and Malcolm—know one another very well and have read many of the same books. Malcolm is now a philosophy professor at their alma mater, and he takes the lead in the conversations. Each conversation takes place on a different day at the Institute.

Cast of Characters

BRIAN: Brian is a Catholic priest, who works in the parish where he lives. He studied a lot of philosophy in seminary, earning a master's degree, and has published several articles on religious topics in religious magazines and newspapers in his archdiocese. He is very interested in philosophy of religion issues and is also especially interested in articulating his faith for the modern world.

FRANK: Frank is an engineer. He is an evangelical and has a minor in theology. He regularly reads works of apologetics in his religion. Frank is married and has two children.

3

JEAN: Jean is a housewife and mother, who has little interest in philosophy. She is a strong Baptist. She has a B.A. degree in English and French from the group's alma mater.

JOHN: John is a tough-minded naturalist, who is quite skeptical of religion in general. He has a degree in chemistry and works for a chemical company. He also attended medical school for a few semesters. John is an enthusiastic supporter of atheism, is married, and has one daughter.

MALCOLM: Malcolm is a Catholic and a philosophy professor. He has a Ph.D. in philosophy from a Midwestern university, where he wrote a dissertation, "The Proof of God's Existence." Malcolm's main research interest in philosophy is the philosophy of religion, and he has published several books and articles on this topic. He is a professor at the alma mater of the participants, is married, and has three children.

MARY: Mary is an Episcopalian minister. She has a master's in theology and is a minister at the church in the town where she lives. She is married and has no children.

PATRICIA: Patricia is a high-school teacher and an atheist. Her discipline is history, and she has read widely in philosophy. She is single.

RENEE: Renee is a computer programmer and is a strong member of her Jewish religious community. She is a fideist in religion. She is married and has two children.

SOPHIA: Sophia is a Unitarian minister and is strongly committed to religion. She is a counselor at a large state university and is very interested in philosophy of religion. She is single.

Chapter One

The Existence of God

In this first conversation, Malcolm examines two arguments for the existence of God, the cosmological argument and the design argument, and defends the view that these arguments give us good reasons to believe in God. John and Patricia raise some objections along the way. Toward the end of the conversation some related issues are discussed including the relationship among religion, science, and evolution, and between religion and naturalism. After some preliminary pleasantries, John provocatively opens the discussion.

JOHN: Isn't it true that you Catholics, Malcolm, think you can actually prove the existence of God? Isn't it true that unlike many other religions, which are simply content to believe in God on faith, that the Catholic religion actually offers a proof for the existence of God? Surely you don't think, Malcolm, that there really is such a proof? I mean, isn't that kind of nonsense really outdated?

JEAN: I am very interested in hearing a proof for the existence of God, if there really is one. I am a quite serious religious person, yet I sometimes wonder if my religion makes sense. You know, if my religious beliefs are really true, or if I am just being silly in believing them. But I haven't the time or the energy to read anything on these questions, or to think about them very deeply. Three kids keep you very busy! So, Malcolm, please sketch out for us this proof that John is talking about. And make it as simple as possible. I've done no philosophy since college.

MALCOLM: It is true that the Catholic Church has always insisted that reason can make a contribution to religious belief. Of course, some religious beliefs, such as the Trinity, the Incarnation, and the Virgin Birth, are pure mysteries, and of their nature transcend understanding. But other beliefs, such as the existence of God, happen to be accessible to reason and justifiable by reason, in my view. Such support is called natural theology, the attempt to show that we can examine the world by means of reason and find evidence to support our judgment that God exists.

BRIAN: Natural theology, of course, differs from "revealed theology," in that the latter refers to those mysteries of the faith that reason cannot penetrate. God has communicated or revealed them to us nonetheless. And there is good historical evidence for revelation, though we cannot get into that now.

MALCOLM: It has been suggested that the church does officially claim that the existence of God can be proved, though there is some dispute over how certain church documents are to be interpreted. Regardless, the church has traditionally placed great emphasis on the famous "Five Ways" of St. Thomas Aquinas, a thirteenth century Dominican friar, who is one of the great Doctors of the Catholic Church.

RENEE: Yes, but isn't there a dispute over whether Aquinas really meant the Five Ways to be actual proofs? My philosophy professor said they were probably just meant to be "pointers" or indications that God exists, rather than proofs. I agree with that view myself because I do not think that the proofs work, and I think religion is mostly a matter of faith.

BRIAN: But, Renee, surely religion can't be just a matter of faith? There must be some way of supporting at least some of your basic beliefs with reasons. Otherwise why believe in your religion at all? If religion were purely a matter of faith, then one could believe anything one wished and avoid rational scrutiny.

JOHN: Yes, there are too many people believing in all sorts of irrational nonsense today, and a good many of these people are religious believers!

FRANK: Well, one can appeal to the Bible as one's authority. So one's faith is not without foundation. And before you jump in,

John, there can be good reasons for taking the Bible as an authority. There is a vast literature on this question. I agree that you cannot simply make up what you believe. But I fear that some religions today—even some versions of Catholicism, Brian—are making up their own versions of religion. ← true

PATRICIA: This discussion is very interesting. I believe our minds should always be guided on these kinds of questions by the light of reason. I think that whenever one advocates a view on serious questions having to do with the nature of reality, or the existence of God, or the nature of moral and political value— things of that sort—then one should be prepared to at least *attempt* to justify one's view; this involves showing why you believe it in the first place. You should be prepared to explain the *reasons for holding your view*. That way at least you can have a rational debate. ⌐ & need to back up your beliefs

RENEE: Yes, that sounds very reasonable. But I'm not sure the existence of God is the kind of issue you can have a rational debate about. You simply cannot advance a rational argument that will convince an atheist, like John here, that he is wrong. Proving the existence of God is not like proving that that mountain over there exists. They are simply not the same kind of things. So I think that in matters of religion, it is all right to believe in God purely on faith. I am a fideist myself: I believe that it is perfectly legitimate to commit yourself through faith to belief in God, without entertaining whether reason can support that belief or not. I do not think this means that my belief is irrational. It simply means that rationality is not an appropriate standard by which to judge religious belief.

Renee - it's okay to believe w/ faith alone

JOHN: There are a lot of very interesting points being made here. And although I have very little time for the supernatural view, I am still interested in spite of myself. I am going to order another round of sodas for everyone. And Malcolm, you're the philosophy professor. Perhaps you can sort out some of what we have just been talking about. For example, surely reason is relevant to the question of God's existence?

Patricia & john - need reason

Malcolm = some reason

fideist?

MALCOLM: A lot of issues have been raised—too many for one short conversation. Perhaps we will have a chance to pursue some of them in the days ahead. For example, the *fideist* view expressed by Renee deserves a whole conversation in itself. Let it suffice to say now that I don't see how there could be a genuine faith at all if reason weren't involved on some level. For now, let's just focus on the question of whether one can give good reasons for believing in God.

JEAN: Yes, that is the question I am particularly interested in at the moment.

RENEE: I still don't see what point such a discussion has for belief in God.

MALCOLM: Perhaps this approach will help, Renee. Let me share with you an illustration I use in class to make the point that offering reasons for the existence of God is important. Let me tell you about the Abominable Snowman Worship Society!

RENEE: Kind of a weird example, isn't it?

MALCOLM: That's the whole point. Suppose you discovered a group that worshipped the Abominable Snowman, and let's further suppose that you happened upon them during their annual recruitment drive! Would you join the group? Well, before doing so, you would want to know why the members of the group believed in and worshipped the Abominable Snowman. Now if nobody in the group was interested in this question, and the members of the group simply said they believed on faith and urged you to commit yourself to their faith too, promising that your life would be changed, spiritually renewed, happier, and so on, it is very likely that you would not do it. Suppose you had to pay a $5,000 initiation fee, and you had to write to your bank manager for the money. Would you write the letter? If you did, would it be wise for you to sit back and wait for the check to arrive?

BRIAN: No, obviously not! You would be a long time waiting. Your example nicely shows that, if one can, one should try to give reasons for believing in something, especially something as important as the existence of God. But should *everyone* be able to explain in detail why they believe in God? Most of my parishioners are very sincere religious people, but I doubt if they could do a good job of rationally defending their belief in God.

MARY: And how can they explain it anyway, since it is not possible to have a proof in this domain?

MALCOLM: Brian and Mary have raised interesting questions. I only mean my example to show that the advocates of belief in the existence of God must have some argument to support their belief. But I think it would be too much to expect *every* member of a religious tradition to be familiar with these arguments, or to be capable of explaining them. And Mary raises another point. I do not think myself (though some would disagree with me on this) that it is possible to *prove* the existence of God. I won't be so bold as to offer a proof. I think I can show, however, that God's existence is more plausible than the alternatives, atheism or agnosticism. And I think that if you believe in the existence of God, this belief must be at least plausible, even if it is normally left to the philosophers and theologians of the group to illustrate this.

PATRICIA: I am not fully clear, Malcolm, on the difference between proving the existence of God and showing that the existence of God is rational or plausible. You seem to be making an important distinction here. Could you explain it?

MALCOLM: Yes, it is an important distinction. A *rational* (or plausible) belief is a belief that is supported by good reasons and/or evidence, but one for which we do not have a proof that establishes the belief with one hundred percent certainty. For example, let's take my belief that your car, John, in which we drove here this afternoon, is parked out in the parking lot at the back of this building. This is a rational belief because I have good reasons to believe it: we parked it ourselves, the parking lot is fairly secure, and so on. However, I do not know for certain that your car is parked out there. It might have been stolen since we came into the lounge, or been towed away. So I do not have a *proof* for this belief.

JOHN: I will be back in a minute—I just want to check the parking lot!

MALCOLM: Examples of other beliefs that are rational to believe but that we cannot prove with one hundred percent certainty would include many of our beliefs about the past and about the future, and also many theoretical beliefs, including many in scientific theories. So this is a perfectly respectable set of beliefs. My view is that when we are dealing with theories about the nature of reality, about the nature of human life, and about the nature of moral and political value, the most we can hope for is *rationality* and not proof.

BRIAN: Yes, that is a good way to put it, because in the case of the car in the parking lot, it would be possible to move from rationality to proof by going out to the parking lot and checking. And, of course, we do have excellent proofs in many other areas, for example, in mathematics. So we have *certainty* in that area.

RENEE: I see the point. We cannot achieve such proofs in the case of the existence of God or in some of those other cases you mentioned such as our beliefs about the past or the future, or even about many of our theoretical beliefs.

JEAN: But isn't there some element of faith still involved even in these rational beliefs?

JOHN: There is, but you could call it a *rational faith*; the point is that we have enough reasons and evidence for the belief to make it rational to believe it or commit to it even though the evidence falls short of certainty. Malcolm, I presume you are now going to suggest that we have enough reasons and evidence to argue that belief in the existence of God is a *rational belief.*

JEAN: Let's move on, Malcolm, to the particular belief in question this afternoon—belief in the existence of God.

MALCOLM: Well, there are different ways to approach the attempt to show that belief in God is a *rational* belief. I use the approach called *natural theology,* which we mentioned earlier. It has a long history. It was a strategy made famous by St. Thomas Aquinas (c. 1225–1274). Even those philosophers, such as David Hume (1711–1776), who didn't think natural theology could achieve much, still thought it was the right *approach* to the question of God's existence. Natural theology is the attempt to show that it is reasonable to conclude that God exists based on an examination of the evidence in the natural world and in our experience. This evidence shows, I believe, that it is rational to believe in God, or to be a theist. I use the word "theist" in a general sense at this point simply to describe someone who believes in God.

FRANK: Malcolm, I agree with your approach, but it doesn't always appeal to people who are members of my religion. They are suspicious of it because it gives too much credence to reason in religion and undermines faith.

RENEE: And I, as a fideist, reject the approach of natural theology, because fideism holds that this is not, after all, the right *approach* to the God question.

BRIAN: Let me support Malcolm here. The Catholic Church, mainly due to St. Thomas's influence, is a strong supporter of natural theology.

JOHN: It sounds like a very reasonable *approach* to me. It's the *result* that will turn out to be unreasonable! You look around the world to see if there are any reasons or evidence to suggest that there might be a higher power behind it all. I am anxious to hear Malcolm's actual argument here, since I do not think there is any evidence. Now don't try to blind us with pie-in-the-sky language. Keep it simple and straightforward!

MALCOLM: I will try to keep it as simple as possible. My line of argument is often called the cosmological argument because it argues from the existence of the world (or *cosmos*) back to the

3 step approach for natural theology

existence of God. The argument has a number of different formulations. But basically I follow a three-step approach. My approach, of course, is only one of the various ways in which the argument can be formulated.

BRIAN: Yes, St. Thomas also has a version of the argument, which I hope we can bring up later, Malcolm.

MALCOLM: Yes, in fact, I think that my version of the argument, which is inspired by William Craig, and St. Thomas's version are best presented together, since they reinforce each other, and represent a strong case for the rationality of belief in God. The two versions differ in their respective views of time and causality, as we will see presently. Craig, a contemporary evangelical scholar, has revived an old argument offered by St. Bonaventure (1221–1274), and some Arabian philosophers. The argument is called the *kalam* cosmological argument, *kalam* being Arabic for "speech." But before we get into the heart of the argument, let me begin with my three-step strategy. Step one asks the question: did the universe have a beginning? And the answer I give is "yes." Step two asks: was the beginning of the universe caused? Again, the answer is "yes." And thirdly, I ask: was this cause likely to be something like the traditional God of religion? And again I answer in the affirmative.

1. begin. of universe?

2. was it caused?

3. to do w/ god?

JOHN: Right away, the first step seems problematic. Don't all of these latest discoveries in science—especially concerning the question of the beginning of the universe—show us that the universe might have had no beginning at all? Last summer I read Stephen Hawking's book *A Brief History of Time.* Doesn't he suggest that there might be alternative ways of understanding time, which could alter our whole approach to the question of origins? And there is a good talk on this topic tomorrow night. Check the program. You should go to it!

BRIAN: I think you have to be careful with much of that scientific speculation. Most of it is just that—speculation. And much of it is driven by an antireligious agenda; so I, for one, do not take much of that material very seriously unless there is very good evidence for it. Remember that we are trying to find out whether belief in God is a *rational* belief, and it seems to me that Malcolm's first claim that the universe had a beginning some finite number of years ago is very reasonable.

MALCOLM: Well, let me continue with my line of argument. I begin by focusing on the issue of what caused the events in the universe. For example, what caused the Grand Canyon?

PATRICIA: Well, I suppose we could say the Colorado River caused it?

BRIAN: And what caused that? Is that where you are leading Malcolm?

chain of causes

MALCOLM: Yes. Now we get a chain of causes going. Normally when we ask what caused a thing, we want the immediate or *local* cause. For example, if I want to know what caused your car, Frank, to skid last night, the answer is the rain on the roads. But the cosmological argument is based on a search for the *ultimate* cause of the universe. Now that we have a chain of causes going backwards into the past, the next big question is: how far does this chain of causes stretch back? This version of the argument, unlike St. Thomas's version, which we will discuss later, stresses that the series of causes stretches back in time.

MARY: Perhaps the series stretches back to the Big Bang, which we are hearing so much about these days in the media.

JEAN: What precisely is the Big Bang view?

PATRICIA: It is the view that the universe began when a single point of infinitely dense and infinitely hot matter exploded spontaneously. This point is often called a singularity. It is believed that it exploded with an incredible burst of energy somewhere between 10 and 20 billion years ago. All of our universe, the galaxies, stars, and planets, were formed out of the debris of this explosion. Malcolm, are you saying that the series of causes must go back to the Big Bang?

*[handwritten: 1. universe had beginning
or
2. stretches back infinitely into
the past]*

MALCOLM: I believe there are only two plausible possibilities: either the universe had a beginning, or it stretches back infinitely into the past and had no beginning. Craig presents what I think is a pretty persuasive argument for the conclusion that the universe must have had a beginning. My students have always found Craig's arguments pretty difficult to follow, and even some philosophers have missed the point, so I will try to give a clear, but brief, account of his main points. Basically Craig holds that the notion of an actual infinite series of physical events is a logical impossibility.

JEAN: That's a little heavy for me, Malcolm; could you explain what it means? Remember this is the first time we've heard this argument.

MALCOLM: Let me handle it this way. Craig distinguishes between a *potential* infinity and an *actual* infinity. A potential infinity is an infinity that exists in the realm of thought only, as in mathematics for example; it is an infinity that is an ever-growing set, but which is always actually finite. An *actual* infinity is an infinity that is alleged to exist in the real world. Craig suggests that when you take a good practical look at the latter notion it becomes obvious that it is absurd.

RENEE: This is tough going! So actual infinities don't exist? Mathematical infinities exist only in the mind, because we never actually write out those infinities. We always represent them with symbols, so they do not actually exist. Is that it?

MALCOLM: That's it exactly, Renee, and very well put!

PATRICIA: Are you sure you don't wish to try to support your faith with a little more reason, Renee? But, Malcolm, I have a difficulty. Isn't God supposed to be an infinite Being, and since God exists, he would be an actual infinite, wouldn't he?

MALCOLM: Yes, but you must remember that Craig is only arguing that an actual infinite series of physical events cannot exist; God is not such a series, so the argument does not apply to God.

Craig tries to illustrate his claim by means of four arguments—two philosophical and two scientific. The scientific arguments are well known and need not delay us here. Basically he says that current evidence from the Big Bang Theory and from the Second Law of Thermodynamics clearly support the conclusion that the universe had a beginning.

BRIAN: Yes, I like his approach. So he is actually backing up his argument with scientific evidence, as well as philosophical arguments?

MALCOLM: Yeah! However, he believes that his two philosophical arguments make the case for his conclusion very strong. His first argument is that the notion of an actual infinite simply does not make sense. He illustrates this by means of the "Library" example. He asks us to imagine a library with an infinite number of books and to imagine that the books are stacked in alternate colors, black, red, black, red, and so on. Now, how many books in total are in the library? *[handwritten: = this has no meaning, infinity is nonsense]*

MARY: Well, he has stipulated in the example that the library has an infinite number of books.

MALCOLM: Yes. Now, how many black books, and how many red books?

FRANK: There would have to be an infinite number of black books and an infinite number of red books, since the number of books in the library goes on forever. Which means that the number of black books is equal to the number of black and red books combined. Which is absurd!

MALCOLM: Yes, Craig's point is that when you actually start trying to imagine what would have to be the case for an actual series of physical events to really exist out there in the real world, we begin to see that the notion generates several serious puzzles and simply does not make sense. Craig pushes the example a bit further to ask how many books would be left in the library if we checked out a few, sent some for cataloguing and binding, and so on, and it becomes clear that the notion is very problematic, if not absurd. Remember that Craig is not trying to say that somehow we must make sense of the library example, he is saying that the library example clearly leads to logical absurdities, and this is because the notion of an actual infinite series of physical events does not make any sense. He also refers to an example where the Earth and Jupiter are orbiting the sun from eternity, but the Earth is orbiting at three times the speed of Jupiter. If they have been orbiting from eternity, they will have completed the *same* number of orbits, but again this seems absurd.

PATRICIA: Those are very clever examples! But they are hard to follow and a library is not like the universe. I suspect a trick here! I still don't see why the number of years before this present year could not be infinite.

FRANK: I must confess, Patricia, that I think the suggestion that the number of years before this year might go back *forever* into the past, that there was no beginning, is simply ridiculous!

MALCOLM: Please, there is no trick involved. Craig's second argument might be more appealing to you, Patricia, because it deals directly with the claim that the number of years before this year might have been infinite. This particular argument relies on the impossibility of counting to, or of crossing, an infinity. Craig's argument is as follows: If there were an infinite number of days before today, then today would never arrive. (Because it is impossible to cross an infinity). But today has arrived. After all, here we all are enjoying today! Therefore, since today has arrived . . .

JEAN: The number of days before today must have been finite.

BRIAN: Jean, have you ever thought of going into philosophy!

RENEE: That example reminds me of an old story my uncle used to tell about a schoolboy. This fellow was always late coming home from school, and he always had an excuse! One day, when he got

(handwritten margin note, left side, vertical): "If there were an infinite number of days before today, then today would never arrive."

home from school, his excuse was unique. He told his mother that he had walked an infinite number of steps. My uncle also asked us to work out what was wrong with that remark. And the answer is the same as the point here. Clearly if there really had been an infinite amount of steps between the school and his home, he would never get home.

PATRICIA: But isn't it the case that from any particular point you take in history, and ask how long the distance is—how many days it took—to get to today, the answer will always be a *finite* number. And since all we ever want to know is the distance between individual points in history, I'm not sure his example works.

MARY: Well, Professor?

MALCOLM: What Patricia says is true—the distance between any two points you care to take in history will be finite. But we must also ask—as philosophers seeking the ultimate cause of things—how we (ultimately) got to any particular point in history, and Craig is saying that if the answer is supposed to be that we crossed an infinite amount of time, this is absurd, and so, since *that point* in history occurred, the answer must be that we crossed a *finite* amount of time. More simply put, his example shows that it is impossible to traverse an infinity.

JOHN: By the way, I myself am perfectly happy with the Big Bang view. I happen to agree with Frank on this one. I am perfectly happy to accept the scientific evidence. I believe there was a first event, the Big Bang or whatever it was. But I am trying to probe Craig's argument as far as I can. I remember reading John Mackie in our "Philosophy of Religion" course in college, and if I remember rightly, he thinks the universe might stretch back infinitely into the past, doesn't he?

MALCOLM: Mackie thinks that it is *logically possible* that the universe might have had no beginning. In philosophy, the notion of logical possibility is very narrow; for something to be logically possible simply means that there is no contradiction involved in its assertion. And Mackie thinks it is not contradictory to say that the universe might have had no beginning. Craig, however, takes the opposite view. He is arguing that it is contradictory to say that the universe had no beginning. However, it is important to note that even if you disagree with Craig and think he has not shown that the notion of an actual infinite is absurd, it is still much more *reasonable* to believe that the universe had a beginning than to believe that it might be eternal.

BRIAN: People like Mackie annoy me! Mackie never gives any evidence or argument to show that it would be *plausible* to believe that the universe stretches back infinitely into the past, he just *asserts* that it is a logical possibility. So I think the belief that the universe has a beginning, based on both scientific evidence and philosophical argument, even if you do not think Craig quite *proved* his point, is the most rational option.

MARY: Philosophers like Mackie would entertain the notion that the universe might not have had a beginning for a good reason though. They are trying to block the move from your step one, Malcolm, to your step two.

MALCOLM: Mary, I think you are right, and I think they wish to do this because when you move to step two, the move to step three is inevitable, and the existence of God becomes increasingly more likely.

JOHN: Well, we'll see. It sounds like a leap to me. But let's move to step two, since I certainly agree that it is *reasonable* to think that the universe had a beginning.

BRIAN: Yes, I am fascinated by this issue. The question as I recall it is: Was the beginning of the universe caused? And you said that the answer from your point of view is in the affirmative. Now I know that some contemporary naturalists will want to challenge this step.

MARY: What is a naturalist? Somebody who likes the great outdoors? Or is it one of those people who go around with no clothes on!

MALCOLM: No, Brian does not mean that kind of naturalist! A naturalist in this debate is a person who believes that the physical universe is all there is; that nothing nonphysical exists. This position goes further than atheism, which simply says that there is no God. Naturalism in some people's minds is closely allied with science because a naturalist will usually appeal to scientific evidence to support his view. Though, of course not all scientists are naturalists.

FRANK: I would not be at all surprised to find out that most scientists are religious believers, like John Polkinghorne, for example. But some of the well-known scientists in various fields are definitely naturalists, such as Stephen J. Gould, Francis Crick, and Carl Sagan.

MALCOLM: The main point in the second step is a fairly simple one. It revolves around this question, to put the matter a little more specifically: "Was the first event in the universe, whatever that was, caused?" And the answer to this question in my view simply has to be in the affirmative because of a well-established and much-validated procedure in science, that every physical event has a cause. And so the first event must have a cause. This is a very reasonable answer, the most reasonable answer, and some would say the only possible answer to our question.

JOHN: Is there any alternative, apart from saying that the universe did not have a first event, and is infinite, and so does not need a cause?

BRIAN: I agree with Malcolm; I do not see any possible alternative, and that is why some philosophers are prepared to flirt with the notion that an actual infinite series of physical events might be intelligible—so that they can avoid this step.

MALCOLM: Well, some philosophers might claim that the universe "popped" into existence *uncaused* out of nothing. But I believe this view to be ridiculous, and hardly worth taking seriously. I think it is totally unscientific; it goes against all of our current scientific evidence. Suppose that in all of history we had four examples of events that, taking into account all of our best data, we believed popped into existence uncaused out of nothing, and that all of the other events were caused. Then the probability of the first event being *uncaused* would be very low indeed. But as it actually happens we have no evidence at all of even one event that was uncaused, so the probability of the first event being uncaused is exactly zero without respect to our data. It is incumbent upon any serious thinker to acknowledge that the first event has a cause and then to try to reason out what that cause is.

JEAN: But isn't it possible that they will find out what caused the Big Bang?

BRIAN: Yes, that's entirely possible. But then we will need to find out the cause of that event, let's call it the little bang, which would now be the first event. Malcolm's point is that whatever the first event is, whatever it turns out to be, it must have had a cause. And indeed it is not even necessary that we discover what the first event actually is for his point to be valid.

PATRICIA: What about a point raised by Bertrand Russell, John Mackie, and others, that the universe might be just a "brute fact," that is, something that just "happened," and for which there is no explanation?

MALCOLM: That seems to me to be an *ad hoc* move, developed simply to avoid the conclusion that the universe most likely has a cause, which is outside the universe. I am simply appealing in step two to what is sometimes called the principle of sufficient reason, which states that anything that exists in the physical world must have a *reason* for its existence.

FRANK: Yes, as you pointed out earlier, Malcolm, this move would mean rejecting all of our current scientific evidence, for all of our current evidence points to the conclusion that there is no such thing as a "brute fact." It really does look like an arbitrary move that is motivated by atheism, and which is advanced in order to save atheism as a theory. What about step three?

BRIAN: Well, before we get to that, I would like to discuss St. Thomas's version of the cosmological argument because it adds some points that are new. For a start, unlike Craig, Aquinas is not concerned with a series of events that extends back into the past, or with a first cause *in time*. He is concerned with the fact of the *dependency* of all things in the universe, and he reasons from this dependency to a necessary being outside time. Father Frederick Copleston, a twentieth century philosopher, in his commentary on St. Thomas's work, shows that even if the universe *is* infinite, it still must have had a cause. Have I got that right, Malcolm?

MALCOLM: Yes, Brian, I am glad you brought up that point. Aquinas puts the issue in terms of necessary and contingent beings. He holds that every thing in the universe is a contingent thing, that is, nothing is the cause of itself. Now the universe is made up of a series of events—but it is a *contingent* series, since none of these events is its own reason for being or can account for its own existence. All right so far?

RENEE: Yes, that is plain enough. But where does the necessary being come in, and, by the way, what exactly is the definition of a necessary being?

MALCOLM: We'll come to the idea of necessary being momentarily. Father Copleston next makes a very interesting observation. He argues that if one is dealing with a contingent series of events, then one must look *outside* the series for its cause, *no matter how many members are in the series*. So the temporal nature of the series is not really the issue, for St. Thomas.

JEAN: I see; so he is saying that even if the universe had no beginning—that is, even if the series of events in the universe is an infinite series—that it *still* needs a cause?

FRANK: I think Copleston has an excellent point. In other words, if we wish to find the cause of the series of events in the universe—whether it be a finite series or an infinite series—we must look *outside* the series for the cause. It cannot contain its cause within itself; the series cannot provide its ultimate explanation from within itself.

• even if the universe is infinite
it still needs a cause

MALCOLM: Excellently put, Jean and Frank. I hope my students next semester can see the main points that fast and express them so well! Copleston uses the example of a series of chocolates as an analogy. He points out that even if the number of chocolates we are considering is infinite, we still would not think that the ultimate cause of the chocolates could be found within the series of chocolates itself. It is the same with the series of events in the universe. Another example I often use is that of adding plumbing to your house. You lay all the pipes, and connections, and get everything in place, but even if you were to extend the pipes to infinity, that alone would not get *water* into the system. This will have to be supplied from outside the system of plumbing. It is the same with the dependency of all that exists in the universe. We must appeal to something *outside* the universe to account for the dependency of all things *in* the universe.

MARY: So either way—whether the universe is finite or infinite—it still needs a cause that is outside the universe? Where does the necessary being come in?

MALCOLM: That's right, Mary. Of course, Copleston believes that God is the cause of the series of events in the universe. God is a necessary being, that is, a being that is uncaused, is eternal, which did not come into existence, because this being always existed. His point is that—if we seek an ultimate explanation—we must eventually stop at a necessary being. To find the cause of a contingent series we must go outside the series, and we infer the existence of a *necessary* being, for saying that another contingent being is the cause would simply leave us with the same question again. St. Thomas also understands God, the necessary being, to be outside time altogether.

JOHN: So far I will admit that contrary to my expectations you have remained fairly logical! As an atheist, I really do not dispute your first two steps—that the universe had a beginning and that it had a cause. But it is the third step that I would have serious difficulty with. The claim that *God*, or the necessary being, is the cause of the universe is hard for me to swallow!

RENEE: The third step is seen as problematic by many in theology today, and that is why there is not as much emphasis on proving the existence of God as there once was. One of the reasons fideists are suspicious of this step is that they do not think we can arrive at a proper conception of God from this approach, that is, a God who is worthy of worship.

JEAN: Malcolm, so far your ideas have lived up to all my expectations! Please go ahead and elaborate step three.

MALCOLM: Well, again, step three is not all that complicated. I simply draw out a few more of the logical implications, following on from step two. It is important to keep in mind here one very central point. In step three, we are not asking whether the universe had a cause or not—we have already asked that question in step two, and answered it in the affirmative. Our question now in step three is: "what is the cause of the universe like?" or: "what is the nature of the cause of the universe?" Can we establish any of the properties or characteristics of this cause by simply reasoning about it?

FRANK: I have read a number of versions of the proofs, Malcolm, and have not heard that particular point before. Is it essential to the argument?

MALCOLM: Yes, it is. It is an obvious point, but I emphasize it because it is quite common to get some way into the third stage and *then* to hear the objection that we cannot be sure if the universe has a cause. But this issue has been settled in step two; if you move on to step three you have already accepted the conclusion that the universe has a cause. If you do not accept this conclusion, you need to bring up an objection to *step two* that is reasonable.

PATRICIA: I am anxious to see how you reason that God is the cause of the first event, and, therefore, of the universe.

MALCOLM: Well, I will just make one or two points now because it is getting late, and I still want to mention the argument from design. We can have a more detailed discussion tomorrow about the nature of God. I want to argue that—using all of the resources of reason and evidence available—we can very plausibly conclude that the cause of the universe is the Supreme Being. Some of the attributes of the Supreme Being are that he is nonmaterial, powerful, personal, intelligent, eternal, and morally good. And to quote Aquinas: "and this all people call God." I will just comment very briefly on two of these attributes now. Take the fact that God is a nonmaterial being, for example. This is a very reasonable conclusion, given steps one and two. For if you say that God is physical, you have not solved the problem at all.

BRIAN: Yes, the cause of the physical must be *outside* of the physical order. I mean, that's pretty obvious, isn't it?!

MARY: Otherwise, if we say that God is a physical being, we would simply have to ask what caused God—since we agree that every *physical* event has a cause?

FRANK: Wouldn't that be like saying that God is the first event in a way? But, of course, we have already seen in step two that the first event needs a cause.

PATRICIA: But how can we know the cause is nonphysical? Could it not be something else?

MALCOLM: We are trying to reach a reasonable conclusion about what the cause is. And it seems to me that if you accept steps one and two, it is reasonable to say that the cause of the universe is nonphysical. If you think it could be something else, it is incumbent upon you to say what. And you can't just arbitrarily rule out that it is a nonphysical cause. So I do not think that conclusion is very controversial; yet it is quite significant because, if you accept it, you are committing to the view that naturalism is false, since you now believe that something nonphysical exists. The universe is now "ontologically haunted," as Dallas Willard puts it. I also think that it is not very controversial to say that the cause of the universe must be very powerful indeed, since the universe is a very complex and sophisticated place. It must have taken enormous power to create galaxies, planets, rocks, not to mention life itself, and logic and rationality. "Only God can make a tree," as they say. But we can discuss all of this tomorrow.

JOHN: I would like to raise a question about the argument from design and then one about the problem of evil. Although the argument from design is an interesting argument, didn't Hume raise some very good objections against it?

JEAN: I knew you would want to focus on the objections!

MALCOLM: According to the argument from design, the universe shows clear evidence of design or order, and it is reasonable to conclude that this design or order was planned by a mind, that is, by God. The argument is an argument from analogy. That is, it argues from a comparison between the order in the universe and the order in the objects produced by human beings to a God who designs the order in the universe just as human beings design the order in the objects they create. John has alluded to criticisms of this argument by Hume. Some of these criticisms hold for earlier versions of the design argument, such as William Paley's (1743–1805). But they do not hold for more modern versions of the argument, as Richard Swinburne, a contemporary philosopher, has shown. I would like to concentrate on the more modern version of the argument.

BRIAN: I didn't know there were different versions of the argument, Malcolm. How does the modern version differ from the earlier versions?

MALCOLM: It is necessary to distinguish between two meanings of design or order so that we can appreciate the difference. The first meaning is that when we say something is designed or ordered we mean that *it looks designed to us;* it looks to us, on the surface, as it were, as if it is following a pattern or is ordered in some way; examples of this kind of design would include a steady downpour of rain, a car engine, or the human cell. The second meaning of design or order means that something is designed or ordered *if it obeys, or if its behavior can be explained in terms of, the laws of physics.* Of course, everything in our physical universe (with the exception of the human mind, in my view) is following the laws of physics, and so is designed in this second sense.

FRANK: So what you mean is that even though we might come across something *that does not look ordered to us*—for example, a random mix of chemicals in a dish—it would still be ordered in the sense that it would be following the laws of physics?

MALCOLM: Absolutely right! Now since everything in the universe is like this . . .

RENEE: Except for the mind . . .

MALCOLM: Except for the mind . . . our next big question is: Why is the universe following laws? Why is it lawlike, and not lawless or chaotic? Why, for example, when you throw a stone up in the air does it not float off into space occasionally, instead of *always* falling to the ground? Why do the laws of science always hold? And, of course, the answer is: The universe is lawlike because it was designed that way by God, just the way a car engine is ordered because it was designed that way by man. So the modern version of the design argument stresses this kind of order, whereas the earlier versions, such as Paley's, tended to stress the fact that many features of the universe looked ordered to us.

JOHN: Yes, I admit that the argument from design, especially Swinburne's version of it, is interesting, but I know that Hume raised some excellent objections against the argument. It's been a while since I looked at them, but I do remember one in particular. Hume suggested that, in an argument from analogy, it is not possible to reach a conclusion about an object if it is the *only* one of its kind, as the universe is. I have always thought he raised an interesting point. The design argument might have some merit if we had several other worlds that we knew had been designed by a powerful designer. Then we could be more confident in our speculation that our present world was also designed.

MALCOLM: Yes, Hume did raise a number of interesting objections to the argument from design. However, Swinburne deals with them all very effectively in his recent work on the argument. We do not have time to mention them all now. But you have raised a well-known one, John. Swinburne replies by simply saying that Hume is wrong about his claim that one cannot reach a conclusion about an object if it is the only one of its kind. Scientists, he points out, reason this way all the time—both about the universe and about the human race. So it is quite reasonable, if you have one object that shows evidence of design, to conclude that it probably had a designer.

BRIAN: Another objection of Hume's is his suggestion that in order for the design argument to be plausible, we also would need to explain the *designer*. Isn't that a reasonable objection, Malcolm?

MALCOLM: Well, the issue of the nature of the designer is undoubtedly an important issue, a fact that the theist does not wish to deny or downplay. And we have already agreed to get into this issue further tomorrow. However, it is not a good objection against the argument from design that we cannot explain the designer. The need to explain the designer is a secondary question; even if we cannot explain the designer it is still reasonable to conclude that there *is* a designer. Swinburne expresses this well when he points out that it is no objection to explaining X by Y that we cannot explain Y. Science has always accepted this practice, and to reject it would be to reject science.

PATRICIA: Listening to these objections, I am reminded of another one from Hume. He argues that if we can appeal to the analogy of the human mind designing things as a basis for our argument that God is the designer of the universe, why not go the whole way and say that God is like man?

MALCOLM: Well, let me appeal to Swinburne again on this objection. He replies by saying that when we argue that God designing the world is analogous to human minds designing things, we do not mean that they are alike *in all respects*. This is a truth about all arguments from analogy. Remember we said the hypothesis that the universe has a designer must explain the scientific laws that operate in the universe. Now if God had a body like man, then he would be confined to a part of the universe, and those laws outside his domain would have to operate independently of him. Hence, a God with a body would not explain how scientific laws operate in all of the universe. So the hypothesis that God is disembodied explains more than the hypothesis that God is embodied. If we were to conclude that God is completely like man in all respects, this would be to arbitrarily and unnecessarily weaken the argument from design.

JOHN: Perhaps so. But isn't this where evolution emerges as a powerful explanatory theory? Haven't we shown that evolution can explain the design in the universe without bringing in God? For example, don't we now know that the apparent design in the habitat of, say, the greenfly—the fact that the greenfly's habitat looks perfectly designed for a greenfly to live and flourish in—don't we now know that this was brought about by the processes of natural selection, adaptation of the species, and survival of the fittest, and so on?

FRANK: I am not very convinced by the evidence for evolution. Like Peter van Inwagen and Philip Johnson, I think much more is claimed for the theory than the evidence actually warrants. I have particular difficulty in believing in macro-evolution, the idea that simple life-forms evolved into more complex life-forms. I also have great difficulty with the lack of evidence from the fossil record. And since the implications of subscribing to the theory of evolution are so great, especially for my religion, which holds to a literal view of Scripture and especially of *Genesis*—I will not subscribe to it until I see good evidence. But, John, on your specific example, how does the theory of evolution explain the design of the habitat of the greenfly?

JOHN: The theory of evolution claims that all of the present species in the world evolved from common ancestors, reaching all the way back to one-cell organisms about three billion years ago.

Over billions of years our current, more complex life-forms gradually evolved from earlier, more simple life-forms. One of the key ideas in the theory is the process of natural selection—the idea that the process of evolution favors those life-forms and subspecies best able to cope with their particular environments. That is, those that are the "fittest" survive best. The evidence for the theory—despite what you say, Frank—is seen in the clear similarities in anatomy and molecular chemistry found among the diverse life-forms and also in the evidence from the fossil record.

MALCOLM: A very nice summary of the theory, John. Can you show how it works with the greenfly example?

JOHN: Well, I am no expert on this, but, as I understand it, the basic idea is that millions of years ago there were many different *types* of what we now call the greenfly, and they had different characteristics than our present greenflies have. For example, they were not all colored green. The theory of evolution says that over millions of years those greenflies that had an advantage—who were the fittest—survived, and those who did not have this advantage did not survive. For example, when greenfly predators came along, the flies colored green had an advantage because they could blend in with the green plants; so the predators ate the black, red, and yellow flies because they were easier to see, and so on. A host of other factors was involved too, of course, but the idea is that eventually after millions of years there were only greenflies left.

MARY: Oh yes. And although it looks like the greenfly and its habitat were perfectly designed for each other they were not; it just evolved that way over time.

PATRICIA: Yes, and that is why, to take another example, the cheetah has just enough speed to escape its predators; because all of the slower cheetahs, over millions of years, were caught and killed. Since parents tend to pass on their characteristics to their children—the offspring of the fast cheetahs generally had the gift of speed as well. If by some chance they did not, they were killed off. Eventually we had only fast cheetahs left. Of course, many species did become extinct.

FRANK: Yes, that's all very nice, John and Patricia, but isn't it all speculation? Is there any hard evidence that any of that actually happened? That's a question van Inwagen discusses.

RENEE: Well, this is fascinating! Now Malcolm, if that is a plausible story, is it not an interesting argument against design? Doesn't it show that order comes from disorder and that it was not orchestrated by a mind?

MALCOLM: Actually no, it cannot function at all as an argument against the fact that the universe is lawlike. Evolution is a theory about how things change or evolve over time; for example, a theory about how A evolves into B. *But A and B are still following the laws of physics, and, remember, it is these laws that we have to explain.* In short, we need to explain why the universe is following laws and not why things look designed to us. It is true that evolution can explain, in the way that John and Patricia showed, why some things *look designed to us,* but it cannot explain *why things are following laws in the first place.* And this is the key issue raised in the design argument, as Swinburne and others have pointed out in recent literature.

BRIAN: I read Richard Dawkins's book *The Blind Watchmaker* over the winter, and he actually claims in that book that evolution can explain how order came out of chaos. What about that claim, Malcolm, from a highly qualified, well-respected, and well-known scientist?

MALCOLM: Yes, Dawkins is an example of how a highly qualified scientist can make an elementary mistake in logic. And we must be careful not to allow the fame and expertise of these scientists to blind us to the need to examine their arguments carefully on important issues. Dallas Willard has pointed out well the mistake Dawkins makes. Dawkins uses the example of pebbles floating around in the waves by a beach and then being thrown out onto the beach by the force of the water. He says that *in the waves* the pebbles are chaotic in the sense that there is no order or pattern to their movement. But because the pebbles respond differently to the motion of the waves, according to their size, *they land out on the beach in a pattern,* that is, lightest ones in a row near the water, next lightest ones in a row a little farther up the beach, and so on. Dawkins then concludes that in this case order came out of disorder and no mind planned it.

MARY: Yes, that is a silly point by Dawkins in the light of your distinction between the two different meanings of design. It is clear that the pebbles in the waves—and on the beach for that matter—are still obeying the laws of physics, and so are ordered, because this is what we mean by ordered. What Dawkins means when he says the pebbles in the waves are chaotic is that *the pebbles do not look ordered to us.* Yet they are still really ordered because they are obeying the laws of physics. Right?

BRIAN: Right! Saying that the pebbles in the waves are disordered would be like saying that if we went into a lab and saw a dish with loads of stuff floating around in it in a chaotic way, that this stuff would be disordered. But this would only mean that *we* could not see the lawlike operation of the particles, but their operation would be lawlike nonetheless.

MALCOLM: Exactly! So this type of appeal to evolution does not touch the need to explain the order in the universe. And I am arguing that to explain this order it is very reasonable to bring in God. And this is the point of Paley's famous watch example; in order to explain the order present in a watch, that is, its lawlike behavior, it is very reasonable to conclude that a mind planned it. In fact, it would be irrational to imagine that it has just happened by sheer chance, which is what the naturalist has to say about the order in the universe.

FRANK: And we must not forget to point out that, as Willard says, evolution, either cosmic or biological, *logically cannot* explain the existence of the first event in the universe, though some naturalists often talk as if it can. Because in order for A to evolve into B, A must first exist, and the theory of evolution cannot explain the *existence* of A. Evolution also cannot explain the origin of life, though, again, naturalists like Dawkins talk as if it can.

PATRICIA: But evolution, Frank, does disprove your version of religion, since I believe the theory is true, so the biblical story in *Genesis* cannot be true. And perhaps scientists will eventually discover a chemical origin of life.

MALCOLM: It is helpful here to distinguish between three quite different positions on the origin and nature of the universe. I make these distinctions in my classes. Creationism I, simply stated, is the view that God created the universe and all life according to a particular design or with a particular purpose in mind. The development of life happened in whatever way science tells us, and at present this appears to be according to evolutionary principles. Human beings, however, at the top of the evolutionary tree by far, have a special place in the universe. I contrast this view with your view, Frank, which I call Creationism II. Creationism II is very similar to Creationism I, except for its position on evolution. Creationism II denies that evolution took place and holds that the species were created individually by God just as described in *Genesis*. But Creationism II agrees with Creationism I on most of the other key points.

RENEE: Creationism II then is what we normally call "Creation Science," and Creationism I would be the mainstream Catholic view, as well as the view of many forms of Protestantism and Judaism?

MALCOLM: Yes, that's right. But both positions are to be contrasted with what I call Darwinian Evolutionary Naturalism. This would be the position of Sagan, Crick, Dawkins, and other naturalists. They hold that the universe came into existence uncaused out of nothing (or some version of this), that this occurred accidentally, that simple life-forms emerged out of the primordial soup, again by chance, that more complex life-forms evolved from these (and here we all are!), and that there is no purpose or ultimate meaning to the univese. My own view is that this position is not as plausible as Creationism I.

JEAN: I have to say that I think Malcolm's argument is very good and very believable.

MALCOLM: I must add that I would present the cosmological and design arguments as a part of a package of arguments, which, taken together, constitute a very good cumulative case for the rationality of theism. Other arguments in the overall cumulative case would include the argument from religious experience, the moral argument, the argument from mind, the arguments from history and miracles, and so on. We will discuss several of these arguments in our future conversations, no doubt. I am claiming that theism is the most rational explanation for the universe and human life; I believe that, given the initial evidence we have considered, it is the best available explanation and is superior to naturalism.

JEAN: It's quite a convincing argument, Malcolm, and it clearly shows that religious faith is not irrational superstition at all, but is in fact a perfectly reasonable worldview.

MALCOLM: I think one will find it a pretty good argument if one approaches it in a fairly neutral manner. In fact, I think that overall the evidence is clearly in favor of theism. If, however, one approaches my arguments from an already entrenched position of naturalism or atheism, then my reasons in favor of theism might not appear so strong. But this is not because the arguments themselves are weak. What do you think, John?!

JOHN: Well, Malcolm, your moves in step one and two are okay in my view, and I can see some of the points you are making in step three, and some seem possible—I won't say reasonable. But my biggest problem with your view of God is the problem of evil in the world, which I would now like to discuss. ↖ good point

MALCOLM: I agree that it is a significant problem and not one to be taken lightly. It is regarded by many as one of the biggest obstacles to a philosophical demonstration of God's existence. But it is a very large topic, and we must leave it for another day when we will have time to have a detailed discussion of that issue by itself.

RENEE: Yes, I need to stretch my legs. How about going for a walk down into the valley?

The friends adjourn for the day.

Key Terms and Distinctions

Reason vs. faith
Fideism
Rationality vs. proof
Natural theology
Theist
The cosmological argument
(two versions)
Local cause vs. ultimate cause
Potential infinity vs. actual
infinity
Logical possibility

Naturalism
Atheism
Principle of sufficient reason
Contingent being vs. necessary
being
Two meanings of "design"
Argument from design Evolution
Creationism I
Creationism II
Darwinian evolutionary
naturalism

Questions on Chapter 1

1. Compare and contrast theism with atheism or naturalism, and assess the *rationality* of each view.
2. Discuss the relationship between religious belief, atheism, and science that has emerged in the first conversation. Be sure to address the question of whether a scientist can be a religious believer and vice versa.
3. Are religion and science compatible?
4. Which step of Malcolm's three-step approach do you find the least convincing? Explain why, and consider how he might respond to your criticisms.
5. Discuss the relationship between religion and evolution in the light of the issues raised in the first conversation.
6. Would a rational argument such as that offered by Malcolm actually lead one to become a religious believer?
7. Discuss the distinction between rationality and proof, and explore some areas of life, including religion, where it functions as a useful distinction.
8. Is it possible for some people to believe in God based on reason—to have a rational belief in God—but to be unable to explain or defend their view very well? If so, should we take their belief seriously?

9. Explore Renee's point that the arguments of natural theology might not lead to belief in a God who is worthy of worship.
10. Explore further John's argument that the theory of evolution can explain the apparent order we see in the universe.
11. Explore the relationship between reason and faith in religious belief.

Bibliography

Aquinas, St. Thomas, *Summa Theologiae,* Part 1, Question 2, Article 3, in *Introduction to St. Thomas Aquinas,* ed. Anton C. Pegis (New York: Random House, 1945).
Copleston, Frederick, *Aquinas* (Harmondsworth: Penguin, 1955).
Craig, William Lane, *The Kalam Cosmological Argument* (New York: Harper & Row, 1979).
Dawkins, Richard, *The Blind Watchmaker* (New York: Norton, 1986).
Hawking, Stephen, *A Brief History of Time* (New York: Bantam, 1988).
Hume, David, *Dialogues Concerning Natural Religion* (original edition, 1779), (Indianapolis: Hackett, 1980 edition).
Johnson, Philip, *Darwin on Trial* (Downers Grove, IL: InterVarsity, 1993, second edition).
Kant, Immanuel, *Critique of Pure Reason* (original edition, 1781), trans. Norman Kemp Smith (New York: St. Martin's, 1965).
Mackie, John, *The Miracle of Theism* (Oxford: Oxford University Press, 1982).
Paley, William, *Natural Theology* (original edition, 1802), (Indianapolis: Library of Liberal Arts, 1963).
Polkinghorne, J.C., *The Faith of a Physicist* (Princeton, NJ: Princeton University Press, 1994).
Russell, Bertrand, *Why I Am Not a Christian* (London: Allen & Unwin, 1957).
Russell, Bertrand, and Copleston, Frederick, "A Debate on the Existence of God," in *The Existence of God,* ed. John Hick (New York: Macmillan, 1964), pp. 167–191.

Swinburne, Richard, *The Existence of God* (Oxford: Oxford University Press, 1991, second edition).

Van Inwagen, Peter, *God, Knowledge, and Mystery* (Ithaca, NY: Cornell University Press, 1995).

Willard, Dallas, "The Three-Stage Argument for the Existence of God," in *Contemporary Perspectives on Religious Epistemology*, ed. R. Douglas Geivett and Brendan Sweetman (New York: Oxford University Press, 1992), pp. 212–224.

Chapter Two

The Nature of God

Everyone who participated in the discussion about God's existence found it stimulating and provocative. Renee encourages them to pursue the discussion further, now taking up the question of God's nature. John and Patricia point out what a difficult, if not impossible, question that would be for the human mind to entertain. Malcolm and Brian agree that it is difficult but disagree that it is impossible. If the natural theologian reasons carefully, they explain, she or he can attain some speculative conclusions about what the divine nature is like. They argue, moreover, that the divine nature must be something like the God of the Judeo-Christian tradition.

RENEE: I'm glad we got to have that rousing discussion yesterday. I had been wanting to think through some issues about the existence of God for some time. You guys gave me some motivation and some nice direction on dealing with that question.

JEAN: Yeah, it was very interesting. But, you know, I found it a little frustrating too.

MARY: Oh, why is that?

JEAN: Well, we focused almost exclusively on evidence for the existence of God. But I'm not sure I have much of an idea of what God is. I guess I would like a little more talk about God's nature.

MALCOLM: That's a good point, Jean. But, after all, we can only do so much. We've got to take these issues a step at a time. Taking up each issue in its proper order and giving each its due is the mark of a good philosopher. So, having worked through the question whether God exists, it seems that we are now prepared to talk about just what God is. Just what or who is this being whose existence we tried to justify yesterday?

JOHN: You're pushing it, Malcolm. You naively think that we can talk about God like we can talk about a tree or a chair or a soda pop can. You don't seem to appreciate that the human mind is only acquainted with sensible, physical objects. Speculating about the existence and nature of God is not within its range, I'm afraid.

MALCOLM: I admit you've brought up a very important point here, John. Everyone who takes seriously an intelligent philosophy of God is obligated to discuss it.

PATRICIA: Yeah, it's a darn good point, John. It reminds me of those remarks Ivan Karamazov made to his brother, Alyosha, in Dostoevsky's great novel, *The Brothers Karamozov*. You remember the discussion, I'm sure.

JEAN: Could it be, you're fishing for an invitation to recite it, Patricia?

RENEE: No, she's not going to recite it. She's going to read it! I was with her at the book store. She bought a copy of the novel just this morning. She has been itching to quote a passage here and there to make Malcolm squirm.

MALCOLM: Always up to your tricks, eh, Patricia?

PATRICIA: Now that you've found me out, let me read you a brief passage where we find Ivan Karamazov speaking to his brother, Alyosha, a Christian monk: "I have a Euclidean earthly mind, and how could I solve problems that are not of this world? And I advise you never to think about it either, my dear Alyosha, especially about God, whether he exists or not. All such questions are utterly inappropriate for a mind created with an idea of only three dimensions."

JOHN: Well said, Ivan. That would make a nice epitaph for natural theology. Don't you think so, Malcolm?

FRANK: I'm not sure I get it. What's the point?

JOHN: It's simply this: the human mind is not adequate to speculate about metaphysical things, like the nature of God or angels, or souls, or any such spooky stuff. Our minds are constrained to know physical things. We have to be content with that and not pretend we can contemplate nonphysical objects.

MALCOLM: Ivan makes a powerful point. But I think there is still a reply to him.

MARY: Something told me you were going to say that.

MALCOLM: The human mind, no doubt, is strained to its limits in metaphysical speculation. That's why analogical language is essential to the task of metaphysics. But while such speculation is tested, and perhaps taxed, it is not bankrupted. I agree with Aristotle that physical, sensible things are the proper objects of human knowledge. But because of our powers of abstraction, of inference, and of analysis of cause and effect, we can ask important questions about the physical things we know. In some cases, we seem entitled to infer beyond physical things to the existence of nonphysical things, as we saw in our discussion yesterday.

JOHN: Well, you natural theologians may feel entitled, but as for the rest of us, I'm not so sure.

MALCOLM: Consider this simple example: when Patricia read Ivan's remark in Dostoevsky's novel, she caused vibrations in the air, right?

JOHN: Yes, she happened to be reading out loud.

MALCOLM: But when I sensed these vibrations, when I heard these sounds, I recognized that they had a certain order, which signaled to me that they were sounds that made up a human language, called English. These sounds were signs of meanings, which signified thoughts in your mind, thoughts that you were conveying to our minds. But neither the meanings, nor the thoughts, nor the minds are (at least not on the face of it) physical

things. Now, it seems to me that once we grant a case like that—
the inference from physical events to nonphysical causes—we have
to grant that it is at least possible that the mind can infer to the
existence of a nonphysical cause that is the reason for the existence of the physical world, and to some of the attributes of this
cause. Ivan is right to the extent it is difficult business. He is wrong
to suggest it is impossible.

JOHN: Even if I agreed with you that inferring to such a being is
possible, it seems to me that it would be pointless to talk about it.
Since it is altogether transcendent and supernatural, how can it be
talked about using our ordinary, natural language?

RENEE: But should we say nothing about God? If he exists, it
makes a difference in human knowledge and in human life. There
is a need to talk about God.

MALCOLM: So we've got this question before us: Having established *that* God exists, can we now ask *what* God is?

JOHN: Yes, that's the question. Even if I granted that you have
accomplished the former, I don't see how we can ever accept that
you can accomplish the latter. To speak in Ivan Karamazov's way,
we may grant that other dimensions exist, but bound as we are by
three-dimensional experience, how could we ever speak meaning-
fully about the others?

BRIAN: Oh, I think there is a way. I think the human mind has
some basis on which to say things about God.

JOHN: You're welcome to try and convince us, Brian.

BRIAN: First, let me summarize Malcolm's argument from yesterday. Last night I reflected on it, and I've been wanting to formulate it myself, just to see if I can. It bears repeating because it
will help me make my case that we can, if very careful, say some
definite things about what God is—I mean about the nature and
attributes of God. By reminding ourselves *that* God is, we will have
some indications of *what* God is like.

PATRICIA: I doubt you can get to first base, let alone second.

BRIAN: Let me run one base at a time. Even when you hit a home run, you have to tag all the bases.

PATRICIA: And when you strike out . . . ?

BRIAN: I'll let you all be my judge as to whether I should be benched. Anyway, let me make this important summary point: It seems to me that evidence for God ultimately comes down to these simple terms, as we saw in our last conversation. We asked the question: Why is there something rather than nothing? While we take the existence of things for granted in our everyday lives, we should not do so as philosophers. We have a duty to ask: Why does the universe exist at all? We ask this in light of what philosophers have called the principle of sufficient reason, which says that anything that exists must have a reason for its being. But when we ask such a question about the universe, we have only three possible answers. First, the universe has existed as an infinite series of contingent beings from eternity. Second, the universe just "popped" into existence out of nothing; in other words, it came into being for no reason and with no cause. Third, a supernatural agent, God, brought it into existence. Of these three options, only the last is plausible. The first is ruled out because it is illogical. We explained this point yesterday. If the universe had an infinite past, we could never reach today, for the universe would have to traverse an infinite number of moments to get where it is now. It is also a weak position in light of the findings of contemporary science, as Craig pointed out. The Big Bang and the Argument from the Second Law of Thermodynamics seem to indicate that the universe has a finite past. The second option is patently absurd. It asserts that something can exist without a reason. There is nothing in human experience or science to suggest that that is so. Thus, we are left with only the last option. It follows that if the universe has not been here for all eternity, it depends for its existence on a supernatural agent. This supernatural agent must be a self-explained or necessary being. Now once we establish that point, we're prepared to say some very important things about this supernatural agent.

PATRICIA: Your argument sounds like a poor man's version of Aquinas's Third Way, the Argument from Contingency.

MALCOLM: As we explained yesterday, Aquinas's version is different from William Craig's, which Brian has just summarized very well. The important point is that Aquinas and Craig both get to the same conclusion: A necessary being exists.

BRIAN: Yes. Once you establish that the universe is contingent, that is, that it is dependent for its being on a necessary being, then you're on your way to showing that that necessary being must approximate the nature and attributes of Judeo-Christian monotheism.

PATRICIA: Not so fast. Why monotheism? I'm not sure you're allowed to make that inference. Why couldn't you have several necessary beings? This is a possibility, which would lead to a polytheism, a position most theists won't stand for.

MALCOLM: Not to worry, Patricia. If you think about it, it's pretty clear that there can only be one necessary being.

PATRICIA: Why is that?

MALCOLM: Because a necessary being must be infinite.

FRANK: Explain, please.

BRIAN: If it is a necessary being, it is its own reason for being. That means it must be fully actual of its very nature. If it is its own reason for being, which is to say that it does not derive or borrow its being from another, why would its being be limited? It must be independently its own basis for being, which is another way of saying that its very nature is to exist. If its very nature is existence, what prevents it from being the fullness of being or actuality? Hence, if it is not dependent on another, it is unlimited in its being. Thus, we recognize that the necessary being is an infinite being.

MALCOLM: Yes. The necessary being's *aseity*, as the theologians sometimes call it, the necessary being's sufficiency to account for its own existence, implies its infinity.

RENEE: Okay, that answers Frank's request for an explanation. But it still doesn't answer Patricia's question. Why can't there be a multitude of these infinite and necessary beings?

MALCOLM: It's because there can be only one infinite. You see, things differ from one another only if one has a property that another lacks or if one lacks a property that another has. But an infinite being has all properties. In the fullness of its actuality, it possesses everything. In order to distinguish one infinite from another, one "infinite" would have to lack a property that the other has. But if it lacks a property, it is not infinite.

FRANK: But can't you have two things that are alike in every way? For example, identical twins. Especially when they're just single cells, they're indistinguishable.

MALCOLM: Oh, they're quite distinguishable, because they occupy different spaces. They are the same in nature, but not in location; so the one does, in fact, have an attribute that the other lacks.

BRIAN: You see, this is a very important finding. The human mind can establish *that* a necessary being exists and can infer readily that such a being is infinite. Since there is only *one* infinite necessary being, we begin to see that it is something like the God of the traditional Judeo-Christian religion.

JOHN: You're going to have to travel a few miles to get us there, aren't you?

MALCOLM: It's a ride worth taking. We're on a path toward saying *what* the necessary being is. If you're curious about what *philosophy* can contribute to this discussion, climb aboard.

JEAN: Well, I'm very curious. I know that theology teaches about the nature and attributes of God. But you're saying that philosophy can determine what he is as well?

RENEE: There you go again with the masculine pronoun to describe God.

BRIAN: God is neither he nor she, but does it really make any difference if we refer to God as he?

FRANK: Jesus called God "Father" in the Scriptures.

MALCOLM: Old habits die hard. For ease of communication, we will stay with the tradition. But your point, Renee, is well taken. As I was saying, it seems that reason, unaided by revelation, can infer from the nature of God's creation, to his existence as a necessary and infinite being. Since God is the cause of creation, it is reasonable to think that perfections in this world exist in God as their source, except that they exist in God in a way appropriate to his nature, which is infinite and perfect. The human mind may not understand the attributes of God in the way we understand attributes of creatures, for, after all, the divine attributes exist in an infinite and perfect being. Nonetheless, we can judge accurately that these attributes belong to him. But the human mind is sufficiently aware of what creatures are like to help us obtain an idea of what God is like.

PATRICIA: Let's grant that you've successfully inferred from the existence of creatures to their Creator. That's a lot to give you, but I'm in an exceedingly generous mood today. For the sake of discussion, I'll grant you that much. But I don't see, as John pointed out earlier, how you can go from knowledge of what creatures are to knowledge of what God is. Creatures are physical, limited, imperfect, contingent—you know, all the things God is not supposed to be. So, doesn't the radical difference between creatures and Creator throw a big wrench into your metaphysical works here?

MALCOLM: You've made a very good point, Patricia. I've addressed it already in my reply to Ivan Karamazov. But I admit it's a

"man was made in the image of God"

difficult and controversial matter. There's no doubt that there is some truth in what you say. It is a challenge that requires a thoughtful response. Let me approach it another way. It seems that there are three ways that creatures can tell us something about God. I think they can do this, in spite of the doubts you've just expressed. The three ways are the ways of *causality, negation, and eminence.* When we know something about God in the first sense—through his causal activity—we know that anything that denotes a perfection in this world, say, wisdom or beauty, must belong to God. God causes all perfections. They must describe him in some sense as well. This is because the reality of an effect depends wholly on its cause. Hence, in some sense the perfection in the effect must already be in the cause. So if creatures are beautiful, wise, and good, then their Creator is beautiful, wise, and good. The creatures (the effects) do not have those perfections except through the Creator (the cause). Still, and this is where negation comes in, we cannot ascribe these perfections to God in just the way we know them, for the human mind is limited and imperfect and knows things as they exist in creatures. Consequently, we cannot understand and express how such positive perfections would belong to an infinite being. As a result, we must always balance our positive ascriptions of God with a denial of the manner by which a finite mind, laboring under the limits of its own knowledge and language, ascribes these attributes. Philosophers call this the way of negation, talking about the Divine Nature more in terms of *what it is not* rather than *what it is.* God is wise and beautiful, to name our examples again, but not in the way that human minds understand wisdom and beauty. In other words, God enjoys positive attributes in an *eminent* or superlative way. Anything attributed of him must be undiminished and unqualified by the limiting nature of matter. Attributes describe him in a way that suits his infinity; thus his attributes must transcend any suggestion of the limitations and imperfections of physical nature.

why didn't God make us perfect

BRIAN: On each account, then—whether in terms of causality, negation, or eminence—God must be talked about in different ways from creatures. Yet there are basic similarities, since perfections, insofar as they are perfections, have their source in God and

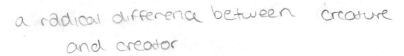

a radical difference between creature and creator

in some ways must be a part of God's nature. They are in God at least *virtually,* that is, in his transcendent power to produce them. Since everything in the effect acquires its reality from its cause, the cause, at least virtually, possesses all that is in the effect. All creation, then, points to something about God, since God is the cause of everything else. Such perfections exist in God in a transcendent way, as befits the infinite mode of God's existence. Hence, when we speak of these perfections in God, we must acknowledge his different manner of existing.

MALCOLM: Yes, to speculate about God's nature is to achieve a balance of what we can say with what we cannot; of what God is with what God is not; of positive with negative theology. I think the remark about negation is especially important. In a sense our knowledge of God is significantly compromised by the limits of our own mind. Ivan Karamazov, John, and Patricia were right to point that out. Still, we seem to have an intellectual right to apply positive ascriptions to God, since he is the cause of them in creation, given that we already have evidence that he exists. As long as we appreciate the role of negative theology in all of this—appreciating what God *is not* along with what God is—we can talk intelligently about the divine nature.

JOHN: It seems to me that you're trying to have your cake and eat it too. You're admitting that God is radically different from creatures. You know that your belief in God's necessity and infinity requires that. Nevertheless, you insist that there is some causal affinity between God and creatures to warrant tomes of theological babble about God. If creatures are finite and dependent and God is infinite and independent, I don't see how you can ever find a similarity between them sufficient to infer God's nature from the creature's nature.

PATRICIA: Yes. The most you can get is necessity and infinity. I don't see how you could get farther than that.

MALCOLM: Admittedly, it is no simple business. You are quite right to stress the radical difference between the creature's mode of existence, which is finite, and the Creator's, which is infinite. Still, there is something that both creature and Creator have in common that entitles the mind to infer from the one to the other. What is common is that they both *exist.* CREATURE VS CREATOR

BRIAN: Right, Malcolm. While the creature and God exist in different ways, they nonetheless both exist. They are both beings. This commonality of being is the bridge enabling the mind to move from creature to God.

JOHN: No. It seems to me the best you can say about God and creature is that their similarity of being is just a *metaphorical* similarity. To say God exists is just poetry for us, because the strain on the language is too great to express the existence of God in a way that accords with our limited, physical, sensory acquaintance with creaturely existents. We may say that "God exists" but that is about as meaningful as saying that "the lion is the king of beasts." It is just metaphor or poetry. It takes an attribute that belongs properly to only one sphere of things and through use of the imagination applies it to another. But it doesn't really belong to the other. Lions aren't really kings, any more than kings—say, Richard—are really lions! Likewise, existence when applied to God is metaphor, for it properly applies only to what we know, and we know only creatures: existents whose modes of being are physical, finite, and contingent. So we're back to Ivan Karamazov. Philosophy of God takes language to the breaking point. So don't pretend that you can talk a blue streak about God's nature once you've established that he exists!

BRIAN: I like your examples to express the nature of metaphor. They make the point very well. A metaphor predicates a term of two or more things when only one properly has the perfection signified and when no relation between the two or more things exists. A similarity is identified by the imagination to express some idea. When I say "My love is a rose," I am not saying that my beloved is *really* a rose, nor even has a relationship to a rose, but that I make a comparison to express my idea or belief about the beauty and pleasantness of my beloved. But this is not always what goes on when we compare God with creatures. Sometimes we use metaphor: "God is my rod and my staff." But metaphor does not exhaust all possible expressions about God. Some expressions capture a deeper, more intimate comparison between God, who causes creatures, and creatures, who are God's effects. Creatures are beings because they have a real relationship to God, on whom they depend as their cause. Without God, they have no being. Hence, we can attribute being to God as the cause of every other being. Philosophers call this kind of analogy, analogy of attribution. This is clearly more than just metaphor.

PATRICIA: But all that gets you is a relationship. You still have no right to say that God is a being just because creatures are beings. It's not enough to say that God is being just because he causes being. I can't say exercise is *really* healthy just because it causes health. I can't say the wind is cold just because it chills me. These are causes, and our language expresses the causal relationship, but it can't do more than that. We aren't entitled to say that the term signified belongs *intrinsically* to both the cause and the effect.

MALCOLM: You're right. Nonetheless, being is such a basic principle that if God is the author of being, he too must exist. Doesn't God have *to be* in order to cause others to be?

BRIAN: I suppose it's true that analogy of attribution can take you only so far. Fortunately, we don't have to rely on that type of analogy alone to secure knowledge of and language about God. There is analogy of proportionality: The creature's existence is to its mode of being as God's existence is to its mode. Granted that God exists, this form of analogy enables us to say something definite about God's way of being. While the creature exists in a finite way, the Creator exists infinitely. His nature is to his existence as a creature's nature is to its existence. This proportionality allows us to say something about God, even though all discourse about God must be limited and properly qualified. At least, it gives us a foothold. Once this foothold is established we can reflect on God's mode of being and draw conclusions about his nature.

JOHN: It sounds to me as though you guys have been reading too many medieval textbooks.

BRIAN: Well, I must admit that my explanations rely mainly on Aquinas and his many commentators, such as Jacques Maritain and Etienne Gilson.

PATRICIA: Somebody hasn't heard that scholasticism is dead.

MALCOLM: It wouldn't be the first time scholasticism survived to bury its undertakers.

JEAN: So, you're saying, Malcolm, that once we establish that God is, we can be certain of a good number of his attributes.

MALCOLM: Yes, but the inferences have to be made very carefully. At each step we have to take note of how God is different from creatures, even if it is the case that God's infinity includes all positive perfections belonging to creatures, such as being, goodness, wisdom, power, and beauty. One thing we have to note especially is that God is not a composite being. This is very mysterious, and it is another expression of negative theology. God is simple. He is not composite, for if he were, he would be dependent on some principle to bring his various parts into composition. As the absolutely First and Necessary Being, God is incomposite.

BRIAN: This means that God's nature is not different from his existence. For if his nature were not the same as his existence, he would be composite and there would be no necessity in his existence. He would have to be made to exist by an external agent, if his nature were different from his existence. His nature would be a mere potency, awaiting actuation. This would make God just another contingent being. Hence, God would not be the first and necessary existent. But we've already shown that the cause of the universe must be a necessary being. Surely, then, God's nature is to exist. There is, then, no real distinction between God's essence and his existence.

MALCOLM: This, again, makes God unique. He is necessary, infinite, simple, and pure actuality, having no essence that is distinct from his existence. This is the primary truth about God: he is pure existence, utter and complete actuality. From this all other characteristics of God flow.

BRIAN: Interestingly, this philosophical excursion into God's nature vindicates the remark in *Exodus* (3:14), where God tells Moses that he is to be called "I am." "Tell the Israelites," God commands Moses, "that 'I am' has sent you." Just as revelation says that God is, he is named "I am," so philosophy now justifies that God is the act of existence, pure actuality.

JOHN: I guess it's now where the God-talk really begins. Go ahead. Spin out all those divine attributes. I'll lean back and sharpen my Ockham's razor, if you don't mind?

MALCOLM: Not at all. We've got our razors too! It's just that we don't use ours indiscriminately.

BRIAN: It does happen that a number of divine attributes become apparent once we establish by negative theology that God has no sort of composition—that he is pure act of existing.

MALCOLM: Yes, it's obvious that God is perfect, for example.

MARY: Why is that exactly?

BRIAN: God is perfect by virtue of the full possession of existence. Complete actuality is God's, since he is his own existence.

MALCOLM: God's perfection also entails that he is morally good and incapable of evil. Hence, he is a being supremely worthy of worship.

JOHN: Now, isn't that a funny use of the word "perfection"? Why is it that just because God exists he is perfect? You're assuming that where there is being, whether in creature or Creator, there is perfection. Why should I accept that assertion?

MALCOLM: Well, we can be sure of this much. Being is the basis of all perfections. There can be no perfection attained except through being. Take, for example, the human perfection of kindness. To possess this perfection is *to be* kind. It is by this act of existing that there is kindness. Keep in mind that it is because someone acquires being, say by becoming kind, that he or she gains a degree of perfection. It doesn't happen the other way around: Somebody doesn't gain a degree of being by gaining a degree of perfection. No, somebody acquires a degree of perfection by gaining a degree of being. Every existent is more or less perfect because it more or less *is*. If so, then, that being which is existence itself is absolutely perfect.

JOHN: But, sure, if you use an example like kindness, your point seems to be supported. But what about something negative. I mean some things seem to be worse, that is, imperfect, because they exist. For example, cancer cells exist in some patients. Wouldn't it be better that they didn't? Isn't that an argument by counter-example against your position?

MALCOLM: It seems to me we have a right to say that to the extent the cancer *exists* it has a kind of perfection. It is something, not nothing. The separation of something from nothing is a remarkable thing that finds its explanation in the act of existing. What could be more significant than the difference between existence and nonexistence? To be something and not nothing is, from the point of view of existence, a perfection.

JOHN: Are you begging the question here?

BRIAN: Perhaps this distinction might help: that anything exists at all, whether cancer cells or something less undesirable, it has perfection in the sense that it is actual, real, existent. *What* kind of existent it is determines whether or not it is perfect in some appetitive sense—that is whether we *want* it to exist or not for other reasons or in certain contexts. Perhaps we can distinguish between *existential* perfection—a kind of metaphysical perfection evident in the fact that anything exists at all, no matter what—and an *appeti-*

tive perfection—a kind of moral perfection evident in the fact that this or that existent satisfies a particular desire.

MALCOLM: Good distinction. In light of it, we can say that even things we don't want still exist and to think of them purely in that light—to think of them just existentially, that is to say, in terms of their actuality, their difference from nothingness—is to think of them as having a perfection: being as opposed to not-being. Since being is an existential perfection in its own right and since being is the ground of all other perfections, we can say that God is perfect since complete actuality. All perfections, both the existential and appetitive types, belong to God since he is infinite.

JOHN: But if God is infinite, wouldn't undesirable things have to be said of him as well? Good point

BRIAN: Perhaps another way to handle this would be to argue that undesirable things, that is, evil events, are not things in their own right but privations. They are not existents; they are not actual things; instead they are absences within the order of actual things. Evil, like the evil of cancer, is not a positive something in its own right; instead it is a disorder, a disruption, a deficiency within things that actually exist and are good. Perhaps all evil is like tooth decay, vitamin deficiency, or disease—an absence within an order otherwise good. If all evil can be explained, or explained away, in this fashion, then the act of existing will always surely be good, never evil. As Pure Existence, then, God is Pure Goodness.

MARY: Perhaps we should have a discussion on the problem of evil. Maybe we could discuss whether evil and imperfection in the universe undermine belief in an infinitely good God.

MALCOLM: Maybe we could take up the problem of evil in our next conversation.

JOHN: Well, I'm not sure I'm willing to go along with how you explain evil as an absence. It's one thing to say such an explanation can be given; it's quite another to provide it.

BRIAN: It's a challenging issue, I admit.

FRANK: What about old fashioned attributes like spirituality and eternity? How does one justify these attributes?

MALCOLM: Quite obviously, a number of attributes follow from God's self-subsisting existence; that God exists in and of himself. Spirituality and eternity are among them.

BRIAN: You can see how God's independent existence entails spirituality. God is immaterial, because if he were physical, he would be composite. Physical beings are composite; they have parts outside of parts. As composite, they are contingent, dependent on external causes to maintain their existence. We also saw yesterday that if God—the First Cause—were physical, the universe could not be explained. Physical things do not exist in and of themselves. Since God is his own reason for being, he is necessary, infinite, and simple, as we have seen. Now, we can add the attribute of immateriality.

MALCOLM: Surely God is also omnipotent. If God is the fullness of being, He is omnipotent, because actuality grounds possibility. Since God is being itself, that which is purely actual, he is all-powerful. He is able to cause anything that is possible.

he is all powerful

PATRICIA: If God is omnipotent, how do you explain evil? Couldn't God always do something about evil? If so, why does it happen?

MALCOLM: You've asked a very important question, Patricia. You've just brought up again the problem of evil. As it requires a whole day to do it justice, why don't we reserve it for another time, as I suggested a few minutes ago? I promise we'll get to it, maybe tomorrow. I'd like to hear what you all have to say about that classic problem.

FRANK: What about God's omnipresence. I'm not sure I fully understand that one.

JOHN: Yes. That one seems contradictory to me. How can God be in any place if he is not physical? It looks like theists again are not able to accept the implications of their own position that if God is spiritual, he must altogether transcend this world. He must have no location and can have no relationship to the physical.

BRIAN: True, God is not in place, because location requires matter, the references of bodies to each other. Since God is non-physical, he cannot have location. Nor does God relate to physical things. That would mean that God is dependent on things. Since he is infinite, God is independent of all things. Nonetheless, while God does not relate to physical things, the latter do relate to God. They depend on God for their existence. In this way, on account of the creature's dependence on God, God in a sense is *present* to it. Omnipresence refers to God's active power producing creatures and conserving them in existence. As God gives existence to everything that is, so God's power is *present* to that thing, no matter what it is, whether archangel or stone. In this way, God is everywhere or omnipresent.

MALCOLM: Another important attribute, of course, is immutability. Since God is already complete as a being, since he is all-perfect, God is fully actual. Since change implies potentiality, change cannot apply to God. God cannot become, since he lacks nothing. What need has God of change or further perfection?

PATRICIA: Sounds like a pretty static and lifeless God to me.

BRIAN: That criticism is sometimes made about divine immutability. But that criticism fails to appreciate the divine actuality, the fullness of God's perfection. If God is perfect and actual, he is fully life. That he doesn't change is a sign of his completeness of existence and life, not a sign of imperfection. It is only because we think of life in purely physical, mutable terms that we fail to appreciate how God's transcendent life and perfection requires immutability.

MALCOLM: Of course, God's immutability requires that he is eternal. If God is unchanging, then God is not in time. Time attempts to quantify motion. But there can be no motion where there is no potency or change. Since God is immutable, God is timeless.

BRIAN: This means that there is no succession in God. He does not experience events one after the other as we do. He comprehends all experience, all being, all actuality in one present moment, an "eternal now" as philosophers have sometimes called it.

MALCOLM: Further, if God is infinite, God is all-knowing, or omniscient. Knowledge consists in possessing the intelligibility of something. Now, God possesses all intelligibilities, since he is the source of all that is and can be. Accordingly, God knows everything.

JOHN: I have a problem with God's knowledge. God knows everything creatures are and do. But some things, of course, creatures haven't done yet. God will only know them when the creatures do actually this or that. But doesn't that undermine the radical independence of the divine nature?

RENEE: What do you mean?   *not all knowing?*

JOHN: Since some things don't exist yet, God can't know them. He, like us, is forced to find out about them when they happen. But this means God is dependent on the events of creatures—a circumstance most unbecoming for a perfect deity. God cannot be dependent on creatures. If so, God is just another contingent being.

MALCOLM: In your own flippant way, you've lurched into the problem of divine foreknowledge! God is not forced, like you or me, to find out what happens only when it occurs at this or that particular time. God knows from all *eternity* what is happening and what will occur. Remember, it is something of a misnomer to speak of God's "foreknowledge." This has been explained clearly in works by past philosophers such as Boethius (c.480–524), Augustine (354–430), and Aquinas (1225–1274). They point out that there is no "before" or "after" in God. He doesn't come to know things successively. His eternal vision of all possibilities and actualities makes him aware of what all creatures will do. God knows this by knowing himself. Within his own mind he sees the existence or life or destiny of all creatures.

PATRICIA: Well, even if we allow your explanation that God's knowledge of creatures doesn't imply dependence, there still remains another problem. Among the things that can be are future events, that is, events that someday will actually come to pass. Some of these include events resulting from the free choices and actions of human beings. Doesn't omniscience require that God knows from all eternity what each human being is going to do, now and in the future? But if God knows everything we're going to do, how can we be free? *this is the free will*

JEAN: Yes, I've thought of that before myself. Brian, you said that God is all-perfect. That means he cannot make a mistake. So if God knows what I'm going to do at a given time, I can't do it freely.

FRANK: I don't get it. Why can't you do it freely?

JOHN: Because freedom means you have the ability to do otherwise than what you do. But if God knows for all eternity that you are going to do 'x,' and God doesn't make mistakes, then it is necessarily true that 'x' will happen. Well, if your actions happen of necessity, then you are not free. See the problem?

FRANK: Perhaps it's not so much a problem as a mystery.

MALCOLM: No doubt, we can never fully explain how divine foreknowledge is compatible with our freedom, but I think we can show that in principle the two are not incompatible.

BRIAN: Yes. You have to remember that knowledge is not the same as causation. Just because I know something is the case or is bound to happen, it doesn't follow that I cause it to happen. It doesn't follow that my knowledge cancels out your freedom. I know John very well. But just because his decisions and actions are predictable doesn't mean that they aren't made freely.

Well even though God knows what we're going to do, don't we still do it freely?

JOHN: But you can't compare human knowledge with divine knowledge. With the best inductive evidence behind them, humans still can make mistakes predicting decisions and actions of others.

MALCOLM: Still, it seems to me that *in principle* complete knowledge and prediction need not preclude free decision-making.

BRIAN: I heard it once put this way: God's knowledge of future events is like our knowledge of the past. From the vantage point of the present moment, I know retrospectively that the Battle of Hastings occurred in 1066. But my knowing that does not cause it to happen. Harold and William fought that battle of their own choosing. It was not determined by my knowledge. Likewise, God from the vantage point of his nonsuccessive, eternally present life knows that human beings will act successively in this or that manner. But his knowledge does not cause it to happen, even though each known event is or will be necessarily true. God does not err. So these events will surely happen. They are necessarily true in that sense. But they do not happen "of necessity," which is the phrase John used earlier. In other words, human events are *not* necessarily true in that they are *determined* by God. It is our freedom that causes them. God just happens to know what our freedom will decide.

JOHN: So God does not cause what we do?

MALCOLM: No, he just happens to know what we will do.

JOHN: And we do not cause what God does?

MALCOLM: Correct. God is not caused by anything.

JOHN: Why, Malcolm. How can you say such a thing? Don't you believe in prayer?

MALCOLM: You crafty devil! I see where you're taking us.

MARY: Yes, I do too. You're saying, John, that God must be

influenced by us. We influence him in prayer. We petition him to help us in our lives or in the lives of others. This means that God depends on us. We affect God!

BRIAN: You've brought up an interesting area of theological speculation, John. Prayer is a very mysterious thing.

JOHN: You may call it mysterious, but that won't be enough for you to salvage your philosophy. You see, the God you've described thus far is independent of any influence from contingent beings. If God is affected by contingent things, his necessity is undermined. But doesn't this pose a big problem for your belief in prayer. In order for God to hear or answer your prayers, he has to become aware of them. This means that there was a time when God was unaware of a prayer, then became aware of it. And he must also choose how to answer the prayer, if at all. This means that God changes; that there is a before and after in God. Your whole scholastic philosophy of God comes tumbling down. Or are you willing to give up your belief in prayer just to keep your scholasticism?

MALCOLM: Granted, John, you've brought up a challenging point. But I think it can be answered. I believe that human beings have a relationship with God and that prayer is one expression of that relationship. You assume that God has to be in time to hear and answer prayers. You assume that God must first be ignorant of a prayer and then come to know it. But God is not involved in temporal succession. Nor does prayer require that he is. God can know and answer our prayers from his perspective in eternity and thus not be under the influence of change, time, and contingency.

JEAN: How is that possible?

MALCOLM: God knows from all eternity what your prayer is going to be. From all eternity he has taken it into account and has decided to answer it one way or the other, perhaps affirmatively, perhaps negatively.

BRIAN: In this way God remains perfect and cognizant of our

prayers. If God did not know our prayers, he would not be perfect. In fact, it is precisely because God is perfect—hence omniscient— that he can be aware of our prayers for eternity. God is fully providential and responsive to our prayer life and still remains the God we have identified: the Necessary, Infinite Being.

RENEE: I'm not sure I am comfortable with that. Some people who hold the fideistic view believe that God is not completely perfect. God needs human beings, and God wants them to respond in prayer.

PATRICIA: Could I ask one last question?

MALCOLM: Go ahead, Patricia.

PATRICIA: It has to do with this emphasis on God as infinite. I think God's infinity might lead to a consequence that you and Brian might not fully realize. Doesn't God's infinity lead to *pantheism*?

MARY: What does that word mean exactly?

MALCOLM: Pantheism is the view that God is nature, the sum total of everything in the universe. Pantheism holds that God is identical with his creatures; that there is no real distinction between God and everything else, even though it appears that way.

PATRICIA: Right. And pantheism seems to follow from your philosophy of God, Malcolm. If God is infinite, then he is everything. Doesn't it follow that God has to be creatures too. Creatures have to be a part of God, encompassed by his infinite nature.

JOHN: That's quite a problem for your religion, isn't it, Malcolm? Don't you Christians, unlike followers of certain other religions, especially Eastern ones, maintain that God is really *different* from creatures? Don't you insist that God and his creation are separate beings? As a result, doesn't pantheism, which seems to follow from your philosophy of God, actually undermine your Christian faith?

MALCOLM: Clever try, John, but the answer is "no." Just because God is infinite and is the cause of all other existents, it does not follow that he is the same as his effects in existence or nature. Everything depends on God for existence. Each thing exists precisely through God's active causality. But this dependency is not identity. That things derive their existence from him does not mean that they are part of God's nature or that they are projections or manifestations of God—things really reducible to God in the last analysis. No, God is God distinctly. His infinity is unique. His infinity is his own. It does not encompass creatures. They exist because he elects to bring them into being through his power. He is present to them as his power conserves them in existence, but God remains really distinct from them. He *is* existence; they *have* existence. God is Pure Actuality, whose nature is to exist. Creatures in their nature only potentially exist; their natures become actual only as God gives them existence. Accordingly, God and creature are by no means the same. There is all the difference in the world between that whose nature is to exist and that whose nature is not to exist. Hence, pantheism doesn't follow even though the former is infinite in his nature.

MARY: It always happens. Talk about pantheism makes me hungry and tired.

RENEE: Before we go feed Mary, I'd like to ask something. If you're right that the necessary being approximates the Judeo-Christian God, what does this mean for all the other religions in the world? Does this count them out? I'm very uncomfortable with that implication.

MALCOLM: That's a very important question, Renee. That's the problem of religious pluralism. Perhaps we can get into that discussion at a later time. Believe me, it takes more than a few minutes to explore it!

FRANK: Come on, everybody. Mary's about to leave without us. The bistro beckons.

Key Terms and Distinctions

Analogy	Spirituality
Cause and effect	Simplicity
Principle of sufficient reason	Omnipotence
Monotheism	Omnipresence
Infinity	Immutability
Aseity	Eternity
Causality, negation, and eminence	Omniscience
Virtual perfection	Divine foreknowledge
Positive vs. negative theology	Necessarily true vs. true of
Metaphor	necessity
Analogy of attribution	Pantheism
Analogy of proportionality	

Questions on Chapter 2

1. What does Ivan Karamazov mean when he says that questions about God "are utterly inappropriate for a mind created with an idea of only three dimensions"?
2. Why is ordinary language significantly challenged when applied to God?
3. How does analogical language attempt to partly remedy problems of language about God?
4. Brian insists that one must first establish that God is a necessary being before uncovering the divine attributes. Why does he insist on this first step?
5. Why does divine infinity follow upon the fact that God is a necessary being?
6. Why can there be only one infinite being?
7. What are the ways of causality, negation, and eminence?
8. Can one say that certain perfections found in creatures exist in God? Why or why not? What does it mean to say God possesses these perfections *virtually*?
9. Select one (or more) of the attributes of God defended by Malcolm and Brian, and critically assess their argument.
10. What is the problem of divine foreknowledge?
11. How does the realization that there is no "before" or "after" in God help solve the problem of divine foreknowledge?
12. Why doesn't God's infinity imply pantheism?

13. If God is perfect in the sense explained by Malcolm is Renee right when she suggests that this kind of God would be too remote for prayer to be meaningful?

Bibliography

Adler, Mortimer, *How To Think About God* (New York: Macmillan, 1980).

Aquinas, St. Thomas, *Summa Theologiae,* Part I, Questions 3–25, Blackfriars Translation (New York: Benziger Brothers, 1947), pp. 14–141.

Augustine, *The Confessions* (original edition, 400), (Indianapolis: Hackett, 1993).

————, *On Christian Doctrine* (New York: Bobbs-Merrill, 1958).

Bobik, Joseph, *Aquinas on Being and Essence* (Notre Dame, IN: University of Notre Dame Press, 1965).

Boethius, *The Theological Tractates and The Consolation of Philosophy,* ed. H.G. Stewart and E.K. Rand (London: Heinemann, 1978).

Garrigou-Lagrange, R., *God, His Existence and Nature* (St. Louis: St. Louis University Press, 1934).

Gilson, Etienne, *Being and Some Philosophers* (Toronto: Pontifical Institute of Medieval Studies, 1952).

————, *The Christian Philosophy of St. Thomas Aquinas* (New York: Random House, 1956).

Maritain, Jacques, *Approaches to God* (New York: Harper & Brothers, 1954).

Mascall, E.L., *Existence and Analogy* (London: Longmans, Green, and Company, 1949).

————, *He Who Is* (London: Longmans, Green, and Company, 1943).

McInerny, Ralph, "Can God Be Named by Us?" *The Review of Metaphysics,* 32, no. 125 (September 1978): 53–73.

Owens, Joseph, *An Elementary Christian Metaphysics* (Milwaukee: Bruce, 1963).

Sillem, Edward, *Ways of Thinking About God* (New York: Sheed and Ward, 1961).

Smith, Gerard, *Natural Theology* (New York: Macmillan, 1951).

Sweeney, Leo, *Authentic Metaphysics in an Age of Unreality* (New York: Peter Lang, 1988).

Chapter Three
God and Evil

The topic of this conversation is the problem the fact of evil in the world raises for belief in an all-good and all-powerful God. Two versions of the problem of evil are discussed, with John arguing that evil gives us a good reason not to believe in God. Malcolm defends the theistic response to the problem of evil. The chapter concludes with a brief discussion of Augustinian and Irenaean theodicies.

MARY: These recent conversations, along with some of the meetings I've attended at the Institute, have really got me thinking these last few days.

FRANK: I know what you mean. Last night I kept going over some of the things we talked about yesterday. I haven't felt this intellectually challenged in ages!

JOHN: We raised good points on all sides, but there are some things still bothering me. I guess good intellectual conversations often prompt further questions.

BRIAN: I wonder if we could discuss today the problem the existence of evil in the world presents for religion and the existence of God? I am drawn again to this problem, especially after watching that movie, *Schindler's List,* about the holocaust this morning. The problem of evil has always bothered me. As a priest I see up close the reality of evil in human experience all too often. People often come and talk to me about the tragedies in their lives and ask me to explain how God can allow such awful things to happen. And what can I say? This is a very difficult part of my ministry. Just last week a very devout lady, whose son is a drug addict, asked me why God created a world in which such things happen. And the horrors of an event like the holocaust, captured so well in the movie, raise the same question.

yes, where was God?

If I were God, and I knew this was happening, I'd do something!

64   *Chapter Three*

RENEE: Yes, it is a very disturbing movie. I think that of all the possible objections to the existence of God, the problem of evil is probably the strongest, and the one with which the theist should be most concerned. It certainly bothers me a lot. It seems that evil is always with us, and it is so intrusive in all our lives. Do you agree, Malcolm?

[handwritten: most of the world is suffering]

MALCOLM: Yes, I do. Evil is a very difficult reality to come to terms with, and even if you do think you can reconcile it with the existence of God, which I do, it still does not seem to make the *fact* of evil all that much easier to deal with sometimes.

FRANK: I remember, though, when my uncle was killed in a car accident several years ago, our family's faith in God helped us through this very difficult period, except for his brother, who almost gave up his faith because of that tragedy. Don't you often feel, though, that faith in God—especially faith that there will be eternal happiness in the next life—is the only real way that one can cope with the problem of evil? I'm not saying that we should believe in God for that reason, but, given that there is other good evidence for the existence of God, as I think we have seen in the last few days, then doesn't the theistic response offer the most fruitful way to make sense of evil, even if it does not *completely* solve the problem? I often wonder, for example, how an atheist can make sense out of the reality of evil. At least the Christian has the hope that it all somehow makes sense.

[handwritten in left margin: good point; but what kind of God are you praying to?]

PATRICIA: Well, Frank, I think the fact of evil in the world is one of the best arguments against the existence of God. I have friends who do not believe in God for that very reason. My friend, Joe, for example, abandoned his religious faith altogether when his six-year-old daughter died of cancer. And it wasn't just because of grief or anger; it was because he really came to believe that an all-good God would not allow this to happen. So I'm not sure that Christianity can offer us any hope here. There is simply too much pointless evil in the world.

JEAN: My neighbor almost gave up his faith when his twenty-year-old daughter was killed in a car wreck. I wonder if we could begin our discussion, Malcolm, by stating what exactly we mean when we speak of evil and "the problem of evil" and how this problem is supposed to count as evidence against the existence of God? I raise this question because a friend of mine is fond of saying that a lot of what we call evil is really our own fault and that we shouldn't blame God all the time!

~ but why weren't we created so we

MALCOLM: You raise good questions, Jean, for there are a num- *couldn't* ber of important distinctions to be made in the discussion on evil. By an evil event, we usually mean an event that causes human or *be?* animal suffering or pain, for example, earthquakes, disease, mur- *evil?* der, mugging, and so on. The problem of evil, as it is usually described in the philosophy of religion, is the problem of how to reconcile the fact of evil in the world with the existence of a God who is supposed to be all-powerful, all-good, and all-knowing.

JOHN: I believe it is very reasonable to ask why God does not prevent evil if he is all-powerful.

PATRICIA: And since God is all-good, wouldn't he *want* to prevent evil? Surely, he does not enjoy watching people suffer, does he? *maybe*

he's a

BRIAN: We could solve the difficulty by saying either that God is *sadist* not all-powerful—that he doesn't have enough power to prevent *lol* the evil that does occur—or we could solve it by saying that, although God has the power, he will not prevent the evil from occurring because he is not all-good, that is, he enjoys evil! But neither of these answers is acceptable to the traditional Christian believer. This is why critics of theism who appeal to the problem of evil usually argue that the existence of evil makes it very likely that there is no God at all.

FRANK: Yes, evil is often presented not just as a problem for the religious believer, but as an argument not to believe in God at all. I think you're right, Renee, that a lot of people, including religious believers, do have difficulty with the existence of evil.

but why even though we have free will, why weren't we made to be more selfless?

why do these exist? our free will has nothing to do with this

MARY: But is it fair to blame God for all of the evil? Don't we have free will? Isn't a lot of the evil that occurs in the world our own fault? Last week, they caught a guy breaking into our house. Luckily, we were not there at the time. He was trying to steal money to buy drugs. Wasn't his act of wrongdoing *his* fault, not God's? Isn't he fully responsible for this evil deed?

MALCOLM: That is a good point, Mary, and leads me to introduce an important distinction. Philosophers usually distinguish between two kinds of evil, natural evil and moral evil. Natural evil would refer to evil events that seem to occur naturally in the world such as earthquakes, floods, famines, and disease. Moral evil refers to the evil actions of human beings, such as murder, rape, torture, robbery, and so on. The distinction is important because any proposed solution to the problem of evil must deal with the question of how an all-good and all-powerful God can allow *both* kinds of evil.

BRIAN: I remember from my reading on this topic, Malcolm, another distinction that seemed important. It was between what the author called the "logical" problem of evil and the "evidential" problem of evil. I couldn't quite grasp what was meant by the "logical" problem of evil. Could you explain the difference between these two different versions of the problem of evil?

JEAN: Well, Professor, you are on the spot again!

MALCOLM: I don't mind being put on the spot, as long as I know the answer! Brian, I am glad you brought up that distinction. It is an important one, and we need to introduce it before we move on to discuss some of the ways in which theists can respond to the problem of evil. Proponents of the "logical" problem of evil claim that the existence of an all-good and all-powerful God is *logically inconsistent* with the existence of evil in the world. This argument is interesting in that it is not making the weaker claim that the existence of God is *improbable* given the fact of evil, but the stronger claim that it is *logically impossible* for God to exist if evil exists.

FRANK: My brain is fuzzy today! I'm still not fully clear on what "logically inconsistent" means here.

RENEE: Someone bring Frank a cup of coffee!

BRIAN: Well, from my readings on this topic it seems to me that if we say that two statements are logically inconsistent, this means that if <u>one of them is true</u>, then the other <u>one cannot be true</u>. Have I got that right, Malcolm?

you can't have
both evil &
god?

MALCOLM: Exactly right, Brian!

RENEE: Brian, can I have your autograph!

MALCOLM: An example from ethics will help us understand the distinction. A typical criticism of moral relativism is that it is usually developed in a logically inconsistent way. This is because while the moral relativist says that moral values are relative to the individual or to the society and that no-one can impose his values on anyone else, at the same time the moral relativist usually wants both to advance moral absolutes and to impose these absolutes on others, for example, that murder is immoral, that racism is immoral, and so on.

PATRICIA: So the statement that "moral values are relative" is contradicted by the moral absolute that "racism is morally wrong"?

FRANK: Yes, and this contradiction is a common mistake made by those who engage in the rhetoric of moral relativism.

MALCOLM: Those who advance the logical problem of evil—such as John Mackie—argue that it is logically contradictory to say, on the one hand, that God is all-good and all-powerful, and to say, on the other hand, that God allows evil to occur. Philosophers like Mackie are suggesting that the existence of evil is logically incompatible with the existence of the traditional theistic God. He is not simply saying that because of the fact of evil the existence of the theistic God is *unlikely*.

JEAN: He is actually saying that it is logically *contradictory* for there to be the theistic God I believe in and for evil to exist in the world at the same time? I must say that I do not see the contradiction myself. It is not all that obvious, if it is there. Why then do so many believe in God despite evil? I mean, couldn't God have some *reason* for evil, which is why he permits it?

PATRICIA: I think Mackie has a point, though, for what reason could God have for evil, given that he is supposed to be all-good and all-powerful? Couldn't God prevent earthquakes? Does he have to allow murders to occur? Surely not?

MALCOLM: A well-known response to the logical problem of evil is what has become known as the "free will defense." Proponents of this argument, including St. Augustine (A.D. 354–430) and, more recently, Alvin Plantinga and John Hick, argue that the highest gift that God can give to his creatures is free will. This includes the freedom to do what we choose, including rejecting God. But free will comes with a price—it means that human beings can choose evil if they wish. The point is that it would not be possible for God to always *prevent* human beings from choosing evil, and yet at the same time ensure that they are fully free beings with a *genuine choice* between good and evil.

PATRICIA: Good point. I have heard that argument before, and it is an interesting one. So if God causes us to always make the right choice, then we are not really free. But if God is all-powerful isn't it possible for him to do anything? In particular, why couldn't God create human beings who are completely free, and yet who *always* choose the right thing to do instead of sometimes choosing wrongly?

JOHN: There is another difficulty for the free will defense. It is offered as an explanation for moral evil, but how would it explain natural evil such as earthquakes, famines, and disease? How can these be explained through free will?

MALCOLM: We can come back to your excellent question in a minute, John, when we return to the "evidential" problem of evil. But to address your concern first, Patricia, philosophers have usually argued that an omnipotent being is not a being who can do anything at all. There are some constraints even on omnipotence, as I mentioned in our conversation yesterday. Philosophers working on the problem of evil have often maintained that God cannot do what is logically impossible. He cannot square the circle for example, and he cannot create genuinely *free* beings who always at the same time choose the right path, and never the wrong path.

FRANK: Yes, that makes sense. If God wants to guarantee that human beings always choose the good path, then he would have to *cause* us to choose that path. But if he continuously forced us to select certain options, then we would not be really free. He wants me to *freely* choose helping Mrs. Jones across the road rather than leaving her stranded. But this is incompatible with *forcing* me to make this choice.

JEAN: I suppose it's like a parent who wants a child to choose correctly, but wants the child to do so freely rather than to force the child. I want my son to see that bullying kids at school is wrong and to freely choose not to do it. Right now, though, I am having difficulty with getting him to see that—and am simply forcing him not to bully kids!

MARY: Could you remind us again, Malcolm, of how the free will defense is a rejoinder to the logical problem of evil?

MALCOLM: Yes, it is a very good rejoinder, in my view, because it shows that a perfectly good and all-powerful God might create a world in which evil existed as a result of free human actions. This is because when God had the option of creating either beings whom he could cause to always choose the right path or genuinely free beings who will inevitably sometimes choose the wrong path, he chose the latter. Because freedom is the highest gift God can give to us. Jean makes this point well. A world in which we had no free choice would not be as good as a world in which we have free choice. It would be a world of robots and puppets.

PATRICIA: Okay, but how is this compatible with another belief about the nature of God—that he knows the future. How can he know what we are going to do, if he *doesn't* cause it?

JEAN: I am glad that I am not answering these questions.

MALCOLM: Well, as the U.S. Marines say, we do the difficult immediately, the impossible takes a little longer! We got into that issue a little bit yesterday in our discussion of the problem of the compatibility of God's foreknowledge (his knowledge of the future) with human freedom. The key point for our discussion is that perhaps *God* could know the future *without* causing it to happen, especially if he is outside time, as I argued yesterday. So if God does know the future, this would still not compromise the freedom of persons. It is true that human beings could not know what was going to happen with certainty unless they took steps to cause it to actually happen, but perhaps God could know the future without causing it.

MARY: I think the free will defense is a pretty good reply to the logical problem of evil. It does seem to show that God and the existence of evil are not logically incompatible. But the evidential objection is more serious, isn't it?

BRIAN: I have always found it to be a very clever argument precisely because its proponents usually don't claim to *prove* that God does not exist, only that it is *probable* that he does not exist. And while I do not accept that conclusion, I do admit that the argument has some merit and is not nearly as weak as some of the attacks on the cosmological argument are.

MALCOLM: Yes, the important move in the evidential argument is not only the attempt to prove that the existence of God is implausible due to the fact of evil in the world, but the similar claim that it is *rational* to be an atheist because of the problem of evil. This is an argument that William Rowe makes. Rowe is a contemporary philosopher who has had significant influence on current debate.

JEAN: I'm not sure evil can make it rational to be an atheist. I mean are you not throwing the baby out with the bathwater? What exactly is Rowe saying, Malcolm?

MALCOLM: He is making a more modest claim than those philosophers who advance the logical problem of evil. And yet he believes he has a *stronger* argument for atheism as a result. He is not claiming that the existence of evil definitely shows that there is no God. He knows this would be difficult to prove. He recognizes that a religious believer could still plausibly believe in God despite the fact of evil. He claims only that the existence of evil makes it *rational* to be an atheist. That is to say, because of evil, atheism is a reasonable or plausible position to hold.

JOHN: So he is not saying that evil makes it irrational to be a religious believer? Only that one could look at all of the evil in the world and plausibly conclude that there is no God, even if one could not quite prove this?

MALCOLM: Yes, that's it. In fact, he describes himself as a "friendly atheist" precisely because he believes that theism may well be a rational view as well. Rowe chooses to interpret the evidence as leading to the conclusion that there is no God, but someone else might interpret it as leading to the conclusion that there still very probably is a God despite the evil. He simply wants to establish that the atheistic response is a *plausible* response.

BRIAN: The intriguing part about this approach is that the religious believer usually does not want to grant the conclusion that atheism is a *plausible* response to the fact of evil.

MARY: How does Rowe develop his argument?

MALCOLM: His argument is pretty straightforward. He focuses especially on cases of apparently pointless or gratuitous evil. The response of theistic philosophers to the problem of evil usually must include some general argument stating only that God has a reason for evil, but not saying what that reason is. This approach is called a *defense*. Some philosophers such as St. Augustine go further and try to offer a theory to explain what God's reasons are for allowing evil. These theories are called *theodicies,* and we can come back to some of them in a little while. Rowe focuses on two features of the atheistic response to the theist's defense that there must be a reason for evil. First, he suggests that there are too many obvious cases of *pointless* natural evil in the world. The second point is a variant of the first: it suggests that there is *too much* natural evil in the world—surely God could have achieved his aim in allowing evil by allowing far less of it than we actually have? After all, look at all of the wars and horrors of human history, the pain in the animal world, and so on. Rowe especially emphasizes the pain in the animal world as a fairly clear case of excessive pointless evil.

MARY: But how does he know that there *really are* cases of pointless evil or gratuitous evil? Maybe cases that he thinks are pointless are really *not* pointless at all.

JOHN: Do you mean, Mary, that some good must come out of them? Would this good effect, if you like, be something we would know about, or would God conceal it from us?

MARY: I'm not sure about that, John, it is a good question. And it is still quite early in the day for me to answer difficult questions. I guess what I am saying is that in any given case of evil, some good might come out of it, and in some cases we might recognize this goodness, and in some cases we might not. But even in those cases where we do not *recognize* any goodness as coming from an instance of evil, there still might be some good that comes out of it. And my question is: How does Rowe know that no good comes out of those cases he is describing as "pointless?"

FRANK: An example here would help a lot. Let me introduce one that I remember my professor used in our ethics course in college. A drunk driver whom he knew personally killed a guy one day while driving under the influence. The drunk driver was so devastated at what had happened that he reformed and founded an organization to combat drunk driving. This organization even-

tually succeeded in getting a state law passed m
send drunk drivers to jail. And the good thing
that over the course of several years, the number
related to drunk driving went down dramatically
new law. This is a clear case of good coming out
from one point of view, much of human history is   __, ui progress of this kind where we introduce improvements to minimize
human suffering by learning from past mistakes.

BRIAN: That is a brilliant example, Frank. The problem for me
as a priest is when I am called upon to explain all of those *other*
cases where we can see no obvious good resulting from an evil
happening. All of those cases, to continue with your example,
where evil incidents related to drunk driving *do not* seem to produce *any* good.

JEAN: And, of course, a mother who has just lost her son is not
going to be too pleased with the view that this is for the greater
good of others.

RENEE: To go back to the *logical* problem of evil again, Malcolm,
the theistic philosopher, as I understand it, claims that God could
not prevent evil incidents like this without compromising free will?

MALCOLM: Yes, that's correct. But the *evidential* objection asks
why could God not have created a world in which incidents like
this were minimized and where those that do occur all have an
obvious point to them so that at least we would not come to
believe that much evil is pointless.

JEAN: But to repeat Mary's question, how can Rowe argue that
some incidents of evil *are* pointless? They might seem pointless to
us, but really have a point after all.

MALCOLM: Well, in a way that is where the strength of his argument lies. Let me illustrate with his example of a fawn trapped in a
forest fire and horribly burned. The fawn lies in agony for several
days and eventually dies. Rowe suggests that this evil is apparently

pointless, as far as we can see. Now he does not argue that it definitely is pointless, only that it is reasonable to look at this incident and the millions of similar occurrences and to conclude that they are pointless, and this supports the view that there very probably is no God.

JEAN: But couldn't there be a reason for the suffering of the fawn that we do not know about?

MALCOLM: Rowe acknowledges that there could be. He doesn't claim to *prove* that there is no reason for the suffering of the fawn. He simply says that it is very reasonable to conclude that there is no reason for it. Since it is pointless and it would make no sense to say God allows pointless evils, the conclusion that there is no God is rational.

BRIAN: But another person looking at the *same* case and concluding that nevertheless there still is a God would also be making a rational decision, according to Rowe?

MALCOLM: Well, he thinks they might be because just as the theist cannot prove that these evils are definitely not pointless, Rowe cannot prove that they definitely are pointless. The theist would believe in God not on the basis of cases of evil like this, of course, but by considering all of the evidence, including the arguments of natural theology, and concluding that, on the balance of the evidence, God exists. But I suppose Rowe might add that the theist still believes in God *despite* the problem of evil, whereas Rowe chooses not to believe in God *because* of the problem of evil. Though I would like to come back to that point momentarily when we consider some of the theistic replies.

JOHN: I think Rowe has a very strong argument. His claim that a lot of evil appears pointless is very plausible indeed. I mean what is the point of allowing little children to die of disease, just to take one example? It really seems pointless. Malcolm, how does the *amount* of evil in the world figure in his overall argument?

MALCOLM: He doesn't deny that in some cases we might be able to show how some good comes out of evil. For example, perhaps in a particular case of an animal suffering in the forest, a person walking by might hear the animal screaming, realize that the forest was on fire, alert authorities, and have the fire put out, thereby saving the nearby town from being burnt down. Rowe acknowledges that some cases of evil can have good effects, but he argues that it is very hard to believe that this is the case for *all* of the millions of cases of evil that have occurred in history. So it is very reasonable to disbelieve in God because of the amount of apparently pointless evil in the world.

RENEE: Even if there is a good effect in some cases, there is the added problem that Jean referred to earlier of using some people as *means* to that end. It is not much consolation to the person who actually does the suffering, like the person killed in our earlier drunk-driving example or even the actual fawn who suffers in this present example, to know that some good is coming out of it.

PATRICIA: Yes, I believe that Rowe has presented a reasonable case for the rationality of atheism. Has the theist any reply to these problems, Malcolm?

MALCOLM: I thought you would never ask, Patricia! The theist has several lines of response, and perhaps we could finish off our conversation by going through a few of them. One line of response is to suggest that it is a mistake to look at the problem of evil *in isolation* from all of the other evidence and arguments for the existence of God. It is a mistake to make a decision about the existence of God based on the fact of evil alone.

FRANK: Yes, I was just thinking that when I consider the whole issue of evil, I already have good evidence that there is a God. And how does evil invalidate that evidence? When you say "in isolation," I presume you mean in isolation from the cosmological argument?

MALCOLM: Yes, and from all other evidence and arguments that might bear on the existence of God question. What the theist might say is that when you look at the example of the fawn in the forest, you must take into account when you are weighing up the evidence, not only the apparently pointless suffering of the fawn, but also the question of where the universe came from, the questions of the origins and purpose of human life, and so on. And the theist argues that when you take all of that into account, the claim that the apparently pointless evil makes it likely that there is no God becomes much *less plausible* than it originally appeared.

RENEE: So theism in a way is regarded as the best explanation—for which there is good evidence like the cosmological argument, religious experiences, and so on—for all that exists, including, perhaps, evil?

MALCOLM: Well, most theists would say that theism is the only view within which the fact of evil can make sense. But my point here is that when looking at all of the evidence as a whole, even if one were to count the fact of evil negatively, the balance of the evidence still supports theism rather than atheism.

RENEE: There is another point that we haven't mentioned. If evil counts negatively against God, might not goodness count positively in favor of God? And there is more goodness than evil in the world. So that would have to be factored into the weighing of the evidence when one is judging the rationality of theism or atheism.

MALCOLM: Great insight, Renee. C.S. Lewis makes a similar point in his work on the problem of evil.

FRANK: You raise an interesting point, Malcolm, about atheism, or perhaps we should call it naturalism, since that is the most popular version of it today. I hope we can discuss the whole question of the meaning of life in more detail in a future conversation. But I have often wondered if not believing in God because of the *fact* of evil helps us very much. After all, it still doesn't explain the *fact* of evil. It makes evil even more pointless, because at least on the theistic view we have the hope and expectation that evil ultimately has a purpose, even if we cannot discern what that purpose is in this life. And if there really is an eternal paradise awaiting us in the next life, then perhaps evil will not look quite so bad from that vantage point. But on the naturalistic view, everything—not just evil happenings—seems pointless, since the universe and our place in it are simply accidental occurrences, and are part of no larger purpose or plan. In fact, it's difficult to see how a naturalist could even describe an event or happening as *evil,* given their worldview.

MARY: Your point, though, Frank really depends upon having a good reason to believe in God based on the cosmological argument or some of the other arguments. Because otherwise it would simply be a form of wishful thinking.

FRANK: You're right about that—but the cosmological argument is a very strong argument, I believe. I believe it does provide sufficient evidence to make theism a very reasonable hypothesis about the nature of reality.

PATRICIA: I think a key issue in the whole discussion is the problem of *natural* evil. I can see how the free will defense might be regarded as a good reply by some to the problem of moral evil, but I think that philosophers like Rowe have constructed a very good argument by appealing to natural evil. And I don't see how you can handle it, Malcolm.

MALCOLM: Yes, this is where theodicy comes in, though not all theistic philosophers agree that theodicy is a worthwhile or necessary enterprise. Some theists, as I mentioned earlier, believe the most we can say is that we have good reason to believe there is a God, and so there must be some good reason for evil, but we cannot work out what this reason is. Some would go further and say there is not even much point in speculating about what the reason might be because there is such a disparity between our mind and God's mind, among other things, that such speculation would be of little use. However, other philosophers such as St. Augustine, and more recently, C.S. Lewis and John Hick, have tried to go further than just saying that the existence of evil does not make the existence of God unlikely. They have tried to actually explain why evil exists—both natural and moral evil.

BRIAN: I have always been interested in St. Augustine's view, Malcolm, which I studied while in the seminary—the view that evil is a privation of goodness. I used to have long discussions with my fellow seminarians on this issue. Didn't he hold that the universe was in a fallen state, and then try to use this claim to explain evil?

MALCOLM: Yes, he wanted what most theodicists want—to explain the existence of evil without making God *directly* responsible for it. He did this by arguing that everything that God creates is good, and so if evil occurs, it must be explained as a privation, or lack, or deficiency in something that was originally good. He then argues that the reason we have evil in the world is because of free will. This argument for him explains both moral and natural evil. It explains moral evil because human beings are free and sometimes choose the bad. Augustine accepted the doctrine of the fall of man from an original ideal state and the doctrine of original sin and linked them to the notion of free will.

JOHN: How can this view explain natural evil, though, such as earthquakes and disease?

MALCOLM: St. Augustine believed that natural evil is the work of fallen angels who are free beings, such as the devil and other evil spirits. These are beings who have continued their rebellion against God even in the afterlife. More recently, Alvin Plantinga has offered a similar kind of argument and also links it to the free will defense. Augustine also believed that some natural evil was God's punishment for sin.

PATRICIA: Oh, puh-leeeeze! It is one thing to offer arguments for the existence of God, but surely one can no longer believe in the devil? Augustine accepts Christian theology too literally and too uncritically. His explanation of natural evil may have been all right in his own unenlightened time, but it surely cannot be an explanation of natural evil today.

MARY: I really think the idea of the devil, and eternal damnation, and all that stuff is out of date. You're right about that, Patricia. I believe God would never allow someone to suffer for all eternity anyway, and if he did, he would not be the kind of God I believe in. Such a God would be a tyrant. And the idea that evil is a punishment for sin is very implausible. Look at all of the innocent people who suffer!

FRANK: How do you know they are innocent?

JEAN: If you believe in God, then surely the existence of the devil is a possibility? Perhaps the existence of the devil might not turn out to be plausible philosophically or theologically, but even that conclusion must come at the end of the inquiry. To rule out the existence of the devil from the beginning is simply to assume naturalism.

JOHN: Well, one could simply reject St. Augustine's theology though, especially the doctrine of the Fall. To criticize him one simply has to refuse to concede to him the view that human beings were originally perfect. He has a problem with this anyway, it seems to me, for it doesn't explain why God allowed us to *fall* from our originally perfect state into an evil world. God is surely still responsible for setting things up this way. There is no way to get God off the hook, Malcolm. Even if St. Augustine changed his view to say we had a choice between good and evil right from the very beginning (that is, before the Fall), he still can't explain natural evil, without God turning out to be responsible for it.

MARY: You're wrong there, John. It would be explained by the free will defense.

JOHN: Yes, but God could still have prevented the devil or evil spirits from continuing to exist in the afterlife and committing acts of natural evil. That was my point.

MALCOLM: Other philosophers have maintained that evil—natural as well as moral—is necessary in order to recognize, understand, and appreciate goodness. That if we had a perfect world, at least some good actions and purposes, and perhaps even goodness itself, would not appear to make much sense. Versions of this argument have been advanced by St. Thomas Aquinas and by Richard Swinburne. Justice and compassion, for example, seem to make sense only when contrasted with injustice and hardship.

JEAN: Yes, I think there is something in that, especially as a way to understand moral evil. It might be difficult to appreciate good human conduct if we did not occasionally have bad conduct as well.

MARY: We would not be able to make improvements in the future, either, if we did not see how things had gone wrong in the past. My only worry with this view, though, is this: Is there not *too much* evil in the world for this to be a good suggestion as to why evil exists?

BRIAN: Too much natural evil or too much moral evil? Remember that the free will defense explains pretty well the existence of moral evil, no matter how much there is.

FRANK: Well, there is still a lot of natural evil though. We mentioned all of the evil in nature over millions of years, all of the countless tragedies involving human beings, and happenings of that sort. And it is only lately, don't forget, that we have been able to do much about some occurrences of natural evil, for example, disease. It is only in the last century or so that we have made significant medical advances. Before that people suffered badly, and the mortality rate was very high across the whole population. Why did God allow all of that?

JOHN: And don't forget, as John Hick has pointed out, that most of the human beings that have lived have died in infancy. What is the point of that? The answer to all of these questions is obvious: There is no God.

MALCOLM: There is a certain blurring of the line between natural and moral evil today, at least in some respects. For example, in the fourteenth century, the plague known as the Black Death wiped out almost three quarters of the population of Europe and parts of Asia, and we could do nothing about it. But what about today? Sometimes the spread of disease today is often our own fault, either individually or as a nation. If a million people died in the tenth century because of famine, this is clearly a case of natural evil. But if the same tragedy happens today (and it has), is it natural or moral evil, given that we have the knowledge, the resources, and the technology to prevent it?

MARY: And what about earthquakes? I mean, how can people live in California! If people are killed today in an earthquake, is that a natural evil or is it our own fault for living in cities that are built upon earthquake faults? Yes, Malcolm, I think you are right: The line is blurring. But what conclusion can we draw from this point?

MALCOLM: Well, it is too early to draw any substantive conclusion from it. But it could be that God is giving us the means to minimize natural evil. Or that more of the evil today is the product of free will, and so can be explained by the free will defense.

BRIAN: Malcolm, let us not finish without mentioning John Hick's explanation of evil. I have been reading his book *Evil and the God of Love* recently. I think he has an interesting approach.

MALCOLM: Yes, he has been an influential contemporary thinker on the problem of evil. His view is often called the "soul-making" theodicy or Irenaean theodicy and is interesting for its novel explanation of natural evil, though many think his view overall is quite speculative and not much supported by argument. He has been influenced by the writings of St. Irenaeus (A.D. 130–202) and offers his view as an alternative to St. Augustine's. He adopts the free will defense for moral evil. But he argues that the reason for natural evil is that God has created a world in which our purpose is to become morally and spiritually mature. For that reason, the world is full of spiritual and moral challenges, and natural evil plays a key role in these challenges. In the end, according to Hick, everyone is saved, because this is part of God's plan. Hick, however, realizes that many people do not appear to be in a state of moral or spiritual health when leaving this present life, so he is forced to speculate that the soul-making process continues after this life, and he even suggests that people may be reincarnated in future lives so that soul-making can be completed.

RENEE: So if you are raped, for example, as well as this being an evil happening, it would also be of benefit to you? Because it would help form your character? I don't want to be flippant, and I know his view is more sophisticated than we have time for here, and I assume he is talking about developing your character over the long term, but isn't this far-fetched? Wouldn't it be far better all round if there was no rape committed in the first place, both for the victim and for the rapist?

JOHN: It sounds even more speculative than St. Augustine.

MALCOLM: The main criticisms against it are that it is speculative with very little, if no, evidence to support it. Also, there seems to be far too much evil used by God in the attempt to develop our moral character. The means seem too excessive for the ends.

BRIAN: What struck me about his view is that he doesn't give sufficient weight to the countless cases where evil appears to destroy people and the cases where it clearly corrupts and certainly does not reform. In general, certain kinds of evil seem to corrupt more than they reform. I am particularly interested in whether he would have to regard the increase in crime today as perhaps a good thing? It could be argued on his view that crime gives all of those involved—both the victim and the perpetrator—an opportunity to build character, the former by making them stronger and the later by making them repent.

JEAN: Doesn't his view also imply what Augustine was trying to avoid: that evil is directly created by God to make us suffer, even if it is for a good purpose?

MALCOLM: Yes, his view would appear to be vulnerable to those good criticisms. However, he agrees with John that Augustine's view is no longer tenable today, and he thinks we need to offer some explanation for natural evil, in particular. He does make a good point about the natural world, one echoed by Swinburne. The natural world, according to Hick, operates according to physical laws, and these physical laws must hold consistently if we are to live in a stable universe. A stable universe is one in which much of benefit would accrue to us: For example, because the laws of physics always hold, we can build bridges, airplanes, and computers. But stability comes with a price, which is that sometimes natural evil occurs, for example, a rock falls off a mountain and crushes a house, killing the occupants.

JOHN: I do not see why God could not have built a natural world that mostly followed the laws of physics but that did *not* contain natural evils. Why, after all, when you are creating the world should you allow earthquakes to occur? Why not create a set of physical laws that allow us to have all or most of the good things but to have none of the bad effects? I do not think you can argue that this is logically impossible.

PATRICIA: And in those cases where natural evil is about to occur, why doesn't God intervene and prevent it? For example, if a bridge is about to collapse under the weight of a train, why doesn't God directly intervene and prevent the bridge from collapsing?

FRANK: Well, in some cases that might interfere with free will. For example, if the engineers who built the bridge had been deliberately negligent. That happened in my hometown a few years ago. A shopping center collapsed, and it emerged in the investigation that the engineers had deliberately cut costs, and they took huge risks to save money. So this evil event occurred because of free will.

MALCOLM: You all raise good points, and I don't think the theist wants to minimize them only to insist that they are not sufficient to disbelieve in God and that there is a good reason for them within a theistic worldview, even if we cannot discern that reason now. But it is only within a theistic worldview that there is any hope for an explanation. The atheist usually insists that evil happenings are so severe, and so numerous, and so apparently pointless that the fact of evil by itself at the very least makes atheism a rational option. But the theist argues that evil is not sufficient to disbelieve in God and that if we confine ourselves to the question of the rationality of both views, theism is clearly the more rational view, since it provides a plausible explanation for much of our experience, whereas atheism explains little or nothing. We have covered the key issues, I think, in this discussion on the problem of evil, and have we settled it?

RENEE: Does anyone here believe in lunch!

JOHN: I want to offer a defense of the view that at this time lunch is a rational option. . . !

FRANK: Would this be a moral or a natural lunch?

JEAN: Oh, puh-leeeze!

Key Terms and Distinctions

Evil	Evil and the rationality of atheism
Problem of evil	(Rowe)
Natural evil	Gratuitous evil
Moral evil	Natural theology and evil
Logical problem of evil	Augustinian theodicy
Evidential problem of evil	Irenaean theodicy
Free will defense	

Questions on Chapter 3

1. Could God have created a world in which human beings were genuinely free and in which there was no moral evil?
2. Is it necessary for evil to exist so that we can recognize, understand, and appreciate goodness?

3. Is natural evil, in particular, a special problem for the religious believer? If so, do you think the religious believer has a plausible way of dealing with this problem?

4. Compare and contrast the approaches of the free will defense and theodicy as ways of trying to deal with the problem of evil.

5. Compare and contrast the logical problem of evil with the evidential problem of evil.

6. Could God have (a) minimized moral evil more than he has without compromising human freedom, and (b) created a universe in which natural evil never occurs?

7. Is theism our only hope for dealing with the fact of evil?

8. Discuss the question of whether the problem of evil makes it rational to be an atheist.

9. Discuss the question of whether the problem of evil makes it irrational to be a theist.

Bibliography

Aquinas, St. Thomas, *Disputed Questions on the Power of God,* Part III, Article 6, in *The Pocket Aquinas,* ed. Vernon J. Bourke (New York: Washington Square, 1960).

Augustine, St., *On the Free Choice of the Will,* trans. Thomas Williams (Indianapolis: Hackett, 1993).

Hick, John, *Evil and the God of Love* (San Francisco: Harper & Row, 1978, revised edition).

Lewis, C.S., *The Problem of Pain* (New York: Macmillan, 1962).

Mackie, John, *The Miracle of Theism* (Oxford: Oxford University Press, 1982).

Plantinga, Alvin, *God, Freedom and Evil* (Grand Rapids, MI: Eerdmans, 1977).

Rowe, William, "The Problem of Evil and Some Varieties of Atheism," in *Contemporary Perspectives on Religious Epistemology,* ed. R. Douglas Geivett and Brendan Sweetman (New York: Oxford University Press, 1992), pp. 33–42.

Swinburne, Richard, "Some Major Strands of Theodicy," in *The Evidential Argument from Evil,* ed. Daniel Howard-Snyder (Bloomington: Indiana University Press, 1996), pp. 30–48.

Chapter Four

Life After Death

Forced inside by a midafternoon Rocky Mountain rainstorm, the friends enter into a discussion on immortality. Malcolm has given special attention to the subject. Patricia and John criticize Malcolm's arguments from the standpoint of naturalism. Malcolm assesses evidence found in the science of neurology to support his view that the mind is not reducible to brain and central nervous system; thus he defends the position that immortality is possible, that the mind could survive bodily death. He takes up the classic argument from concept formation to support his nonreductionist thesis as well. The dialogue ends with some reflections on the nature and significance of near-death and out-of-body experiences.

JEAN: Well, now that we're all here sitting around with coffee cups in our hands, why don't we engage in another discussion. I know just the topic, unless Renee finds it too sensitive and personal.

RENEE: No, not at all, Jean. Jean and I were talking this morning as we were walking the trail overlooking the cliffs. I talked about some personal things. As you know I lost a dear friend of mine this past year. And while at the funeral, hearing the pastor's sermon, I had some real pangs of doubt about whether I would ever see her again. I mean I had always believed in life after death, but when death confronts you in very personal terms, it takes on a new significance. Immortality is no longer just something you recite as part of the creed. It becomes a central test of one's hope and faith. Anyway, I'd really like to talk with you about it. Jean suggested I bring it up, if I got the chance.

PATRICIA: Are you sure you want to talk about it? I'm afraid some of us, if we were to speak frankly, would try to encourage your doubts. But I don't really want to do that. I mean I don't like to be in the business of upsetting people. You seem to find a lot of comfort in your faith. I'm not sure I feel comfortable undermining your hopes about the afterlife.

JEAN: Undermining my faith is not something you seemed to care about in our earlier discussions! I don't expect you to cut me any slack now. I'm a big girl. Besides you and John have not been successful in your efforts. My faith has only benefited by our conversations. I have a feeling, in spite of your doubts, Patricia, that my belief in life after death will also be strengthened by our discussion now.

JOHN: Well, I guess I can see why someone's belief in God might be helped by our discussions about God's existence, even if I'm not convinced, but this business about life after death seems clearly to be in the realm of sheer superstition. Life after death flies in the face of an obvious fact: When a person dies, he's a corpse. Corpses are not alive. Death is final. The brain dies. You're extinct. End of story. What's there to debate about that? To talk about life after death not only goes against science, it goes against common sense.

PATRICIA: I'm afraid I'd have to agree with John. I don't see how a modern, educated, intelligent person can believe in immortality. It's just medieval superstition. Oh, we might speak of life after death in metaphorical ways, but to suggest that one's consciousness, one's intact personality, survives beyond the grave is nonsense. If one clings to that belief, one holds to something irrational.

RENEE: Still, it's a very mysterious world. And I don't think you should just dismiss such things.

JOHN: You're not about to tell us you believe in ghosts too, are you, Renee?

RENEE: No. Well . . . maybe. I mean you can't just go around dismissing issues because they don't seem to fit in with what you regard as the "scientific" view of things. I'm not sure the questions of death, afterlife, and human destiny are scientific questions.

PATRICIA: Well, I see Malcolm over there sipping his Kona

blend, looking like a bemused despot as we all talk about this business. Maybe we should solicit his expertise. And I'd like to hear from Brian too. Isn't he in the business of preparing people for the great beyond?

MALCOLM: I must say, I've had a strong interest in this question. And it didn't develop because I teach a philosophy of mind class in which I have the students discuss immortality. No, my interest is personal. I woke up one morning and realized that someday I was going to die. From that moment, I became passionately focused on the question of immortality. It became for me one of those "existential" issues, as some philosophers like to say. I have now spent many years obsessing about the issue, and I have concluded that the arguments put forward by some philosophers that man is just a body and therefore will not survive death are unconvincing. I'm inclined to agree with many of the philosophers of old, among them the greatest, who have tried to defend the thesis that human persons can survive death. I think a case can be made for it. Does that mean, Patricia, that I can't qualify as a "modern, educated, intelligent person"?

PATRICIA: We might just have to consider you an exceptional case, Malcolm.

JOHN: Your arguments will have to be exceptional too. I for one would like to hear them, but I have to say beforehand that it seems to me you're just denying the obvious. After all, what's more obvious than a corpse? Show me corpses up walking around, then I'll believe in life after death.

PATRICIA: Yeah, that's what we'd call a miracle. And that's what it'll probably take to get me to change my mind about life after death.

MARY: Now, now. You don't want to close your minds before we get started. If you keep a little window open in those heads of yours, you might see things in a different light.

MALCOLM: To get started, let me sum up your view, John, and I presume it is also yours, Patricia. In short, you reject life after death on grounds that it contradicts empirical and scientific research.

JOHN: And don't forget ordinary experience too. I mean there is no evidence whatsoever to suggest that when a brain dies consciousness can continue. True, biology and neuroscience have advanced the hypothesis that the human mind is just the functioning of the brain, a physical organ. But you don't have to be a brain scientist to know that your mind is dependent on your brain. You hit somebody in the head with a rock, you can injure his brain, and that upsets the way his mind works. We've all seen the soap operas, where people have a head injury and end up in a coma or with amnesia. And taking it a step further, when the brain is completely destroyed, so is the person. Point me to someone without a brain who is still alive, conscious, and fully functioning, and I'll believe in life after death.

PATRICIA: That means that we should invest our hopes and energies in the here and now—you know, while we've got our brains.

JEAN: But don't you find life, then, a rather depressing and hopeless mess? I find it very dismaying to think that all we know and do will ultimately just perish.

PATRICIA: No, no. In a way, it makes life more precious. It makes you appreciate those you love and all the blessings of life, because you know it's brief and will end. This may come as a surprise to you, Jean, but I think a lot of people become indifferent to the significance and treasure of life because they believe in immortality. It makes them sort of lazy about the here-and-now, living on a kind of postponement plan. They don't put enough effort into seeking life's immediate rewards because they buy the idea that true meaning will be found in the hereafter. It's like a perverse form of deferred gratification.

JOHN: I couldn't agree more with Patricia. My guess is that this postponement of the meaning of life on the expectation of a hereafter is a source of considerable human misery. Because it's an excuse for people not to care for each other in this life. Marx thought religious teachings about the hereafter were the main reasons that people did not attend to their present, desperate economic plights. I think he was right. Remember that line from John Lennon's song, *Imagine:* "imagine all the people living for today." What a wonderful world this would be if people quit religion and gave up their superstitions about the afterlife.

RENEE: Well, if there is life after death, it certainly ought to influence what we think about and what we do in this life. Some people would say that their faith in the afterlife is what gives their life here and now meaning and hope. It's what energizes them and makes them productive in the here-and-now. It's also their consolation. Without that belief, they'd have nothing. Belief in the afterlife has a profound, practical impact on those who accept it, because they also doubt that life has meaning if there is no life after death. At least, life can't have any ultimate meaning. Doesn't science tell us that someday the whole solar system will fall apart? Where's the meaning of your life in the face of that sad finale?

MARY: Christianity certainly teaches that immortality ties in with the meaning of life. I have a suspicion that one of the reasons people are reluctant to believe in life after death is that it suggests that their life may be judged; that they're morally accountable. This they want to avoid. They want to live without answering to any standards but their own.

MALCOLM: Mary's made an interesting comment here, tying in immortality with morality. Her response further illustrates why religious believers have taken immortality seriously. But for now I'd prefer to separate the question of morality and the meaning of life from the debate about immortality. Let's defer those discussions to a later time. In order for us to keep matters philosophical and scientific, I think that we should discuss immortality without any appeal to religious assumptions or beliefs. I want to avoid the risk of confusing what we're doing with religious issues. I think it's very instructive to see whether one can marshal a purely *philosophical* defense of immortality. I think this will keep the waters from getting muddy.

JEAN: Fair enough.

MALCOLM: To begin, I think we should analyze John's and Patricia's dismissive assertion that life after death is nonsense. Let me ask some questions so as to get clearer on your position. Would you go so far as to say life after death is impossible?

JOHN: No, I wouldn't go that far. I wouldn't say it's contradictory to believe it. I suppose, if there were a God (whose existence I doubt, by the way), he could either resurrect the bodies of some of his creatures after they die or create them in the first place containing some spooky, spiritual stuff that survives death. So I'd grant that much: It's possible. But I'm not yet at all prepared to say that, even if God exists, there is any evidence that he made us immortal. Immortality might be logically possible, but there is no evidence for it, no reason to believe it's true. That's my position. When faced with a situation where all the evidence says that something is one way and not its opposite, it's not rational to believe the opposite. Well, all the evidence points to man's mortality. Hence, a rational person—one who believes things because of evidence rather than wishful thinking—must dismiss life after death as superstition.

MALCOLM: And your purported evidence is that, since our bodies die—specifically our brains and central nervous systems—then our minds and personalities perish, for our conscious life is only brain states and activities?

JOHN: Nicely summarized, Malcolm. You'd get an "A" in your philosophy of mind class for that pithy summary. You've expressed my view exactly: We're only flesh and bone, and when our bodies die, so do we.

MALCOLM: Your view tries to take the high-minded tone of obvious fact and natural science, but I think it really only declares an assumption as though it were established fact. You may not realize it, but your view begs the question; that is to say, it assumes a conclusion without really proving it.

᾽ more obvious than that people die?

᾽y die physically, but that doesn't end
᾽here it starts. Just saying that physi-
᾽ssion begs the question. You can't presup-
᾽ supposed to prove, and that's what you do when
᾽ıe matter with the evidence of physical death. You see,
᾽ believer in immortality holds that it is possible that human existence might mean more than just physical life. So the real question is whether physical death is completely and absolutely the end of life and personality?

PATRICIA: You talk about *our* assumptions masquerading as facts! It's the immortalist that has to come up with some evidence. We physicalists—we might call ourselves "mortalists"—have done our job. We observe and respect nature. And nature tells us in merciless terms: "People die."

MALCOLM: Again, I fear that you and John are doing what physicalists typically do. They grant brain death as evidence to deny immortality. But that is not to engage the debate. That is simply to assert and reassert your conclusion. You have to take up the challenge whether brain death is *sufficient* evidence that human consciousness has perished. If the human person need not exist entirely in physical form, then it is possible for him or her to survive the death of the body. You have to show that this is impossible or implausible. You can't just rule it out of court.

BRIAN: That's good, Malcolm. Yeah, the reason skeptics like John and Patricia can get away with snidely brushing off immortality and other religious truths is that the prevailing "climate of opinion" supports their view. Hence, in many circles there's nobody to protest their view publicly. So the impression is left that their view is the only respectable, intelligent one.

JOHN: Well, as I said before, I'm willing to grant that it's possible, in some purely logical sense, for there to be life after death.

But it's facts, empirical evidence, that tells the tale on questions like this, and a rational examination of the facts makes only the mortalist conclusion plausible. So I'll take your bait, Malcolm. Yes, immortality is very implausible. When we die physically, we also die psychically.

PATRICIA: It seems to me, Malcolm, that you're cleverly trying to shift the burden of proof to us. We've already done our job. We've given evidence—corpses, dead brains—as data persuasive of mortality. In the face of this evidence, belief in immortality is so implausible as to be counterintuitive. If the immortalist thinks otherwise, then it is he or she, not us skeptics, who have the burden of proof.

FRANK: I must say I've never fully appreciated the point that John mentioned earlier that when a person's brain is damaged, their mind, their conscious life, even their perception, is affected. The dependence of the mind on the brain is pretty clear by that example. Doesn't that pose a serious challenge to the immortalist? Doesn't that make it implausible that a mind could survive death? When death comes, don't they both die—the mind and its brain?

MALCOLM: I like the way you put that: "the mind and its brain." That expression reminds me of John Eccles's classic book, which he wrote with Karl Popper, entitled *The Self and Its Brain*. Eccles's point is that, while indeed there is dependency of the mind on the brain, there is likewise dependency of the brain on the mind. This last point is important. No sound philosopher would ever deny that there's some interdependence between mind and brain. But the mind's dependency on the brain does not necessarily imply that it is nothing but brain activity or its by-product. Perhaps I could make the point by putting it this way: the brain is a *necessary* but not a *sufficient* condition for mental life.

JEAN: What do you mean by that, exactly?

MALCOLM: An example should make it clear. A wheel is a necessary condition for a bicycle, but a wheel alone does not produce a bike. Many other components must be present. When enough are present, and when they are put in a right relationship, when these sufficient conditions are met, then you have a bicycle.

JOHN: But you can't use "sufficient conditions" as an excuse to believe just anything. In the spirit of Ockham's razor, I prefer not to admit any more entities than one has to in order to explain something. Neurology has shown that brain states and activities are *sufficient* to account for mental life. Since we know brains exist, and since you can explain consciousness in terms of brain function, why posit anything else?

MALCOLM: Well, John Eccles is a Nobel Prize–winning neurologist, and he disagrees. You see, the matter is far more controversial than you seem to realize.

PATRICIA: That's because people like you and Frank and Jean won't let go of your religious beliefs.

MALCOLM: No, no, no! Please get this straight: As I said before, this matter can be handled purely philosophically, and in a way that is sensitive to the scientific evidence. Just by looking at what experience gives us—*without* any recourse to religious belief—a very plausible case can be made for immortality. Moreover, it is a defense that shows your naturalistic view to be counterintuitive.

JOHN: If you're ready to do the honorable thing and take up the burden of proof; if you're ready to make your case that immortality is the more reasonable alternative, in spite of so much evidence to the contrary, then begin. We want to hear it.

PATRICIA: Should we put on the appropriate "new age" music?

MALCOLM: I refuse to be flustered by your sarcasm. I'm having too much fun. I will gladly answer your challenge. I can make a case for immortality by showing that my position, rather than yours, is really more plausible. You'll find my efforts quite interesting as I carefully show how your position—that brain alone ac-

counts for mental life—is exceedingly problematic. I can do this
by showing that there are certain operations of consciousness that
cannot be explained merely in terms of brain function. If there
are certain facts about mental life that cannot be accounted for by
brain states and brain activities alone, then one must conclude
that consciousness is, in some respects at least, irreducible to the
brain. If so, the mind need not perish with the body.

JOHN: Well, I for one would be very interested in hearing what
you have to say.

PATRICIA: I second that. But I should warn you, Malcolm, we're
not going to be content to sit in some medieval schoolroom while
you pontificate about Cartesian dualism or some such old hat.

JOHN: Right, Patricia. Isn't this issue about the mind and the
body really more suitable for scientific research than philosophical
speculation? I mean philosophers are reluctant to admit that science is more and more proving that mental function is just brain
function. As I said before, convince me that the brain doesn't
explain mental life and I'll reconsider the possibility of life after
death.

PATRICIA: Me too. But I'll have to admit that I'm a little jaded,
Malcolm. Years ago I took a philosophy of mind class and the
professor during the whole semester hardly mentioned the science of neurology! He acted as though the mind-body problem
was still just a philosophical dispute about Plato's and Descartes'
views. He occasionally acknowledged a few skeptics, like Hume
and Ryle, but it was clear he knew little about the scientific research on the brain and central nervous system. He therefore
neatly sidestepped any real challenge to his pet dualistic views.

JOHN: As you know, I went to medical school for a couple of
years. During that period of my life, I pored over neurology texts
and spoke to many neurologists. Hey, man, the verdict is in! Mental life is brain function. The evidence is overwhelming. Neurology, since the time of the great Dr. Wilder Penfield, has advanced

by leaps and bounds and is showing that the hypothesis that mind is just brain is the only sound one.

MALCOLM: Well, unlike your earlier professor, Patricia, I've studied some neurology myself. I've already mentioned Eccles. Many of these neurologists do not agree that the case is open and shut. Many of them would not admit that the mind-body problem is really just a body problem—that is, ultimately just a problem to be worked out in time by mapping the physical activity of the brain. You mentioned Dr. Penfield, the father of neurology. Well, he was a scientist who was struck by the mystery of the mind, so much so that he refused to reduce mental life to brain function. His experiments regarding memory, for example, led him to suspect that reductionism is false.

MARY: Could you fill us in?

MALCOLM: Dr. Penfield tried to help patients with epilepsy. Sometimes this required brain surgery. He would often make remarkable discoveries during surgical procedures. One day he found that electrode stimulation of a certain site in the cerebral cortex elicited long-term memories. In light of such an experiment, it would be only natural to conclude that memory has a specific location in the brain and results from the activity of that part of the brain.

RENEE: That would be the only plausible conclusion, wouldn't it?

MALCOLM: As it turned out, when Dr. Penfield excised that portion of the brain, the patient still retained long-term memories. In other words, the brain site is associated with the memory, but it does not seem to be identical with the memory or the cause of it. He was able to repeat this experiment a number of times. So it's a neurological fact: Long-term memory is not necessarily destroyed by damage to the brain.

JOHN: But I recall another study that showed that new memories cannot be formed if the hippocampus and the medial thalamus—

two parts of the brain often studied in connection with memory—
are damaged.

MALCOLM: Yes. I know that study. But *like* Dr. Penfield's experiments, the results show that *existing* memory is not affected by
injury to the hippocampus or medial thalamus. In other words,
injury to these parts of the brain prevent the formation of *new*
memories, but don't destroy memories *already* formed. In the absence of these functioning brain parts new memories are not
formed, but that doesn't mean that it is brain parts that form
memories or even store them. You see the problem?

BRIAN: Yeah, these researchers often confuse correlation with
causation. I mean two things may accompany each other, but that
doesn't mean they're related as cause and effect. When I go
swimming, I always wear blue trunks. But blue trunks don't cause
me to swim!

MALCOLM: A homely analogy, Father, but it'll do. Just because
brain states are associated with memory function, it does not follow that they cause memory or are the same as memory—that is to
say, that memory is *just* brain activity. Penfield's experiments and
these other studies give us good reason to think that correlation
doesn't prove that much.

JOHN: But what about E. Roy John and other neurologists who
have conclusively shown that memory is established by neural
pathways. Neuronal firings explain memory.

MALCOLM: I find it amusing how blithely people appeal to neurons to explain everything. Neurons, no doubt, are in some way
associated with mental life, but to reduce conscious activity such as
memory to neuron firings is pretty implausible. Brain neurons
often fire spontaneously, did you know that? They often fire in the
absence of any stimulus. They will also respond in the same way to
a stimulus relayed by different sense organs. So it's very difficult to
achieve any specificity and predictability in examination of neurons to account for something like memory. Not only is it difficult

to imagine how neurons would form memory, it's also difficult to understand how they would store memory. On this neurological theory, how could someone bring to mind an event that happened years ago without repeated mental attention to it and regular reinforcement? When you consider that the brain's neurological structure is constantly changing under the influence of various stimuli and chemical processes, it is implausible that the brain could store a memory over such a long period with no deviations in content from the original event now being recalled.

PATRICIA: That's a good point, but you've got to connect the examination of neurons with other evidence. I remember studying the work of A.R. Luria and Holger Hyden, who ran experiments proving that there is a purely physical basis for the preservation of memory. Hyden put rats in conditions where they faced the task of crossing a tightwire so as to obtain food. When they learned how to walk the tightwire, he killed them and compared the RNA content of their neuronal cells—the so-called dieters cells taken from the medulla—with a control group of animals that had not learned to walk the tightwire. The trained rats contained more RNA in their neurons than the control group. Hyden concluded that RNA causes memory preservation. This is unquestionably one of the most important discoveries in neurology. It gives powerful evidence for the physical basis of mental life.

MALCOLM: Yes, I'm familiar with these studies. And I find them quite impressive. However, we have to bridle our enthusiasm and not assume such research proves a physical basis for memory when it may not. These studies have been trenchantly evaluated by Robert Geis in his excellent book, *Personal Existence After Death*. I use his book in my class, and much of what I say throughout this discussion relies on his many brilliant observations and arguments. Geis repeatedly cautions us against confusing correlation with causation and identity. Keep in mind that just because two changes occur together, it doesn't follow that the one causes the other. It may be that there is a measurable change of RNA in the brains of rats after walking a tightwire, but this in itself is not evidence that the RNA explained that behavior.

BRIAN: That's what I was thinking. If the RNA change explains how the rat learned to cross the tightwire, what explains how it first crossed it?

MALCOLM: Exactly, Brian. If neuronal cell changes account for a new behavior, how are we to explain the behavior of the rat in first crossing the tightwire? How did it accomplish that feat in the first place? At that first instance, the neuronal change affecting behavior had presumably not yet occurred.

JOHN: Surely the scientists have an answer for that. They just mean that the rat crossed the tightwire more easily after the neuronal RNA change. Without the RNA change the rat would not have acquired its new skill.

MALCOLM: But there you have a problem. You can't just assume it's the RNA change that accounts for that newly discovered agility. You have to prove it. It is just as plausible that the RNA recomposition was caused by the rat's learning to cross the tightwire! Which came first, the learning or the RNA? Once you admit that the rat crossed the tightwire in the first place, that is, before the RNA change, then your position is significantly weakened. If the rat crosses the wire once without RNA being involved, why must its subsequent crossings be determined by RNA? See, you're objecting to my position on the *assumption* that learning and behavioral change are chemically caused. But that's the whole point, whether that's true or not. You have to demonstrate that they're chemically caused, not just assume it.

BRIAN: There seems to be another confusion in that research. They seem to confuse behavior modification with memory. Rats learning a new skill to get to a food source is behavior modification. But it seems funny to extrapolate from that to conclusions about the nature of memory. Long-term memory is not a behavior modification. Changes of behavior do nothing to advance our understanding of how long-term memory might be formed. So scientists drawing conclusions about memory from behavior modification have to justify how the latter is relevant to the former.

MALCOLM: Yes. For example, long-term memory does not usually need reinforcement for retention. Short-term memory—habit and behavior modification—responds to reinforcement. But since short-term memory is quite different from long-term memory, it's not clear that these studies are helpful in an explanation of long-term memory. As Brian points out, establishing a correlation between RNA and behavior modification is a long way from explaining memory in the strict sense, that is, long-term memory. If one is not alert to these differences, one might think these studies prove more than they really do.

PATRICIA: Well, I'm not ready to give up yet. Because I'm convinced that much of this is probably explained on the molecular or atomic levels. There's so much happening on that level, and it's so hard to investigate it and understand it. But I think that if we operate with such a hypothesis—that molecular activity explains conscious life, such as memory—we can make a case for physicalism, the view that there is no soul or mind, just a brain and a central nervous system.

MALCOLM: Okay, let's go with that for a minute. If you explain memories as molecular phenomena, you're obligated to show what kind of brain molecules they are. One thing is certain, these molecules would have to be complex, otherwise they wouldn't be large enough to account for the vast differences contained in the many kinds of memories we have. But this puts the physicalist in a difficult position. The only molecules that could qualify for such an explanation are the macromolecules within the nerve cells. But these molecules do not help the physicalist explain memory. Neurologists tell us that the constituents of nerve cells are proteins and the nucleic acids. The nucleic acids, of course, are DNA and RNA, the ribonucleic acid that carries the gene's DNA message and builds the protein molecules. In light of this fact, the formation of a memory would require the production of a new and distinct protein or RNA molecule; otherwise the memory could not be stored. But in order for new and different RNA and proteins to be manufactured, the neuronal genes would have to synthesize a totally new DNA sequence. Since memories come into being constantly as we experience more and more, there would have to be continuous change in the DNA sequence. But there is no evidence that the DNA of nerve cells constantly changes. To the contrary, neurologists tell us that DNA is stable; it is not replaced from moment to moment. The remarkable constancy of DNA is one of its most striking characteristics. You can read an account of that evidence in Colin Blakemore's book, *Mechanics of Mind.*

JOHN: But admittedly there is still a lot of mystery to the nature and workings of the brain. Neurology is really in its infancy. If we really respect the principle of Ockham's Razor, shouldn't we try first to work out problems using only a physical hypothesis and rely on philosophical explanations and solutions only as a last resort?

MALCOLM: But you can't use hypothetical method as an excuse to avoid criticism or as a rationalization for putting forward claims that don't make sense—claims that appear to be scientific when they're not. You see, John, it's very easy to assert that consciousness is the brain, but it's much harder to prove it or even to show that it is very plausible. And proof is the standard that judges hypothetical method. That's why I said before that when you examine the claims of the materialist, they often amount to little more than question-begging exercises. Let's just take a simple illustration. Where in the brain is located my awareness of this table? Is it a few centimeters behind my left eye? Is it near the parietal lobe? Also, I might ask, how big is it? Further, why doesn't my awareness of the table possess the resistance the table has when I push against it? Do the brain cells take on the characteristic of resistance? The table is solid. But my brain is not, even though Patricia often calls me hard-headed and my colleagues call me tough-minded. But if brain cells are unlike these traits in a table, how does the perception of resistance and solidity arise? See, the physicalist has a problem here. If perception of hardness and resistance is quite unlike brain tissue (which is soft), and if brain tissue is the same as perception or, at least, causes it, then why the difference? Again, we have the physicalist asserting something that he is not prepared to explain, let alone prove. It's one thing to grant that neurochemical processes correlate with conscious states; it's quite another to say they cause them. Everyone grants the former. Only physicalists grant the latter. But physicalists grant it arbitrarily if they can't justify it. And I don't see such a justification forthcoming. Robert Geis puts the matter eloquently when he says: "Might it be that as the notes of a musical score correspond to, but do not cause, beautiful sounds, the electrochemical events of the brain may correspond to, but do not cause, changes in awareness, perception?" So we're right back to granting that brain states are part of the story, but the physicalist has a long way to go to prove that brain states are the whole story.

BRIAN: So, in summary, you're saying that because consciousness appears to be significantly different from material objects, it's implausible to hold that a physical substance, like the brain, can cause consciousness?

MALCOLM: It seems to me to be a fair criticism, a fair question to ask. Physicalists speak as though neurology makes their case for them, but as I have argued, the neurological evidence really complicates their position. When you consider that the brain is bombarded with electro-impulses coming in from the sense organs, that sense activity, in terms of its physical mechanisms, consists of an atomized plurality of chaotic impulses and impressions, but that perception is uniform, coherent, and whole, you have to wonder what physicalism can explain at all about perception. Take this business about neurons firing again. If you study an EEG, the brain waves recorded there show that the neuro-electric charges are not steady. There is, as the scientists say, desynchronicity. Neuro-electric activity is not represented by a single continuous line, but as separate, closely placed lines or segments, signifying the rise and fall of intensity. But here you have the problem: the percept shows no such rise and fall of intensity as its data are given to the senses. This is the kind of thing that has to be explained. For, after all, according to the physicalist, perception is either the same as brain activity or caused by it. But if they're the same, how can they be so different? How can that which is uniform and continuous be the same as that which is discrete and discontinuous? If neuronal firings are the cause of perception, why is the effect so unlike the cause? Perhaps the physicalists can answer these questions, but they seem to dodge them.

PATRICIA: That's an interesting argument. I must say I hadn't thought of that before. But isn't there a way to deflect it. Sure, neuronal firings are different from perceptions in that they're separate, discontinuous firings, whereas perception moves uniformly. But it's important to remember that neurons are all the same in content, that is, in their nature. This is true whether we're talking about spinal or cerebral neurons. These impulses are made up of electrical charges, flows of electrons, and electrons are all the same.

JOHN: Yes, that's no doubt part of the inspiration behind research into artificial intelligence. The assumption is that, just as human consciousness is the result of the neuronal flow of electrons, so a computer might have consciousness, since its software operations consist of the flow of electrons.

MALCOLM: The key word here is "assumption." That human consciousness can be explained as neurons is not plausible. That is just one of innumerable problems with the whole idea of artificial intelligence. It's taken seriously by fewer and fewer scientists and philosophers who look into the matter critically.

BRIAN: I'd like to hear you comment on artificial intelligence. I don't know much about it, but it sounds kind of fishy to me.

MALCOLM: To begin with, the uniform nature of the electrons that make up the electric flow of neurons—to which Patricia cleverly refers as an attempt to escape the problem concerning the separate, interrupted firings of neurons being unlike perception— just adds another complication to the physicalist's task. While perception is uniform, which makes it unlike neuronal impulses, the actual content of perception—that is, what specifically is being experienced—varies from moment to moment. This variation of the content makes perception quite unlike the flow of electrons along neuronal pathways. Those electrons are always chemically and physically the same. How can such sameness account for the flux of perception?

BRIAN: So it looks like you've got the physicalist coming and going.

MALCOLM: As I keep saying, at least the physicalist has a lot of explaining to do.

RENEE: You mentioned that you have other grounds for doubting artificial intelligence.

MALCOLM: I agree with Roger Penrose, John Searle, Stanley Jaki, and other scientists and philosophers who deny that computer function is an acceptable analogue for human consciousness. Penrose, to name one, in his book, *The Emperor's New Mind,* summarily shows that, while research into computers is very worthwhile—computers are wonderful technological tools for human beings—this research will not produce mechanical minds, computers with humanlike intelligence.

RENEE: I'm sure Dr. Penrose has disappointed science fiction enthusiasts everywhere.

MALCOLM: "Fiction" is the proper word. Penrose explains that computerized machines can only process information algorithmically, that is, computationally. Computers perform operations according to set rules and procedures that make up their program. In this way, they are different *in kind* from human minds. While it is true that human beings often appear to process information in this way, we don't always. We are endowed with intuitive powers that often enable us to grasp the truth of things without recourse to algorithms. An example of this is the famous mathematical theorem of Kurt Gödel. I'll spare you the details, but it involves paradoxes in axiomatic systems in mathematics. Once the human mind understands Gödel's explanation, it knows that his claim is true. But it is not true by a demonstration. It is not reached algorithmically or computationally. There is no way a computer is capable of this knowledge by insight, given that the machine, by its very nature, is determined to process information by a computational program. Anyway, you're right, Brian, I'm skeptical about AI research. The so-called cognitive revolution, which is preached by the "cognitive scientists" and the AI researchers, naively presupposes physicalism and, as a result, is philosophically misguided.

BRIAN: You mean a wild goose chase?

MALCOLM: Something like that.

RENEE: So, the mind is a mystery that involves questions that science just can't answer?

PATRICIA: I'm confident that someday scientists will answer most, if not all, of them, just as scientists have been able eventually to explain so many other mysteries.

JOHN: Right, Patricia. All kinds of things in the past seemed to defy scientific explanation—like the changes of the seasons, lightning, the movement of the sun, changes in the tides, the onset of smallpox. But in time science did account for these things. My guess is that the same will happen with the mind-body problem.

BRIAN: Isn't that just another dodge, though? Don't forget, you began by claiming that science had *already* solved the mind-body problem. You can't let the physicalist off the hook just by saying "someday there'll be a scientific answer." Isn't that an argument by postponement? Shouldn't one in all intellectual honesty acknowledge the limits of his position and grant indeed, as Malcolm has argued, that physicalism is the less plausible choice?

MALCOLM: Yes. I have a colleague who refers to Patricia's maneuver as "the scientific faith argument," the view that scientists may not be able to explain something now, but they'll explain everything eventually. Therefore, we should accept physicalism as already true. It's a question-begging argument in the philosophy of mind debate that appears time and again among the writings of the physicalists, and it is especially evident among the AI researchers.

JEAN: I think it's a device for ducking tough criticisms.

MARY: Funny, isn't it. These physicalists don't seem to think it's intellectually responsible for anyone else to operate on faith, but they sure seem to do a lot of it with this—er, what do you call it?—"scientific faith argument."

MALCOLM: Well said, Jean and Mary. You will notice that I've avoided any appeals to faith on my own part. Hard, cold evidence is all that interests me.

JOHN: As far as I'm concerned, you still haven't discovered the "smoking gun" to make your case that physicalism is implausible. Remember, I said I'd be satisfied only when you showed me people without brains who are still alive!

MALCOLM: This may surprise you, John, but that's a challenge I can meet. I've got that smoking gun!

JOHN: You've been putting something strange in your coffee again, Malcolm. You'll be seeing pink elephants next!

MALCOLM: No, I'm serious. Have you ever heard of a neurologist named John Loerber?

JOHN: No. But let me guess. He stole your brain, and you're here to give testimony.

MALCOLM: No, I'm still the first and proud owner of my brain. But let me tell you about Dr. Loerber. Dr. Loerber studied hydrocephalic students at the University of London. The results of his research are discussed in an article by Roger Lewin in a 1980 issue of the journal *Science*. Dr. Loerber discovered that many of them had virtually no brains! Their heads were filled mainly with cerebrospinal fluid. His research found that the cerebral mantle of these hydrocephalic students had been so desiccated that they were left with virtually nothing but brain stems. Yet some of them were honor students with very high IQs! Again, we have a case of the facts contradicting neurological dogma: A profoundly damaged cerebrum should impair intellectual and perceptual function, but in these hydrocephalic patients, such is not the case. So there's the answer to your claim, John, that the brain is everything in conscious life. There appear to be fully functioning human beings without brains after all!

JOHN: Get a grip, Malcolm. I'm sure Lewin wrote that article tongue-in-cheek.

PATRICIA: Besides, that's not such a shocking study. Scientists have performed experiments on rats in which they remove parts of their brain, and if it's done gradually, the rats continue to function pretty well. And that's analogous to what happens under the pathology of hydrocephaly. The brain sort of dissolves away very slowly. It's sudden, catastrophic damage that is the problem. With sudden trauma, the brain doesn't have time to compensate for damage by transferring the function of the injured area to neighboring parts. So it turns out that Loerber's research fits in with neurological "dogma" in spite of what you say.

JOHN: Yes. I remember reading about that sort of thing in medical school. Neurologists refer to the capacity of one part of the brain to compensate for loss in another part as "redundancy." Another part of the brain gradually recircuits and takes up the activity of the damaged tissues. The brain is amazing. It can do that.

MALCOLM: This redundancy thing is kind of tricky.

PATRICIA: I knew you were going to say something like that.

MALCOLM: You can't get much out of this redundancy hypothesis. Sometimes redundancy presumably works after brain damage, sometimes it doesn't. It then lacks predictability and loses explanatory power, becoming, in a word, an *ad hoc* explanation—a cavalier attempt to save the physicalist's hypothesis against contrary evidence.

JEAN: Could you explain that further, Malcolm?

MALCOLM: Notice how the physicalist argues in his appeal to redundancy. He says, first, that in those instances where brain damage does not produce impaired consciousness that redundancy occurred. In other words, some other area of the brain took over and compensated for the impairment to the original site. Secondly, the physicalist says that where brain damage does indeed produce impaired consciousness redundancy did not occur. The other brain tissues did not take over for the impaired site. But this explains nothing! If the redundancy hypothesis is really *scientific*, that is to say, if it has real predictability and explanatory power, it must also *account for why* redundancy did not take place in those cases in which it did not. But that would involve identifying precisely what happens in the brain to explain such cases. The physicalist does not provide this kind of evidence. He just says "redundancy occurs" or "redundancy does not occur." But he has to do more than that. He has to explain why!

PATRICIA: I'm confident that as scientists run further experiments on the brain, they'll come to better understand how such a phenomenon as redundancy occurs and why.

JOHN: Yes, it's the experimental method that will set the physicalist free.

MALCOLM: I hate to be the bearer of bad news, guys, but as I read summaries of the experimental research, the evidence seems to worsen daily for the physicalist. For example, ever hear of Benjamin Libet?

PATRICIA: Yes, I've read about his experiments in Daniel Dennett's book, *Consciousness Explained*. My nephew read it in college. I looked it over once while he visited me for the holidays.

MALCOLM: Libet is another prominent neurologist. He's been able to repeat the results of this study many times. This experiment really throws a grenade in the bunker of the physicalists.

Daniel Dennett, as Patricia mentions, spends almost a chapter trying to cope with Libet's findings. Dr. Libet stimulated persons' hands when undergoing brain surgery. He attached electrodes to their cerebral cortices in order to see how the brain registered the cause-effect relationship of brain and stimulus. Of course, according to orthodox neurology, the cerebral cortex should register activity and the experience of the stimulation should follow. But what in fact happens is that the patient reports a conscious event—feeling the hand stimulation—a full half-second before there is corresponding registration in the cerebral cortex. This means there appears to be powerful experimental evidence that conscious activity—in this case, perception—can occur independently of cortical activity.

PATRICIA: But as Dennett argues, perhaps another part of the brain, not the cortex, is responsible for the stimulus. If I recall, he suggests that maybe the limbic system regulates neural perceptions of temporal events in a way different from the cerebral cortex. Perhaps it is through the limbic system that the cause-effect relationship is taking place. If so, that would account for the apparent temporal disparity. True, orthodox neurology may have to be adjusted, but brain alone could still account for the experimental results. But again, as I said earlier, we'll have to wait and see.

MALCOLM: Well, at least these experiments show that the physicalists still have a lot of explaining to do. I think we can say this much: reductionism of mind to brain is not so obvious as the physicalists would have us believe.

BRIAN: I, for one, think that Malcolm has given us good reasons to think that survival at death is quite plausible.

PATRICIA: Even I have to admit that you've assayed the neurological evidence in a very provocative way.

JOHN: I would like to compliment you too, Malcolm, especially in the way that you did not haul out all the old philosophical blunderbusses to criticize our position.

PATRICIA: Yeah, you spared us all the droning on about universals, intentionality, personal identity, first person subjectivity, and all that jazz.

MALCOLM: I must say that I do find all those standard philosophical arguments convincing. But I've found that when you're discussing the mind-body problem with die-hard physicalists, it's best to target the neurological evidence.

FRANK: Time has just flown by. I'm enjoying this discussion too much to bring it to a close. So please, Malcolm, what are some of these classic philosophical arguments that Patricia just referred to?

MALCOLM: If we move outside the realm of neurology and handle the mind-body problem purely philosophically, we come across long-standing arguments that call into question physicalism. I'm not going to discuss all of them. But I will summarize my favorite one—the argument from concept formation, which Patricia hinted at by using the word "universals," a word that stands for concepts, an argument that goes as far back as Plato and Aristotle. Many philosophers still find it persuasive. I give it considerable attention in my philosophy of mind class, so it's still fresh in my memory, since I just finished teaching that course this past semester.

JOHN: Okay. Let's hear it. Or should I say I'm all ears, to keep things as physical as possible?

MALCOLM: Be patient. It'll take me a few minutes to present it fully. This argument appeals to the human intellect's unique capacity to form concepts. In general syllogistic form, it goes like this: if human beings can form concepts, then they have a faculty (namely, the intellect) that is nonphysical. But human beings can form concepts; hence, they have a nonphysical cognitive power (the intellect). One can draw the obvious consequence that, if we're endowed with a nonphysical power, then why must it perish with the body?

PATRICIA: Of course, you'll have to say far more to convince us.

MALCOLM: I know. I gave you the argument in general outline just to make clear its basic content and aims. But I think I can discuss the issue with you specifically so as to make it clear and convincing. Let me first say this: No object known by our senses is general in nature. Sense experience acquaints us only with physical things, which are always particular, always singular.

MARY: When philosophers start talking about the general versus the particular, the one and the many, and all that sort of thing I want to go on to other things. Can you give us some examples? Maybe that would help.

MALCOLM: For example, I perceive such physical things as *this* tree, *this* dog, *this* triangle, *this* man, *this* horse, and so on. These are particulars, sensible objects. And these physical things always have spatio-temporal determinations.

BRIAN: That's just a fancy way of saying that they are located in space and time.

MALCOLM: Right. Sensible objects are also divisible, having parts outside of parts. Questions of space, time, and divisiblity, accordingly, are relevant and coherent when asked about singulars. But not all awareness is of what is singular. In addition to knowledge of singular objects, I am also aware of *general* objects.

PATRICIA: This might be where we will disagree.

MALCOLM: Surely. But these general objects are really known. These are awarenesses derived from my knowledge of traits common to sense objects. By focusing my awareness exclusively on traits common to sense objects and by ignoring altogether the particulars to which these traits belong, I have the power to form general objects of knowledge, in a word, "concepts."

PATRICIA: Boy, you really are reaching into the past. No philosophers that I read believe anymore in such odd entities as universals or forms. That went out of philosophical fashion centuries ago.

JOHN: I knew it. We've matriculated into that medieval school-room!

MALCOLM: Hey, I told you this argument was a golden oldie. Anyway, I'd rather call these general awarenesses "concepts" rather than "forms" or even "universals." That way you won't make the mistake of thinking I'm some kind of Platonist.

JOHN: If you ask me, you're taking us on a ride in Mr. Peabody's "Way-Back Machine" by talking about this kind of stuff. It's down-right archaic!

MALCOLM: Well, I stubbornly refuse to give up principles that make sense just because they conflict with prevailing intellectual fashions. Trends come and go. The truth remains. I refuse to be a slave to the former at the expense of the latter. Having expressed my indignation, let me continue. This operation whereby I focus my awareness on traits of particulars while remaining indifferent to the particulars themselves is called abstraction. These general no-tions (concepts), which result from the activity of abstraction, have a basis in sense-experience, but they transcend sense-experience in that they are general. As a result, questions of space, time, and divisibility seem irrelevant and incoherent when asked about them. The mental content of a given concept captures a sameness about things, irrespective of the particulars to which it may be ascribed. Consequently, it is a kind of knowledge that is nonsensory.

RENEE: Could we beg you for some examples again?

MALCOLM: As an example, take the term "animal." This term signifies a concept that differs sharply from physical, sense-particu-lars in an evident way. No physical existent possesses the attributes "dog," "horse," "hawk," "lungfish," "beetle," "snail," and "lizard." No singular happens to be all of these things at once. No physical thing really has the traits that make both a lizard and a hawk, for example. But my concept of "animal" is under no such restriction. In precisely the same sense my concept of "animal" applies to "all living things capable of locomotion and sense-knowledge." Moreover, I can think of the meaning of this concept without any regard for its instances at all.

FRANK: Interesting, but how does this all apply to the mind-body problem?

MALCOLM: I can explain. In light of what I've said so far, my mind apprehends general objects or concepts. These objects are called "intelligibles," and my cognitive power that grasps them is correspondingly called "intellect." Concepts, then, are not known by the senses but by the intellect. But concepts or intelligibles, since general (or nonparticular), are nonphysical. Since my intellect grasps the nonphysical, it must itself be nonphysical. Immaterial activity cannot be caused by matter. Matter is bound by the laws of physics. Matter has spatial and temporal properties. How can it produce something that has no such physical constraints? The nonphysical has a kind of perfection, freedom from physical constraints, that does not belong to matter. An important conclusion follows. Given that something cannot come from nothing, material being cannot produce immaterial being. This means that conceptual awareness is evidence that the nature of the human knower is in part nonphysical. And this shows that the human intellect is not a bodily organ, which may imply also the possibility of its survival after bodily death.

JOHN: There's only one problem with this argument: There aren't concepts. Concepts or what you medieval types used to call "universals" are fictions. Philosophers in the old days fooled themselves into thinking there are such things. Language misleads us. Because we speak in general terms, or use terms that don't refer to any one particular thing—like when I use the word "man" and don't mean Patricia here or Frank—we mistakenly conclude there are general natures, or forms, or universals. But this is all a mistake.

MALCOLM: Well, I agree to this extent: There are not *real* universals, that is, universals that exist independently or outside of the mind. But still, there is a foundation in real things for these universals, what I call "concepts," that we form by abstraction—you know, when we separate in our thinking the sameness of traits in an individual from the physical conditions that make it an individual. And this sameness at least enables us to form universals or concepts *in our minds*. And that's what counts for purposes of this discussion. After all, my point is that a certain feature of our mental awareness—namely, our knowledge of general notions or concepts—establishes that our minds are not altogether physical. And that conclusion opens the door to the possibility of immortality.

RENEE: I think I figured out what Malcolm is trying to say. Now, you've confused me, John. What do you mean when you say philosophers like Malcolm have "fooled" themselves?

JOHN: Well, I'm saying that there aren't these so-called "universal" or "general notions" anywhere, whether inside or outside of the mind. Philosophers like Malcolm have been misled in their thinking and their language. They conclude mistakenly that there are such generalities. But there's no need to think these things exist somehow in our minds. Our minds only know sense-particulars. But our minds have organizing powers whereby through habit and custom we develop behaviors in which we apply names in a general way. The names don't refer to general objects, as Malcolm would have it; they just are associated with certain behaviors that enable us to refer to groups or representations of such groups without referring to anyone particular in the group. For example, I use the word "mammal" to refer to a class that certain particulars might belong. But mammal isn't a general notion or nature, it's just a naming device that helps us know that some particular animals—fur-bearing ones, for example—can be represented by it and some cannot. But it derives from conventional usage, not by some kind of unique awareness of general natures or concepts or whatever. Names don't refer to anything but particulars or to ways of organizing particulars. To think otherwise is to fall victim to the errors that gave rise to medieval metaphysics.

RENEE: But if you can think of the name independently of its particulars, isn't that to make Malcolm's point for him?

JOHN: No. I can focus on the name and its usage but this

doesn't mean it signifies general objects. The name may carry with it the suggestion of some vague particular, but not of a general object. Having a vague particular in mind is all that is needed to apply names to what we call classes of things. The vague particular represents all the others, enabling classification and other types of general usage. This is a far cry from saying that general names refer to universals.

MALCOLM: Your reply is quite clever, John. It's essentially David Hume's argument against universals. His view and yours is called "nominalism," after the Latin word, *nomina,* which means names. Unfortunately, it does not succeed. Why? Because it's self-refuting. It presupposes precisely what it denies. The problem for nominalism is this: We have a *reason* for applying the names correctly, and that reason is that certain particulars have things in common. You presuppose this yourself when you give a reason—a common trait—to specify the reference of "mammal" to animals that are fur-bearing. Also your reference to a "vague particular" further makes my case. It's vague because the mind is really not thinking of particulars primarily but of what they have in common. And that's my point. The mind is not limited to just having particulars as its objects.

MARY: Oh, I see. We know not to confuse the name "mammal" for the name "fish" because what's common to those particulars called "mammals" is not what is common to those called "fish." Because sameness of traits is the basis for the correct application of names, the nominalist implicitly accepts what he denies: There are in things common traits, the foundation for the formation of general notions, concepts, like "mammal" or "fish," or "animal."

JOHN: I think you've underestimated the power that custom and habit exercises over people's behavior.

MALCOLM: No, I think you've overestimated the power of convention. By appealing to convention to explain away general awarenesses, you've refuted yourself again. Because convention is always applied with a criterion. But a criterion establishes a *same-*

ness that runs throughout different instances, different appropriate applications of the conventional usage. Therefore, by appealing to convention, you've again made my case for me. That's why the custom or convention of using certain names for certain types of particulars came up in the first place.

RENEE: Can we take a recess now and step outside the medieval schoolroom. Let's leave this discussion about universals for you philosophers to work out later. In the meantime, would you comment, Malcolm, on near-death and out-of-body experiences. I've read a lot about that in newspapers and magazines. I've even read some of Dr. Raymond Moody's books. I find it all very fascinating. I would like to hear what you make of it.

FRANK: Yes, I would too.

MALCOLM: I've read some of the literature myself, especially the work of Dr. Kenneth Ring at the University of Connecticut. He's a tough-minded empiricist who tries to determine whether there is anything we can learn scientifically from these events. His book, *Heading Towards Omega,* was the first text I read on the subject, and I found it totally fascinating. Afterward, I looked into the work of Raymond Moody, a philosopher and a medical doctor at the University of Georgia. His book, *The Light Beyond,* is very instructive. I'm also familiar with Michael Sabom's book, *Recollections of Death: A Medical Investigation.* His contributions are helpful. He is a very cautious interpreter of the evidence. Most recently, I read Dr. Melvin Morse's book, *Closer to the Light,* a poignant study of children who report having had NDE's and OBE's. There's a lot of interesting research being done on these phenomena. Researchers going into the subject rather skeptical are often so impressed that they become convinced that these experiences are authentic. Moody and Morse, while initially skeptical, have both changed their minds and are convinced that these experiences are veridical.

RENEE: Which means that they believe that the NDE and the OBE indicate that there is life after death?

MALCOLM: Yes.

JEAN: What exactly is the difference between the NDE and the OBE?

MALCOLM: The NDE refers to an experience at the moment or near the moment of death that is characterized by an ecstatic sense of well-being. The experience typically involves a variety of features. For example, people who have had these experiences and have come back to tell about them report that they, upon death, floated through a dark tunnel, toward a brilliant light, which emanated warmth and love. This light was a person, communicating universal knowledge as well as love, enabling the deceased to review his or her entire life, including a moral evaluation of it. The light made clear what was most important in life, and now having experienced it, the deceased wanted to be with it forever. In fact, most persons who undergo the near death experience are genuinely upset when they discover that they have come back to this life, back to earthly consciousness.

FRANK: And the OBE?

MALCOLM: The OBE might be thought of as a special part of some NDE experiences. Kenneth Ring found that 37 percent of NDErs experienced an OBE. The out-of-body experience consists of a sensation of being separated from one's body and, like a detached spectator, viewing it from a distance. The deceased is aware of being separated from his body and is aware of having now a different kind of consciousness—a nonbodily consciousness.

JOHN: You don't really take any of this stuff seriously, do you Malcolm?

MALCOLM: I wouldn't go so far as to say the NDE or the OBE proves immortality, but they are evidentiary. They provide further evidence that challenges those that deny immortality. They add other data that the physicalist has to explain away.

JEAN: It's important to appreciate that these experiences definitely happen. The question is how to explain them.

JOHN: But they are pretty easily explained away, aren't they? I mean notice how the experience is phrased: it's not the "death-experience," it's the "near-death-experience." Remarkable things, no doubt, happen to our brains near death. For example, if you start dying during an operation, the anesthesia and other pharmacological influences are likely to affect what you experience. This doesn't mean any of it is real.

PATRICIA: That's a good point. I've read accounts of some of these people who report these NDE's. None of them, as I recall, were unambiguously dead. Show me somebody, like Lazarus, who experiences *rigor mortis* and then gets up to report what happened to him and you'll get my attention. As it is, I don't take this stuff seriously. John's explanation is probably correct. The NDE is just the body's response to chemicals. It's also possible that it is simply a defense mechanism that we have evolved in order to adapt to life's last moments. In the closing minutes of life, if we can feel like we're in paradise, we can cope better.

JOHN: Yes. One can explain these phenomena naturally. For example, Susan Blackmore, a British scientist who has researched into the NDE, suggests that the experience of floating through a tunnel is nothing more than the brain operating with its last remaining tissues, the oxygen animating only the interior of the brain which has tunnel-like dimensions. The shape of the inner brain is what we're experiencing, not the route to heaven!

MALCOLM: Dr. Blackmore's explanation is probably the crassest physical explanation of a conscious event I've ever heard. In light of all we said earlier about how conscious events are totally unlike physical ones, I'm not sure Dr. Blackmore's remark deserves a reply. Let it suffice to say that Moody reports that some patients have reported NDEs and OBEs when coincidentally their brains were being measured for oxygen uptake. Some patients have recorded unusually high oxygen suffusion to their brains during the experience. That may undermine Dr. Blackmore's thesis that oxygen deprivation or increased carbon dioxide is responsible for these experiences. But I will concede the point made both by you and Patricia that the NDE is perhaps more an event involving "clinical" rather than unequivocal death. For that reason, I'd be cautious about investing too much in it to make a case for immortality.

RENEE: Still, if I read the literature correctly, aren't the researchers reluctant to write it all off to anesthesia, drugs, or hallucinations?

MALCOLM: Right you are, Renee. Dr. Ring, for example, in his book, *Life at Death,* gives considerable attention to this question and concludes that the NDE in its nature and texture seems to be quite different from what those under the influence of drugs or psychosis experience. Other researchers, like Carol Zaleski in her book, *Otherworld Journeys,* back up Dr. Ring's conclusions. No doubt, the controversy will continue. Regardless, I'm not willing to make my case on the NDE alone. It's the OBE that provides compelling evidence for life after death.

FRANK: Why do you say that?

MALCOLM: In a word, the OBE contains evidence showing that human consciousness can exist in a nonbodily state. For you see, during the OBE people acquire new awarenesses. Kenneth Ring and others have documented that certain patients who were pronounced dead by hospital doctors and who then experienced an OBE reported the details of resuscitation attempts on their behalf that eventually succeeded. These reports were corroborated by the medical personnel and were checked to see if they accorded with hospital records. Now, when a deceased patient acquires new knowledge undergoing an OBE, you've got to admit, that that counts as evidence.

PATRICIA: Pshaw! The patient could have just been dreaming, or pieced memories together based on what he or she heard during a comatose state.

MALCOLM: Sometimes the patients report having no auditory

experience at all. The experience is primarily visual. And they insist it was no dream. They are alive, in a nonbodily condition, completely aware of their surroundings, and acquiring new information. Now that has to count as evidence against physicalism, if one's senses are shut down, and one still has perceptual experiences.

RENEE: Yes, I see. A comatose body, a body clinically dead or at least unconscious, cannot have the kind of experience that the OBE reports relate.

MALCOLM: Exactly. Ordinarily, the only pathways for bodily awareness are the senses. But if an unconscious, perhaps clinically dead, patient claiming an OBE gave an account of her resuscitation treatment and surroundings derivable only from bodily sense operations, her claim to being out of the body could not be flippantly dismissed. If she has an awareness of events in the absence of sensation, she has had it without the body. Now that seems to me to be powerful evidence.

JOHN: A lot might depend on the reliability of these testimonies. Is there fraud involved? Are the methods of investigation reliable? Are there variables that the scientists are overlooking?

RENEE: Well, it'll be interesting to watch what's reported about these OBE's in the future. I know there is one emergency room in which the hospital staff have placed a teleprompter on a panel well above the heads of working personnel. Each day a different message is programmed into the machine. This way they'll have a real test for evidence. If a patient reporting an OBE can repeat the teleprompter's message—a message she would presumably see as she floated in the room high above her body—then that would be, on the face of it, irrefutable evidence that the OBE really happened.

PATRICIA: Latest bulletin: no teleprompter message has been reported yet!

BRIAN: I have a bulletin, too. We should bring this conversation to a close, so that Malcolm can relax.

RENEE: I think I can speak for all of us in saying that we are grateful for your instructive and hopeful remarks about immortality.

FRANK: I agree. But you must be exhausted, Malcolm. Those were some tough mental gymnastics you displayed. You're lucky you were drinking something with caffeine.

MALCOLM: Yeah, but now it's time to see my trainer. I've got a neuronal cramp that needs massaging!

MARY: Hey, good news everybody! I've just stepped onto the porch. I see blue sky!

FRANK: The sun is breaking through. Come on, Mary. Let's resurrect our plans to play some tennis.

Key Terms and Distinctions

Mind-body problem	Artificial intelligence
Miracles	Scientific faith argument
Necessary vs. sufficient condition	Concept formation
Ockham's razor	Universals
Dualism	Abstractions
Reductionism	Nominalism
Memory	Near-death experience
Correlation vs. causation	Out-of-body experience

Questions on Chapter 4

1. In your own words formulate the mind-body problem.
2. Explain how one's belief in immortality is influenced by one's solution to the mind-body problem?
3. Reductionism and dualism are opposing solutions to the mind-body problem. How exactly do they differ?
4. What does Malcolm mean when he says that brain and central nervous system are necessary but not sufficient conditions for conscious life?

5. Do you agree with John and Patricia that neurology is incompatible with dualism?
6. Malcolm argues that machines could never be made to think. Do you accept his criticism of artificial intelligence?
7. What is the argument from concept formation? How does it show that the intellect is nonphysical? If nonphysical, can't the intellect survive death of the body?
8. What is nominalism? On what grounds does Malcolm charge that nominalism is self-refuting?
9. Can one make a plausible case that near-death experiences are a glimpse of an afterlife?
10. Do you agree with Malcolm's argument that the out-of-body experience is powerful evidence for dualism?

Bibliography

Aquinas, St. Thomas, *Summa Theologiae,* Part I, Questions 85–86, Blackfriars Translation (New York: Benziger Brothers, 1947).
———, *On Being and Essence,* trans. Joseph Bobik (Notre Dame, IN: University of Notre Dame Press, 1965).
———, *On Truth,* trans. Robert W. Mulligan (Chicago: Henry Regnery, 1952).
Aristotle, *De Anima,* trans. W.D. Ross (Oxford: Oxford University Press, 1955).
Atwater, P.M.H., *Coming Back to Life: The After-Effects of the Near-Death Experience* (New York: Dodd, Mead, 1988).
Blackmore, Susan, *Beyond the Body: An Investigation of Out-of-the-Body Experiences* (London: Heinemann, 1982).
Churchland, Paul M., *Matter and Consciousness: A Contemporary Introduction to the Philosophy of Mind* (Cambridge, MA: MIT Press, 1988).
Dennett, Daniel C., "Can Machines Think?" in *How we Know,* ed. M. Shafto (San Francisco: Harper & Row, 1986), pp. 1–26.
———, *Consciousness Explained* (Boston: Little, Brown, 1991).
Eccles, Sir John, and Popper, Karl, *The Self and Its Brain: An Argument for Interaction* (New York: Springer International, 1977).
Geis, Robert, *Personal Existence After Death: Reductionist Circularities and the Evidence* (Peru, IL: Sherwood Sugden & Company, 1995).
Hume, David, *A Treatise of Human Nature* (original edition, 1740), ed. L.A. Selby-Bigge (London: Oxford University Press, 1968).
Jaki, Stanley, *Angels, Apes, and Men* (Peru, IL: Sherwood Sugden, 1983).

————, *Brain, Mind, and Computers* (Washington, DC: Regnery Gateway, 1989).

Libet, Benjamin, "The Timing of Subjective Experience," *Behavioral and Brain Science*, 12 (1989): 183–185.

Lewin, Roger, "Is Your Brain Really Necessary?" *Science*, 210 (1980): 1232–1234.

Moody, Raymond, *Life After Life* (New York: Bantam, 1976).

————, *The Light Beyond* (New York: Bantam, 1988).

Morse, Melvin, and Paul Perry, *Closer to the Light* (New York: Villard, 1992).

Ring, Kenneth, *Heading Towards Omega* (New York: Harper & Row, 1982).

————, *Life At Death: A Scientific Investigation of the Near-Death Experience* (New York: Coward, McGann, and Geoghegan, 1980).

Sabom, Michael, *Recollections of Death: A Medical Investigation* (New York: Harper & Row, 1982).

Swinburne, Richard, *The Evolution of the Soul* (New York: Oxford University Press, 1986).

Zaleski, Carol, *Otherworld Journeys: Accounts of Near-Death Experiences in Medieval and Modern Times* (New York: Oxford University Press, 1987).

Chapter Five
Religion and Morality

Three issues are the focus of discussion in this chapter: the divine command theory of ethics; the relationship between secular ethics and relativism; and the question of whether it is possible for religious believers and atheists to discuss and debate moral issues in a meaningful and productive way, given their radically different starting points. After some initial criticisms of the divine command theory, the participants take up the issue of the ultimate justification of morality, considering Kant's view along the way. The conversation ends with a discussion of religious morality versus secular morality and considers some implications for church-versus-state matters.

RENEE: I have always been fascinated, and, I must admit, a bit puzzled too, by the relationship between religion and morality. I mean we have all of these debates today about moral issues. And many of them seem to involve religion as well. Just last week my friend Alice was criticizing liberals for attempting to force their views on abortion on everyone, and we got into a very interesting discussion about whether the arguments against abortion were primarily *religious* arguments or not. We didn't really resolve the matter though; we could have done with your input Malcolm!

JOHN: It is one thing to criticize liberals, but what about those religious people who are trying to force their religious morality on everyone else? Several people on our school board are like that. Every year several of us get involved in a dispute with them over the curriculum. They want to try to use the curriculum to teach religious ethics, even though it is a public school.

FRANK: But why shouldn't those members of the board support what they believe in? After all, if your view wins the day, won't you then be imposing *your* liberal morality on them?! That argument seems to work either way it seems to me.

PATRICIA: But don't forget that the U.S. Constitution guarantees the separation of church and state. I for one do not want other people telling me what my moral values should be. I want to choose my own moral values. It especially irritates me when people try to impose their *religious* morality on me, when I am not even a member of their religion.

BRIAN: You could do with a bit more religion, Patricia! But, seriously, I think your remarks sound close to moral relativism, a view I hear all the time from the young people at my parish. They like the rhetoric of relativism; though none of them is actually committed to relativism or really believes it, of course.

MARY: I am hazy on this notion of relativism, though I do recognize the kind of language Patricia is using. Malcolm, can you sort out some of these issues we have been talking about? I am getting a bit confused!

MALCOLM: I think one of the main issues behind several of the points made is the fascinating question of the relationship between religion and morality. More specifically, the issue of whether moral values can be justified *independently of religion*. That is a key question. There were some related issues alluded to as well. Perhaps for now it is best to focus on two other questions that I believe were implicit in your remarks and that are very relevant. First, if one rejects religion, can one avoid moral relativism? And second, is it possible in general for religious believers and atheists to discuss and debate moral issues in a meaningful and productive way, and perhaps come to agree on some moral values, given that they are coming from such radically different starting points?

MARY: Maybe we could begin with the first question? Can moral values be justified independently of religion? I believe they can be, because there are plenty of people who are morally good and upstanding people but who are definitely not religious. My next door neighbor for one; he is an atheist, but I would definitely describe him as a good Christian man, if I did not already know that he is an atheist.

JOHN: And there are many religious people too, people who go to church each week and follow all of the other church rituals and rules, but who do not appear to be all that moral. My uncle is like that. Perhaps we have too much religion, Brian.

BRIAN: That's rich, coming from you! But there is a helpful distinction here that we need to make. I am very familiar with it because it comes up all the time in my ministry. I regularly meet people who are lapsed Catholics but who still mostly live by Catholic moral teaching. This has led me to distinguish between *acting morally* and the issue of one's moral values being *justified*. Many of those lapsed Catholics I talk to *act* in a very moral way, but they are often concerned about whether their moral values are or can be *justified*. They wonder if they simply believe in these values because they were brought up with them.

MALCOLM: Yes, Brian has hit on a key point that people often overlook. Our discussion prompts us to confront it. We are not really concerned here with whether people *act* in a moral way or not—be they religious believers or atheists; we are more concerned with the question of whether it is possible to *justify* one's moral values if one rejects religious belief. Immanuel Kant (1724–1804) was a famous German philosopher who believed it was not possible to justify objective morality independently of religion. He criticized the cosmological and design arguments, but he still believed natural theology was possible and that we could develop a moral argument for the existence of God. But in this century several secular humanists like Kai Nielsen and Patrick Nowell-Smith have argued that one can justify morality independently of religion.

MARY: What exactly do we mean by a "secular humanist"? Is it someone who believes that ethics can be done independently of religion?

BRIAN: It is someone who believes that all meaning and value come from human beings alone, since there is no God.

JOHN: Well, that would make me a secular humanist! When you talk about justifying our moral values do you mean giving reasons for why we hold those values, for why they are good things to practice, and for why we think other people should follow those values, and so on?

MALCOLM: Yes; I mean presenting an argument for why you believe human beings should promote certain moral values, for example, honesty and courage, or for why they should not engage in certain behavior, for example, adultery. Here is another example: if you believe it is morally right to treat all people equally then the justification of this view would involve giving an *argument* for why this is morally right, for why people should practice this moral value. Our question is: if one does not believe in God, is it possible to *justify* moral values at all?

JOHN: Well, I do not see why not. Can't I appeal to considerations such as the fact that human life is a value, that we seek happiness, that we are social beings, that freedom and justice are vital in human life, and that we need to treat each other with respect and equality, and so on?

FRANK: But suppose somebody rejects that line of argument and insists on being a racist? You have no *ultimate court of appeal* to justify your moral values, whereas religious people do. Atheists and secular humanists, it seems to me, can simply make up their moral values and are not really in a position to ultimately persuade other people to accept those values. It seems as if they not only have a problem with the justification of their position, but their view is also susceptible to moral relativism.

PATRICIA: Let's not complicate things too much, Frank. Let's come back to the issue of relativism in a little while. But I really do not see how the religious believer is any better off than the atheist. The religious worldview does not seem to provide any more unanimity or agreement on morality than the atheistic worldview. Don't most of the major world religions sometimes disagree with one another on moral issues?

JEAN: My cousin and his wife have different religions; she is a

Catholic and believes divorce is morally wrong, whereas he is a Protestant and believes divorce is morally acceptable. When my uncle got divorced, there was a big argument in our family over the issue.

JOHN: Yes, that's a good example of how religious believers are often in dispute on moral questions. I also wonder how a religious believer can somehow justify his moral values better than an atheist. I do not see how simply saying that your religion says something is right, or that God commanded it, or whatever, gives one any more justification than the atheist has. And don't forget that there are many different religions, all with quite different moral codes. If anything, leaving religion out of morality altogether might be the best way to go—then we could avoid all of these petty and unresolvable arguments between religions and try to arrive at a secular consensus.

RENEE: I am a religious believer, and there is a very strong connection between my religious beliefs and my moral values, so I am inclined to think morality must be linked to religion to make sense. On the other hand, I am not prepared at this point to say that an atheist or secular humanist *cannot* ultimately justify their moral beliefs. Could we explore the issue of how morality is supposed to be better justified if it is based in religion?

MALCOLM: That is a very old question, first discussed in detail in Plato's dialogue *Euthyphro*. Euthyphro, a character in the dialogue, believes that morality derives its authority from the Greek gods, but he does not know how to justify this view. Socrates quickly exposes Euthyphro's lack of understanding of the matter by a series of very penetrating questions. Euthyphro believes that morality is commanded by the gods and that whatever they command is good and whatever they forbid is bad. This is known these days as the "divine command" theory of ethics. Most religions, or at least many religious believers, would be very sympathetic to some version of this view, since they believe that whatever God commands is good.

FRANK: The ten commandments are an example; they are commanded by God, and they are good.

MALCOLM: In the dialogue, Socrates raised what has come to be called the "Euthyphro question," in response to the divine command theory. He asked: "Are actions good because God commands them, or does God command them because they are good?" A proponent of the divine command theory gives the first answer, since he believes that actions are good simply because God commands them. Now Socrates was not satisfied with this answer, and he wanted us to think further about it.

MARY: What does the second half of the question add that is different? Is it not just another way of saying what the first half says?

BRIAN: Actually no, I can see that it raises a very interesting issue. Socrates is asking *what is it* about morally good actions that makes them morally good, and he is suggesting that it is not acceptable to say simply that what makes them morally good is the fact that they are commanded by God. I gave a homily last Sunday in which I argued that adultery is wrong. I was also careful to try to explain *why* it is wrong; I did not simply want to say that it is wrong because God says so in the sixth commandment. One can give a further justification of the matter.

FRANK: I see what Socrates is asking, but is it not just a little arrogant? Isn't God's word enough for us? Shouldn't we simply trust God's law? Otherwise, you seem to be saying that you will accept these commands of God *if* you approve of them after you have examined them to see if they pass *your* moral test. Though, I suppose one could probe the question further simply to improve one's understanding of the issue.

MALCOLM: Yes, that is a good way to put it, Frank. It is not that we are calling God's law into question; we are just recognizing that the reason God ordains certain values can't simply be because he *commanded* them. There must be some further justification to it than that, though I acknowledge it is a very tricky issue. I often use the parent/child analogy here to illustrate the point. When parents lay down certain rules for their kids, the kids often feel they must follow the rules just because their parents say so! However, we all know that this is not the case. The rules embody moral values that the parents believe are right and that they believe can be justified. For example, parents do not want their kids to think that premarital sex is wrong *just because* they say that it is wrong. They want them to be able to see that it is really wrong and eventually to be able to explain why. I think we would all be disappointed if we asked our teenage children why premarital sex is immoral and they answered "because our parents say so"! We are raising the same issue here about God's commands.

RENEE: There is another problem with the divine command theory, and it comes out if you consider the dispute between Jean's cousin and his wife, mentioned earlier. How do we *know* what God commands? I see two problems here. First, there are different sources of revelation in different religions; for example, in the West many rely on the *Bible,* but in the Islamic faith, many rely on the *Koran.* But these "revelations" often command different and even conflicting moral values. Second, there are sometimes disputes *within* the same religion about what God commands. So if we say that morality is simply what God commands, we will still have a big problem trying to decipher what exactly it is that God commands.

MALCOLM: That is an excellent point, Renee, and it gives us a motivation to look elsewhere and to try to justify our morality independently of our religion. Another difficulty that the divine command theory faces is that morality often appears to be *arbitrary* on this view. This is because the theory holds that certain actions are good because God commands them, which means, remember, that these actions are good *just because they are commanded.* But it seems to follow that if God changes his mind tomorrow and commands that adultery is moral, then it would be moral! Adultery would possess that quality that makes actions moral—it would be commanded by God.

FRANK: But God would never do this. I mean that's pretty obvious, isn't it? But I guess the issue is *why* would God not do this, and that question forces us to seek more of a justification than simply saying that it is commanded by God.

MARY: Yes, it would be like your parents suddenly turning around and saying that premarital sex is moral! They would never do that, which means that it is not just *their command* that makes it *immoral.*

BRIAN: But what we are now asking is, I believe, a very difficult question. We are asking *why* does God approve of certain actions, and forbid others? This was Socrates's point in the second half of the "Euthyphro question," when he asked if God approved of certain actions *because* they were moral in the first place. The difficulty I have with this way of putting it, Malcolm, is how, from the religious point of view, could anything be moral outside of God or independently of God?

JEAN: I don't follow that question, Brian; could you explain it?

BRIAN: Well, if God approves of certain actions because they are moral (and not the other way around), then what *makes* these actions moral? Does this way of putting it not suggest that there is a way of justifying moral values independently of God? What I mean is it seems that if you give the second answer to the Euthyphro question, you are saying that certain things are good independent of God, and then God comes along, recognizes that these actions are good, and approves of them. Since I believe that God is eternal and that everything springs from God, especially morality, I do not see how I can accept the second half of the Euthyphro question as the correct answer.

MALCOLM: We need to see if we can come up with a satisfactory answer to the Euthyphro question to help settle this issue. In the *Euthyphro*, Plato implies that the second half of the question is the right answer, but he does not really explain how morality can be justified independently of God. He achieved his aim in the dialogue, though, which was to make Euthyphro realize that his views about religion and morality were quite superficial. However, I believe the solution to the dilemma you raise, Brian, is to be found by introducing the *nature* of God into the discussion. My way of solving the dilemma you raise is to emphasize that God has a certain nature—which is typically described by saying God is all-good, all-powerful, all-knowing, and so on. It is God's good nature that guides him in the selection of the moral values he commands and prohibits, just as it is our parents' nature that guides them in the selection of the moral values they ordain for their children. Moral values, if you like, flow from God's nature; and since God is all-good, then he always commands good values and would never ordain bad things. That is, God is *essentially* good.

JOHN: I understand the argument you are advancing, Malcolm, but the problem with it was mentioned earlier. How do you know what God's nature is?

FRANK: Well, we have already looked at the various arguments of natural theology on this issue, and we also have revelation. And there is general agreement among religions on this question, for a change! So I do not think that is much of a problem.

MARY: Religious believers do seem to be in broad agreement about the nature of God.

PATRICIA: This discussion has taken a very interesting turn, for it now appears that all we have been saying can help us with one of the other questions raised earlier. Remember we asked the question how can religious believers and atheists debate with each other on moral issues?

RENEE: I'm not sure it *can* help us, Patricia, because morality, according to Malcolm's view, is rooted in the nature of God, but you as an atheist do not believe in God. So aren't the atheist and the theist as far apart as ever?

PATRICIA: I do not think so. It seems to me that we have come to the conclusion that even if morality is rooted in the nature of God, religious believers still have to be able to say *why* moral values are right *independently* of religion. They cannot simply say they are right because God commanded them. Wasn't that the conclusion we reached in our discussion of the Euthyphro question? Religious believers, it seems to me, cannot appeal to natural theology either, because natural theology might tell us something about the nature of God, but it does not seem to tell us much about the *specifics* of morality. So they will have to make an appeal to human experience, to an analysis of human life, and so on, to justify their moral values. And this is just what the secular humanist does. Do you see what I am saying, Malcolm?

MALCOLM: Yes, I do. I think you have hit the nail on the head, Patricia. Even if one is a religious believer, one still has to explain why abortion, for example, is morally wrong, and when one justifies this position, one will appeal to the nature of human life to do so. For example, one might give a simple argument like this: An innocent human life morally ought not to be killed; the fetus is an innocent human life; therefore, the fetus morally ought not to be killed. Now notice that this is not a *religious* argument; it makes no appeal to religious matters at all, and it is an argument that a pro-life secular humanist could easily accept.

MARY: Yes, it is a much better argument against abortion than simply saying that abortion is morally wrong because my religion says so.

FRANK: Yes, that is a good point, though I do not think anybody really argues that abortion is morally wrong just because their religion says so. That view is a bit of a caricature. However, the Euthyphro question really does force even religious people to give arguments like the one Malcolm just gave to *justify* one's moral values. It is therefore a very valuable tool. So your point, Malcolm, is that religious believers and atheists or secular humanists could discuss many moral issues by simply discussing arguments in the above form, rather than by appealing to any religious matters?

MALCOLM: Yes, I think they could. I believe they also could make a lot of progress in this manner. I am not saying they will be in total agreement, of course, and I will come back to that point in a moment. But I believe that, just as the advocates of a particular religion must, at least in principle, face up to the question "what makes good actions good?" and cannot simplistically bow to their religious tradition, the advocates of an atheistic view are similarly required to address this question. And when this discussion gets going, both parties will be on fairly common ground and may possibly reach agreement on many issues.

BRIAN: How does this relate to natural law theory, Malcolm, which is an important view in the Catholic tradition, and which was proposed by St. Thomas Aquinas and others? Or does it relate at all?

MALCOLM: I think it does relate in a crucial sense. Natural law theory claims that the natural moral law, which springs from the eternal law of God (not to be confused with the divine law of revelation), is nevertheless naturally known by all human beings through reason and experience, whether they believe in God or not. So, according to Aquinas, an atheist can still recognize the moral law, and debate and discuss it with a religious believer. So in this way the natural law tradition would support the points we have been making in our discussion.

Another important way of looking at this is to highlight the fact that the religious believer can do ethics independently of religion, and yet the results of his philosophical investigation may still accord with the teachings of his religion, at least on the main issues. This is another key point of natural law theory. For example, if a religious believer does not appeal to his religion in his thinking on morality, he will still conclude that honesty, courage, kindness, and friendship are good things, and that murder, adultery, and treachery are bad, and so on.

JOHN: This would not work in all cases, though, Malcolm. These are more general moral values, with which the atheist could easily agree, but there are more specific moral values that appear to be dependent on a particular religious tradition, for example, some religions prohibit the eating of certain foods.

MALCOLM: Yes, there are undoubtedly some moral values that could not be justified without appeal to religion; however, my point is that for many of the large moral issues, one can reach justification independently of religion; indeed, one has to do this, if one is to have an informed view.

BRIAN: This discussion is very important because it shows that religious values can be justified independently of religion and that they are just as well-grounded in reason and experience as secular ethics. This is a point often lost in the contemporary political discussion in this country where the moral values of religious people are often presented as being purely religious, private, even sectarian.

FRANK: A very good point, Brian, with which I could not agree more! But I have another worry about these issues. I want to come back to the point about relativism that was raised at the beginning of our discussion. I understand relativism to mean that moral values are relative to the individual, that no one has the right to impose their moral values on anyone else, because who's to say what is right and wrong? Have I stated that correctly, Malcolm? I hope so, because I have just been reading a book on the topic!

MALCOLM: Exactly right, Frank. The position you describe is what I usually call extreme relativism; it argues that moral values are relative to each individual, which means that each individual can choose his or her own moral values. We can identify another obvious form of relativism, cultural relativism, which holds that moral values are relative to the society; that no society has the right to impose their moral values on any other society. But when you live in a particular society, according to the cultural relativist, you must follow the moral values of that society. Moral relativism, which is a theory about the applicability of moral values, has serious difficulties, not least the fact that it is practically impossible to live by it. For example, one could not condemn murder on this view because then you would be imposing your values on the murderer! But, of course, we cannot go into a detailed discussion of this view now.

FRANK: No, but I want to bring up a particular point. If we try to do ethics independently of religion don't we run the risk of ending up as relativists? In fact, I'm not sure we can avoid relativism. If we try to justify our ethical values by appeal to our experience, human nature, and reason, and so on, isn't it inevitable that many people will all come out with different sets of values, or sets of values that differ in significant ways, at least in different societies? It seems to me that religion guarantees moral objectivity in ethics, which is the view that moral values are objectively true and apply always and everywhere, whether everyone agrees or not. For example, kindness is an objective moral value on my view.

BRIAN: Yes, and if someone disagrees that kindness is an objective moral value, then you believe they are wrong, whereas on the relativist position, if you disagree with someone, they are not wrong in any objective sense. They simply choose to have different values than yours.

JEAN: What a weird view!

MARY: I do not see how doing ethics independently of religion leads to relativism, though. After all, doesn't the religious believer have to do ethics independently of religion, and he is not a relativist, is he? I mean isn't that what we have just concluded, Malcolm?

MALCOLM: Yes, we have been moving in that general direction. However, Frank does raise an important issue, one that is often brought up as a criticism of secular ethics. Many believe that secular ethics must inevitably fall into some form of relativism precisely because one has no higher court of appeal. As the Russian novelist Dostoevsky puts it: "If God does not exist, everything is permitted." If a secular humanist bases her morality on her experience, and reason and human nature, but still ends up disputing at least some values with others, then some argue that it is hard for her to go any further than this. She cannot appeal to a religious tradition, or to a religious text, or whatever, as a guide, since these are all rejected by the secular humanist.

BRIAN: It is true that we see a large drive today in certain circles, especially intellectual circles, away from religious morality, and we do seem to see a corresponding move toward relativism in ethics, as you say Malcolm. I am thinking of the arguments, very common today, that one has the right to choose one's own position on issues like abortion, drug-taking, euthanasia, and so on. And one thing that religious morality is pretty famous for is its certainty on these issues and its near unanimity among believers, at least up until recently; until, in fact, this kind of relativistic language began to become more widespread.

PATRICIA: That is an interesting observation, Brian. But don't forget, as we said earlier, that the old certainties are under threat; there are now many disputes even within particular religions, even on some of these issues, for example, abortion. And, as we mentioned earlier, it is also very desirable, even if you are religious, to justify your moral values independently of your religion.

MARY: Is the fact that the secular humanist cannot appeal to any higher authority, Malcolm, a real problem? Supposing we leave aside for the moment the point Patricia reminded us of—that the religious believer too must ultimately justify why he accepts a religious authority. But is secular ethics condemned to relativism?

MALCOLM: Most advocates of secular ethics, such as Kai Nielsen in his book *Ethics Without God*, would claim that it is not. And I think that you can make a pretty good case that it is not simply because—like the religious believer—the secular humanist has to appeal to human nature, human experience, reason, tradition, and things of that sort. And if the religious believer can appeal to these to arrive at objective moral values, then so can the secular humanist. Though, as you point out, Brian, there is no doubt that secular humanism is nearer to relativism on many issues than is

religious morality, and that the rise of secular humanism has led
to an increase in the rhetoric of relativism, that is, when people
talk as if they are relativists but really are not relativists in the end,
as you mentioned earlier. But there are many things one can focus
on in an examination of morals, for example, the purpose of
human life, the pursuit of happiness, the necessity to avoid suffering, the role of reason and virtue in human experience, the value
of freedom and justice. An examination of issues such as these can
lead to a set of objective values, so Kai Nielsen would argue. The
religious believer is bound to agree since he must appeal to these
too in many cases to explain why God commands as he does, as we
have seen.

BRIAN: You mentioned Kant earlier, Malcolm, and I would like
to recall an idea of his that I have always liked. As I understand it,
he believes that the *ultimate justification* of morality must finally be
based on God's nature and God's kingdom. He believes that only
in God's kingdom can the ultimate *why* of morality make sense
and be explained; also only in God's kingdom will virtue and
happiness correspond with each other. This last point is a crucial
point, I think, in morality in general. I see it all the time with my
parishioners; they realize and are often troubled by the fact that
the moral life is sometimes hard to live, and occasionally does not
seem to pay. Sin often seems attractive! But their conviction that
God exists makes *ultimate* sense out of human morality for them.
Now I think that the secular humanist has a difficulty here.

MALCOLM: Indeed! And although I do not agree with Kant's
particular defense of his argument on these matters, his position
does raise two challenging issues for the secular humanist. One is
the issue of "Why be moral?" since it often seems to be a difficult
choice, and not to pay, and so on. This question is particularly
relevant when we are considering *moral obligations* of various kinds,
duties and the like, with which Kant was much concerned. Most
people, of course, do not have to be persuaded of the correctness
of most objective moral values or of their moral obligations, be
they religious people or secular humanists.

FRANK: I'm not sure about secular humanists on that issue. I think the rejection of religious morals by many people has led to a lot more shrinking of moral obligations and to more selfish behavior. There are several books on that subject.

MALCOLM: Well, perhaps so, but my main point is that if an individual does question certain values, and tries, in particular, to reject his moral obligations, the secular humanist would seem to have a more difficult job than the religious believer of convincing this person *why* he should follow his moral obligations. The religious believer can appeal to the existence of God, God's kingdom, and God's law as the basis for God's moral wishes for human beings, especially in those areas where human reason may not quite give us the justification we need or where there is a dispute about where reason leads. However, the secular humanist can make no such appeal and would seem to have a difficulty in trying to convince those who are tempted to reject moral obligations.

PATRICIA: But how do we know that God exists and what his law is?

MALCOLM: Well, we have revelation to help us. And do not forget our earlier discussions on the rationality of belief in God, and on the nature of God. I believe, as I argued then, that the religious worldview is more rational than the atheist worldview. But this debate focuses precisely the nature of the difficulty for the atheist. It is because the atheist already believes that the universe and human life are the product of chance and have no ultimate purpose or destiny, that he seems to be left with no ultimate court of appeal to justify moral obligations or moral sacrifice and human behavior of that sort.

FRANK: That is one of the reasons that we see more selfish behavior today, I believe.

BRIAN: What about the second point, Malcolm, that comes out of Kant's remarks?

MALCOLM: Oh, yes; I was thinking of Kant's point that in God's kingdom everything turns out all right in the end and everything makes sense. In particular, virtue and happiness are distributed correctly there, unlike in human life where the moral life does not always lead to happiness, though I suppose it does in most cases. However, most people still believe that they should perform their moral obligations no matter how unpleasant these obligations might be occasionally or no matter how opposed to their self-interest these obligations might be. But Kant's point is that in order for human beings to make sense out of morality, it is necessary for us to believe that in God's kingdom the virtuous life will be rewarded. Kant believed this was necessary to provide an ultimate justification for morality. This is the problem the secular humanist may have. It is a problem of *ultimate* justification, and it leads the religious believer to argue that *in the end* you cannot justify ethics independently of religion. Though, as we have seen, it is possible to justify many moral values without appeal to religion, yet one might have to make a final appeal to religion, especially to justify moral obligation and the whole enterprise of morality. Of course, since the secular humanist does not believe in God, he will have little time for this kind of ultimate justification. But here the religious believer and the secular humanist part company!

BRIAN: Since the atheist believes the world is ultimately unintelligible, then it is reasonable to suggest that for him morality must be ultimately unintelligible as well. And if this is a reasonable suggestion, then why be moral?

FRANK: Right on target, Brian! I would like to come back to this whole question some other time if we can. That is, the question of the ultimate justification of morality, and especially the implications this matter might have for the atheist's position on the whole issue of the meaning of life. I think that morality is essential to one's view of the meaning of life, and I feel the atheist might have a difficulty on this matter.

RENEE: We must have a discussion on the topic of the meaning of life before the end of our stay here, especially since this topic is a main focus of the Seminar.

JEAN: We raised the issue earlier of whether a religious believer and a secular humanist can even debate with each other given their radically different starting points. We seemed to conclude earlier that they could, but doesn't our latest discussion indicate that they cannot? I am very interested in this question because I debate with my friend Sinead all the time. She claims she is an atheist, though I have my doubts! Anyway, she persists in taking the humanist line when we get into ethical disputes, and we often seem to come up against a barrier in the form of my religious view versus her secularist view. What annoys me about our conversations is that she then tries to take the moral high ground and insist that I cannot bring religion into the debate since that would be to impose my religion on her.

MARY: That is a very popular argument in our culture today. One hears it all the time on TV and in the media. It is a cultural trend that has upset and marginalized many religious people, but our Constitution does maintain the separation of church and state.

PATRICIA: Yes, and thank God, because as I said at the beginning of our conversation, the religious groups would otherwise try to force their values on the rest of us.

FRANK: Don't forget that the phrase "separation of church and state" nowhere appears in either the Constitution or the Bill of Rights. The First Amendment is concerned with the danger of a theocracy, that is, with the danger of a church established by the state. It forbids that from happening. But it does not say that church and state should be totally separate, or more generally, that religion has no place at all in public life. That is a modern, liberal interpretation of the First Amendment. And, anyway, why should we have to follow *your* values, Patricia? Because that is what it comes down to, especially in the public schools.

PATRICIA: Because they are right!

FRANK: Oh, puh-leeeze!

JEAN: Malcolm, I would like to explore this complicated issue; it is of great personal importance to me and, I think, to the others too?

FRANK: I am irritated by Patricia's position, and she is irritated by mine!

MALCOLM: The whole issue of church versus state is quite complicated, and we do not have time to go into it here in any detail. But a few interesting issues have been raised, and perhaps we might just wind up our discussion by considering one or two of them briefly. One question, I think, that you have raised is: Is it possible for a religious believer and a secular humanist to debate with each other in some kind of *neutral* fashion or on a neutral territory, as it were? What I mean is, can they debate without one side, usually the secular humanist side, somehow ruling that the religious view is out of order? Can we avoid the situation where we simply give procedural control of the debate to the secular humanist, who then appears to be forcing her views on the religious person? That is the issue Jean raised. We also need to avoid the situation where the religious believer imposes his or her religious morality on those who do not accept that particular religion.

I need to recall a distinction here, which I mentioned at the beginning of our conversation today. Not all moral values advocated by religious believers are essentially *religious* values; I pointed out that the argument that, say, abortion is wrong, is not essentially a *religious* argument, although it is an argument advanced by religious people as well as others. What I mean is that religious people need not, and most often do not, appeal to anything specific in their religion to justify their view on abortion. Therefore, they are on a level playing field with the secular humanist in the debate on this issue. They hold that abortion is wrong independently of their religion. However, this issue is more complicated than this, and we must handle it very carefully.

FRANK: I am worried by that approach, Malcolm, because it seems you are saying that a religious believer cannot appeal to his religion when discussing moral questions; yet a secular humanist can appeal to his secular humanism. Why should one be allowed to appeal to his worldview, and the other not be allowed to?

MALCOLM: Yes, an excellent question, and let me use it to elaborate further on some ideas I have on this matter. Suppose a religious believer and a secular humanist are involved in a debate on some moral question. Now the religious believer can take what I call the "simplistic" approach to the debate. When pressed by the secular humanist on why he believes that, say, adultery is morally wrong, he can simply say something like "I believe it is morally wrong because my religion says so." Of course, the secular humanist will respond that since he does not accept that religion, then he does not have to accept that moral value either. The religious believer now has three options. First, he can abandon the debate altogether, which is not much of a solution! Two, he can try to convert the secular humanist to his religion, which will not be easy. Or three, he can move to a more neutral territory and try to justify his belief that adultery is morally wrong *without* appealing to his religion. This is what I call the "sophisticated" approach. In this way, he may be able to make some progress with his friend. The secular humanist is now obliged to debate him and cannot retreat to the argument that he does not accept his friend's religion. We have already agreed that religion in general is obliged to take this sophisticated approach anyway if it is not simply to rely on God's commands.

JEAN: Yes, that is very helpful. But what about the secular humanist? Are you not saying here that the secular humanist's worldview is somehow the *right* one or that religion is almost redundant?

MALCOLM: I am coming to those issues. We now need to look at the issue from the point of view of the secular humanist. And the secular humanist will have the same three options. This is the key point, and it is often overlooked in the contemporary discussion of these matters, which is often more full of rhetoric than reason. The secular humanist can't say "Adultery is morally permissible because my worldview says so" because then the religious believer can make the *same* reply the secular humanist made to him. The religious believer can say "I am not a secular humanist so I do not have to accept that moral value." The secular humanist can then abandon the debate, or try to convert the religious believer to secular humanism, or he can attempt to move to neutral territory and try to justify his view *without appealing to his secular humanism.* Or to put it more accurately: Any point that either of them appeals to in order to advocate a position must be argued for and justified—he must convince his opponent of its truth.

JOHN: How can a secular humanist argue for his view, though, independently of his worldview? The religious believer can do this because, as we have agreed, one can do ethics independently of religion, at least to some extent. But secular humanism is all the secular humanist has.

FRANK: God help him!

MALCOLM: I am trying to get us to recognize that secular humanism, though, is not the default position—it is not somehow automatically true or the preferred option. It must be argued for. My main point is that when a secular humanist debates with a religious believer, the secular humanist is not on the moral high ground he often thinks he is on. He cannot simply say that we can't bring religion into the debate because not all of us accept religion, since this is also true of secular humanism. He must justify every substantive point he proposes, just as the religious believer must do as well when he is doing ethics independently of religion.

FRANK: That is very helpful to me, because what I have often been suspicious of in my debates with secular humanists is something that you have now made clear to me. I am afraid when I suspend my religion, as it were, and move on to more neutral territory for the purposes of debate, that the secular humanist will *not* do the same, and I will be debating in effect from the point of view of a secular humanist, as if I actually were a secular humanist! And that would be to prejudice the debate against me, wouldn't it?

JEAN: Another fear I often have is that if I move on to a kind of "neutral territory," as you call it, I will end up having to give up some of my most cherished beliefs. And it is interesting to hear your points, Frank and Malcolm, because this would particularly trouble me, if it is just me and not the secular humanist, who moves to neutral territory.

JOHN: We must remember that our country guarantees the separation of church and state, despite what you say, Frank. This means that the religious believer may not establish his religious values *in law*. So you would have to compromise on that point because if you establish your values in law you are making others follow your religion, something forbidden by the Constitution. But you can still practice your most cherished beliefs privately, of course.

MALCOLM: To give an example: One could not argue that the Catholic view of the Trinity—that there are three persons in one God—should be placed in the law of the land. But one *could* argue that one's view that abortion is immoral—which one argues for independently of religion—should be placed in law. The important thing in this whole discussion is to avoid making *two* mistakes. The first is the mistake of thinking that (most of) the moral views of religious people are private religious views. The second is the mistake of thinking that the secular humanist does not have to defend the view upon which he bases his moral values and his legislation.

BRIAN: I think some people today deliberately mirepresent religious morality to give the impression that the moral views of religious people are purely private religious views that should not be brought into the public domain. I see this all the time in the mainstream media.

FRANK: Unless we are vigilant, though, it seems to me that it will be only the religious person who is doing the compromising. But surely if the secular humanist moves to neutral territory, they would have to do some compromising too? Also, how can a person practice their most cherished beliefs in a completely *private* way. Don't at least some of our beliefs have some implications for society as a whole—for how we all think people ought to live?

MALCOLM: Well, we have mentioned some of the key questions here. And you have raised several other vital issues. But we cannot get into the fascinating area of church versus state at this time. It would take another discussion in itself. But one can see how our discussion today will have great implications for the whole church versus state debate.

RENEE: I would like to pursue this last issue sometime. It really is fascinating, relevant, and crucially important for my own thinking right now.

MARY: Another time . . . let's go for a swim!

JOHN: You go for a swim. I need an aspirin!

Key Terms and Distinctions

Acting morally vs. justifying morality
Secular humanism
Divine command theory of ethics
Euthyphro question
Natural law
Extreme moral relativism
Cultural relativism

Moral objectivism
Theocracy
The "simplistic" approach
   to moral debate
The "sophisticated"
   approach to moral
   debate

Questions on Chapter 5

1. Do you agree with Malcolm's argument that, at least to a significant extent, religious morality and secular morality are compatible?
2. Do you agree with Frank's point that the secular humanist cannot ultimately justify her moral values? Suppose you are a secular humanist. How would you respond to this objection?
3. Are you convinced by the argument that religion can ultimately justify its moral values in a more convincing way than secular humanism?
4. What do you think of Malcolm's solution to the Euthyphro question? How would you solve Socrates's difficulty?
5. Do you think that a religious believer could simply rely on

revelation to justify many of his moral values and not be concerned with justifying those values independently of his religion? Discuss the advantages and disadvantages of this approach.

6. Select a particular moral issue, and compare and contrast the "simplistic" approach and the "sophisticated" approach in a debate between a religious believer and a secular humanist over the issue you have selected.

7. How might the discussion at the end of the conversation on church vs. state issues continue?

8. Why should one be moral?

Bibliography

Aquinas, St. Thomas, *Summa Theologiae,* Questions 90–97, in *Treatise on Law,* ed. Stanley Perry (Chicago: Regnery, 1970).

Helm, Paul (ed.), *The Divine Command Theory of Ethics* (Oxford: Oxford University Press, 1979).

Hudson, Yaeger, *The Philosophy of Religion* (Mountain View, CA: Mayfield, 1991).

Kant, Immanuel, *Religion Within the Limits of Reason Alone* (original edition, 1793), trans. T.M. Greene and H.H. Hudson (New York: Harper Torchbooks, 1960).

Kierkegaard, Soren, *Fear and Trembling* (original edition, 1843), trans. Howard Hong and Edna Hong (Princeton, NJ: Princeton University Press, 1983).

Nielsen, Kai, *Ethics Without God* (New York: Prometheus, 1990, revised edition).

Nowell-Smith, Patrick, "Morality: Religious and Secular," in *Philosophy of Religion,* ed. Louis Pojman (Belmont, CA: Wadsworth, 1994, second edition), pp. 558–569.

Plato, *Euthyphro* in *The Last Days of Socrates,* trans. Hugh Tredennick and Harold Tarrant (Harmondsworth, England: Penguin, 1993 edition).

Quinn, Philip, *Divine Commands and Moral Requirements* (Oxford: Clarendon Press, 1978).

Chapter Six

Religious Experience

In this conversation, the friends critically examine various contemporary arguments for the existence of God based on religious experience, distinguishing them from the traditional argument from religious experience. They analyze the views of contemporary philosophers Alvin Plantinga, John Hick, and D.Z. Phillips.

MALCOLM: I am surprised to see you all looking so fresh this morning. I thought our long, tiring, but excellent discussion yesterday on religion and morality would have worn you all out. And I thought you would be at church, John!

JOHN: You won't convert me that easily!

JEAN: I am fascinated by how much ground we have covered so far and by how much our discussions are complementing the activities at the Institute. These issues really are quite complicated, and it takes a great deal of patience to work through them. I wonder if we could talk about religious experiences this morning, because they seem to me to be very important. I have a friend who relies a lot on her own personal religious experiences.

FRANK: What about the question of the meaning of life, the subject of that lecture we attended last night. I would like to pursue that particular topic as well. I think you will have a tough time arguing that life has meaning on your view, John.

RENEE: We still have five more days, so we will have plenty of time to discuss all of these fascinating and important questions.

JOHN: Yes, that's right. Maybe we could just stay with the topic of religious experiences today, and come back to the others in the days ahead? Malcolm, perhaps you could begin by giving us an overview of what is normally understood by "religious experiences" and the role such experiences play in coming to believe in God. I should say at the outset that I am very skeptical that there are such experiences.

RENEE: Don't be silly, John. Do you think people make them up? Like the saints, for example, or even Jesus perhaps? My own fideistic view places a very high value on religious experiences.

JOHN: No, I'm not saying that people pretend they are having religious experiences, or anything like that. But I think that people who claim to have had religious experiences are deluded in some way—often in a complicated manner, I would suspect.

JEAN: I find it hard to believe that Jesus or St. Paul or St. Francis of Assisi or St. Teresa of Avila were deluded.

MALCOLM: I find that hard to believe as well. You have all raised good points, but let's not get too far ahead of ourselves. It is interesting that you should raise the issue of religious experiences, Jean, and not just because they have a long history or because many people today in this country, like born-again Christians, claim to have had such experiences. But because there is currently some very interesting and influential work going on in philosophy on this very subject.

BRIAN: I suppose you are referring to the work of Alvin Plantinga, John Hick, and others, Malcolm? Although I agree their work is interesting, I do not find it very convincing myself.

MALCOLM: Yes, I am thinking of Plantinga, an American philosopher, and of Hick, an English philosopher but also of the Welsh philosopher, D.Z. Phillips, who is associated with the movement called Wittgensteinian Fideism, which has influenced Renee.

RENEE: Yes, although I have been personally influenced more by thinkers like the Danish philosopher Soren Kierkegaard (1813–1855) than by Phillips. Maybe we might just begin by discussing Plantinga's view, which I have heard about, but do not know the details.

PATRICIA: Yes, let's hear this new view of religious experiences. I am in agreement with John, though, on this topic. I can see some merit in the rational approach of natural theology to the God question—discussed in our first conversation a few days ago—but so-called religious experiences have always baffled me. I have never had an experience that came even close to being "religious," and I really doubt whether such experiences are reliable sources of religious insight. They seem to be too subjective to be of much value.

MARY: But surely they would be of value to the person who actually had the experience? And, by the way, Malcolm, what is a religious experience exactly—what do we mean by that term? It seems very broad.

BRIAN: Yes, we need to specify what we mean, don't we? We need to be clear about what we are talking about before we launch into a discussion on the topic. I have read many interesting reports of religious experiences—in the lives of the saints, for example—and there often seems to be quite significant differences between their respective accounts. For example, St. Teresa of Avila's description of her sense of the presence of Christ is very different from the awareness of God reported by Nicholas of Cusa.

MALCOLM: There are many different types of experience that can, and indeed have been, described as religious, but it is possible to identify some salient features that arise in many religious experiences. Religious experiences can range from a person's having a vague sense of the presence of a greater Being, beyond the natural order—an experience that some people here have probably had—to a sense of some kind of direct acquaintance with the God of Christianity, as some of the mystics claimed to have experienced, like St. John of the Cross. Religious emotions can be present during the experience, such as feelings of happiness or of hope, or, on the other hand, feelings of abandonment, despair, or sin. Religious experiences may involve sensory awareness of either a public or private object. In the Gospels, the disciples have a public religious experience of the Risen Christ. St. Bernadette, on the other hand, reported seeing the Virgin Mary at Lourdes, but this was a private experience, since the rest of the villagers could not see the vision. St. Teresa of Avila, on the other hand, could not describe her experiences in sensory terms at all.

FRANK: That is a very nice summary, Malcolm, of the different types of religious experiences. Now, how can they tell us whether or not there is a God?

MALCOLM: In terms of these experiences providing evidence for the existence of God, it is necessary initially to distinguish between *two types of argument* based on religious experiences. The first is the more *traditional argument* from religious experience. This argument states that many people have profound religious experiences and that these are best explained by the existence of God. The key point in this form of the argument is that one *infers* that God must be the *cause* of the religious experience. And this inference may not just be warranted only for the person who has the experience. It might be possible to argue from the fact that since we know of many people—either personally or in history—who have had religious experiences, it can be inferred that God is the cause of, or the best explanation for, these experiences. This is a well-established argument, and I think it is a very good argument in favor of the existence of God. Otherwise, one has to conclude that religious experiences are *all* delusions, a view that I believe to be very implausible.

RENEE: Malcolm, could you say more about the role the *inference* plays in these arguments based on religious experience? That seems to be important, and I have often thought about it, for it is relevant to my view. For example, I often think my experience of the world is religious in some sense, but I'm not sure how to explain this. Perhaps some of the others know what I mean.

MALCOLM: Yes, from the point of view of philosophically evaluating whether religious experiences are genuine or not, the role of the inference is crucial. There are two broad positions on this question, as I've said. The first, just mentioned, the more traditional view, holds that one makes *an inference from* one's experiences *to* the existence of God. God is seen as the *cause* of the experience, or the best *interpretation* of the experience, or as the best *explanation* of the experience, and so forth. The second position—we might call it the contemporary argument from religious experience—holds that there is *no* inference involved, that one is somehow *directly aware* of God's presence in the experience.

JOHN: And so the debating point for the first, more traditional view occurs when one considers whether the *inference* from the religious experience *to* the existence of God as its cause is justified? Is that correct, Malcolm, for that is what I had in mind when I said that I was skeptical of this argument? I do not believe that God is the *cause* of the experiences.

MALCOLM: Yeah, that's right on target, John. Proponents of the first form of the argument argue that religious experiences are well documented, have occurred to many good and serious people, including Jesus and the saints, and that the existence of God is the best explanation for such experiences. Christian philosophers and theologians go a little further and argue that it is even rational for a person to come to believe in God on the basis of *another person's,* or on the basis of *many people's,* reports of *their* religious experiences. Richard Swinburne holds this view, for example. And critics of this argument, as you indicate, John, deny that God is the best explanation or the most likely cause of the experience. They hold that people mistakenly (for a variety of reasons) believe that their experiences are "religious," when they really are not.

BRIAN: This is very interesting. What about the second view? Can we discuss that view today? If I read this more contemporary view correctly—Plantinga, Hick, and the rest—aren't these philosophers saying that there is *no* inference involved in religious experiences, that, as you put it, somehow one is *directly aware* that God is present in one's experience? Of course, if they are right, then the person who has the experience could be sure that God existed on the basis of the experience alone.

MALCOLM: Yes, that's it exactly, Brian, and perhaps for today it would be best to focus on the more contemporary version of the argument since the traditional argument is well known. To come back to your point about Hick, Brian, it is not clear that he is doing away with the inference. But let's discuss his view later. I propose to discuss Plantinga's view first, since it is new and influential and has garnered a good many supporters. It will be a good way to probe further many of the issues we have already raised. Plantinga has a kind of love/hate relationship with the kind of natural theology arguments we discussed in a previous conversation. Sometimes he seems to recognize that they can be important in supporting the rationality of theism; on the other hand, he has been much influenced by his distinctive theological outlook and has looked for alternative ways of justifying religious belief philosophically. He has proposed a new approach, called reformed epistemology after the reformed tradition of theologian John Calvin (1509–1564). Calvin believed that God has planted in every human being a disposition to believe in God. This view has been a big influence on Plantinga.

PATRICIA: Let's be clear here! How does he know we have this disposition? Isn't that just question-begging? Wouldn't he have to show that religious experiences are genuine, that is, caused by God, before he could say we have a disposition to believe in God?

MALCOLM: Yes, you raise a difficult problem. Some believe that the reformed view *arbitrarily* downplays reason and elevates faith. But we will come back to that later.

MARY: By calling it reformed *epistemology* it sounds like he is proposing a new way of knowing. Would that be fair, Malcolm?

MALCOLM: Yes, I think it would, though Plantinga often says that he is not really trying to justify religious belief *philosophically* but simply trying to show how faith can be rational for a particular religious believer on the basis of that believer's experiences. I believe, however, that he does intend to justify religious belief philosophically. First, his view is a kind of *indirect* way of justifying religious belief. At the very least he is trying to remove as illegitimate a certain kind of objection to religious beliefs that is based on demanding objective evidence for those beliefs. He calls this the evidentialist objection and tries to show that it is misplaced. And, second, on his view the person who has a "properly basic belief" in God is rational and justified in this belief.

BRIAN: As I understand it, he begins with a critique of traditional epistemology. Is that right? And what is a "properly basic belief"?

MALCOLM: His view is based on a critique of the traditional epistemological theory known as classical foundationalism. Classical foundationalism is a fairly commonsense theory of knowledge. The theory proposes that there are two types of beliefs, namely, basic beliefs and inferred beliefs. Basic beliefs are completely justified beliefs just by virtue of being basic. These would be beliefs like "I am sitting at this table now," "I had breakfast this morning," "2 + 2 = 4," "I have a toothache," and so on; in short, beliefs that are self-evident, evident to the senses, or incorrigible, as the theory puts it. These are basic because they are *not* inferred from any other beliefs. The second type of beliefs—inferred beliefs—are inferred on the basis of other beliefs, namely, the basic ones. For example, my belief that the university where I work is a good university is an inferred belief, my belief that my car will get us through the Rockies tomorrow on our visit to Denver is an inferred belief, and so on.

BRIAN: Could you explain how your belief that your car will get us through the Rockies tomorrow is an inferred belief and how the inferred beliefs and the basic beliefs are related?

MALCOLM: Yes, the difference is important. It's a key point for the development of Plantinga's argument. My belief that my car will get us all through the Rockies tomorrow is inferred from other beliefs that I also hold: for example, my belief that my car has been running well lately, my belief that I just had the engine overhauled last month, my belief that the car is reliable, and so on. Now notice that even some of *these* beliefs are inferred beliefs.

PATRICIA: That's true. Your belief that your car will get you through the Rockies because you got the engine overhauled is based on the prior belief that cars whose engines have been overhauled perform well and better than cars that have had no overhaul done.

MALCOLM: And, according to foundationalism, all of our inferred beliefs are eventually traceable back to dependence upon some set of basic beliefs, to answer the second part of your question, Brian. And the key move in foundationalism for our purpose is that belief in God would be an inferred belief, not a basic belief.

RENEE: Phew, this is getting a little heavy. Let's see if I have this right? If I say I believe in God, a foundationalist will take this to be an inferred belief—inferred on the basis of other beliefs, evidence, and so on—and will ask me to explain the process of inference that led me to the existence of God? Natural theology is, therefore, based on a foundationalist epistemology, isn't it?

JOHN: It obviously is. And I must say that foundationalism seems like the more sensible approach to me. Malcolm, does Plantinga have a problem with this approach?

MALCOLM: Yes. He believes that there is a tacit *criterion* underlying classical foundationalism, a criterion for deciding what would count as a basic belief. And Plantinga does not so much want to attack foundationalism *per se;* he simply wants to *widen* the criterion to allow belief in God *to be among the foundational, or basic, beliefs.*

MARY: That is a bold move, if he can pull it off.

MALCOLM: It is. He claims that classical foundationalism is based on the criterion that "whatever is self-evident, or evident to the senses, or incorrigible" is a basic belief. And any belief not satisfying this criterion would then be an inferred belief, for example, belief in God. According to this theory, a religious philosopher would therefore be required to justify or to give evidence for why he believes in God. This request for evidence Plantinga calls "evidentialism," and he believes it has been a misguided approach in assessing the rationality of belief in God.

JOHN: So he wants to include belief in God in the set of basic beliefs? So if I say "I believe in God," and somebody asked me how I would justify this belief, Plantinga holds that I could simply say it is a basic belief, just like my belief that I am sitting here now? Oh, puh-leeeeze! That seems to be very controversial. After all, my belief that I am sitting here now and my belief in God are two very different beliefs, are they not?

MARY: Yes, surely Plantinga is wrong in his critique of foundationalism? It sounds like a reasonable approach to me. For example, if I said I thought that crime was going to decrease dramatically in the next decade, it is surely a sensible—and justi-fied—approach to recognize that this is an *inferred* belief, which would require me to unpack the inferences that led me to this belief. Isn't it the same with belief in God?

MALCOLM: It might seem so, but Plantinga claims that there is no good argument to support the *foundationalist criterion* for what he calls properly basic beliefs. Recall that the criterion is that "whatever is self-evident, or evident to the senses, or incorrigible" is a properly basic belief, and all other beliefs are inferred beliefs. Plantinga claims that this criterion is self-referentially incoherent because *it itself* is not self-evident, or evident to the senses, or incorrigible.

JEAN: "Self-referentially incoherent"? What exactly does that mean?

MALCOLM: He means that the criterion undermines itself or con-tradicts itself.

FRANK: Because it says we should accept only beliefs that are self-ev-ident, and so on. But then we turn around and accept the criterion itself even though it is not self-evident.

JOHN: That criticism is very soft, I think. Surely the found-ationalist criterion is an *inferred* criterion—a generalization about self-evident beliefs and so on, arrived at by examining many instances of them. This is why a foundationalist accepts the criterion; he does not believe that the criterion is a basic belief.

MALCOLM: Yes, John, for once I think you have stumbled into the truth!

BRIAN: But, curiously, as you mentioned, he is not saying we should reject foundationalism; just that we should widen the net of properly basic beliefs to include belief in God. This seems to me to be a kind of relativism.

FRANK: How so?

BRIAN: Well, it appears that he believes we cannot justify our most famous epistemological theory—called foundationalism—so we can simply believe whatever we like. And if anyone objects to any belief we hold, we can simply say that their criterion for basic beliefs cannot be supported and use that excuse to avoid justifying our beliefs. Whereas I would say that if we cannot prove the exis-tence of something, then we should not believe in it.

MALCOLM: You raise excellent points, Brian. In fact, you identify the two major objections philosophers have made to Plantinga's position. The first objection is that he thinks belief in God is groundless, that we do not need any evidence or reasons to believe in God. We can simply believe, and, when challenged about it, reply that our belief in God is a basic belief. The second criti-cism—a very serious point—is that Plantinga's view appears to sanction just about any kind of belief, no matter how ridiculous, or poorly supported, or even dangerous.

JEAN: Like some crazy wackos could claim that their beliefs were properly basic and therefore justified?

FRANK: Yes, like Jim Jones, or David Koresh, or religious cultists, or leaders of any type of crazy group, religious or not.

PATRICIA: Has Plantinga responded to these excellent objections, Malcolm?

MALCOLM: Yes, he has. And working through his answers will help us to understand his position further. Let us turn first to the criticism that he is really saying that belief in God does not need to be a justified belief. Plantinga replies that this is not so, and he tries to draw an analogy between ordinary perceptual experience and religious experience to illustrate his point. He gives the example of beliefs such as "I see a tree" or "That person is in pain," and he argues that these beliefs are justified *by my experience*. I do not take the behavior of the other person when he is in pain, for instance, *as evidence* that he is in pain. My belief that he is in pain is, therefore, properly basic. The same, he holds, is generally true of memory beliefs as well; my belief that I had breakfast this morning is a basic belief. He concludes by saying that there is *a certain condition in which I find myself, which I recognize, but that is hard to state in detail, and when I am in that condition, I know that my beliefs are properly basic.* Here is another example: if I see a rose-colored wall, then part of the condition would have to be that something appears to me in such and such a way and so on.

JOHN: Come on, Malcolm, that is pretty implausible. I am not sure that all of those beliefs mentioned are really properly basic; I think there may be inferences involved. And my belief that "that person is in pain" is surely based on my seeing him in pain? But, leaving that aside, I can see how what he says might be true of ordinary perceptual beliefs of the kind he mentions, for you can see and hear and touch those things. Yet I do not think his claim that *religious experiences* are similar to these perceptual experiences holds up. Having an experience of God is definitely not very similar to seeing a tree before me now.

PATRICIA: And everybody has ordinary perceptual beliefs, whereas many people do not have properly basic religious beliefs.

JEAN: I bet he is ready with a reply. It's very hard to trip up a philosopher!

MALCOLM: Of course. He argues that many conditions in our experience—such as guilt, gratitude, danger, a sense of God's presence, and so on—call forth properly basic *religious* beliefs, just the way many conditions in our experience call forth properly basic *perceptual* beliefs. He argues that in some cases, for instance, a person might have the belief that "God created this flower" or that "God is near." This experience leads one directly to belief in God. Belief in God is somehow directly carried in the experience. This belief is not based on other beliefs and is therefore a basic belief.

MARY: But what about the fact that many people do not have the belief that "God created this flower" or those other beliefs you mentioned?

MALCOLM: Plantinga might say that that is their hard luck! But the crucial point is that for those who *do* have them, their belief in God is properly basic and justified in just the way our perceptual beliefs are justified.

RENEE: I would like to go back to the point about inferences again. I have had some of the experiences Plantinga is talking about, such as the experience—and then the belief—that God created this flower, but I am sure that I inferred this belief from my general belief in God. Since I believe in God to begin with, I tend to see or interpret the world through "religious eyes," as it were. But that is not what he has in mind is it, if I understand him correctly?

BRIAN: I think Plantinga has to be very careful here. Because there is a clear difference between saying that if one subscribes to—or perhaps it would be better to say if one is committed to—a religious worldview, then one might see the world or interpret the world in a religious way. But this could not be a *justification for accepting* a religious worldview (that is, for believing in God). And, second, it seems that if one takes Renee's route, then the *interpretation* would involve *inferences* as well.

MARY: Could you give an example of what you mean?

BRIAN: Of course, priests are hard to trip up as well! I could report to you my experience of feeling that God's presence is near sometimes, an experience I often have. But perhaps I have this experience *because* I am a religious believer, committed to the religious world-picture, if you like; I tend to see the world in a religious way. So my first point is that I probably could not take this experience of God's presence as a *reason* to believe in God, since I experience the world in this way only because I already believe in God. My second point is that since I am interpreting my experiences in a certain way—under the influence of the religious world-picture to which I am committed—it is safe to say that there is an inference involved from *my actual experience* of, say, the majesty and mystery of the universe and my move to a feeling of God's presence based on this experience.

JEAN: But are you *interpreting* your experiences or experiencing God *directly?* That is a question that bothers me.

BRIAN: Yes it is a key question, and that's why I said "probably" in my example. I'm not fully sure if my experience that God is near arises as a result of my religious beliefs or independently of them. And I am reluctant to say that I only ever experience God as near *because* I am a religious believer.

JEAN: I have read John of the Cross's *Dark Night of the Soul,* and I would find it very hard to believe that he is not reporting that he experienced God *directly.* And I have a close friend who is very religious and who has had a profound religious experience. I trust her very much and do not think she is either lying or delusional.

PATRICIA: Maybe she is deluded, though, and just providing a very subtle *interpretation* of more vague experiences? Her prior background commitment to Christianity—and this goes for St. John of the Cross too—could be influencing her understanding of her experiences.

MALCOLM: Good example, Brian. Maybe you could talk to my philosophy of religion class sometime on this topic. Plantinga is not saying we interpret the world in a religious way; he is saying that we experience God directly in our experience and that on the basis of this experience, our belief in God is rational, and justified, and, therefore, not groundless.

JOHN: I'm still not convinced.

JEAN: I knew it.

JOHN: I do not see how he can avoid the charge that the belief is inferred without giving a *detailed description* of the experience. And it is also very problematic that many people do not have these experiences. One would think—especially given his comparison of these experiences to perceptual experiences—that they should be quite common. This point, I think, further supports the view that such experiences are inferred or involve interpretations and that those who do not have them are people who do not make the inference or the interpretation. After all, he is not talking about mystical experiences, which are rare and do not occur to the common mass of humanity.

FRANK: Plantinga might say that such experiences *are* available to all—for example, of the majesty and mystery of the universe, to refer back to Brian's example—if only people would open themselves up to them. After all, people can close themselves off to much that is valuable in life, such as the spiritual realm. They can do this by committing themselves dogmatically to an atheistic or naturalistic worldview. Can't they, Patricia?!

RENEE: Yes, can't the atheist interpret the world in a nonreligious way based on his prior commitment to his worldview? That would be dogmatic.

PATRICIA: Yes, I think Frank and Renee are right about that, but I have often thought that it is religious believers who are being dogmatic! However, it seems to me to be a mistake to think that an experience of the majesty and mystery of the universe, which is an experience we all probably have had at one time or another, is a *religious* experience of any kind. It is a far cry from this kind of experience to the experience of a sense of God's presence. I think that if you make this extra step, you are certainly making an inference from the more vague experience to the existence of God or are interpreting the experience to be evidence of the nearness of God or something like that. And this apparently is not what Plantinga has in mind.

MALCOLM: No, he is talking about experiences that are more obviously religious in character right from the beginning, such as the experience that "God created this flower."

JOHN: I have never had that kind of experience. I think he owes us a detailed description of such experiences so that we can see how they do *not* involve an inference and yet remain rational and justified.

JEAN: You might have the experience if you opened yourself up to it!

MALCOLM: Let us briefly discuss the second problem we raised earlier for his view, which was the problem of how to place a *limit* on what kinds of beliefs can count as basic beliefs. In other words, isn't there a danger that we could use Plantinga's view to justify any kind of bizarre claim, religious or not?

RENEE: Yes, take Jim Jones, for example, who convinced nine hundred of his followers to commit suicide with him in Guyana in 1978. Suppose he said that he had an experience that "God was talking to me and told me to kill nine hundred people today."

BRIAN: And when pushed on how he could be sure about this or when asked for the justification for this belief, he simply said: "It is a properly basic belief," which means he had a *direct* experience.

FRANK: Yes, that is a crucial point. He is not claiming to make any inference from certain experiences of his *to* the existence of God, an inferential move that could then be challenged. It really does look like any move to evaluate Jim Jones's beliefs has been cut off if he claims his belief is a basic belief.

MALCOLM: Your example is very challenging for Plantinga. His reply is less than satisfactory, in my view. He argues that the proper way to work out whether a belief is a justified properly basic belief is through *induction*. What we must do, he says, is to assemble *examples of beliefs and the conditions in which those properly basic beliefs are called forth such that the former are obviously properly basic in the latter*. For perceptual beliefs, an example might be "I see a tree before me"; we know the conditions under which this belief would be justified even though it is a basic belief. If, for example, you were taking a particularly strong medicine that caused you to have hallucinations occasionally, sometimes of trees, you might doubt on a particular occasion whether you were actually seeing a tree.

PATRICIA: And over a period of time he is saying that we would become familiar with the sorts of conditions in which legitimate— that is, justified—basic beliefs occur. This is what he means when he says that the way to arrive at a criterion is inductive.

MALCOLM: Yes, and he then says that we also know the kinds of conditions in religious communities that call forth basic religious beliefs. For example, in a Christian community people typically have religious beliefs of the sort that "God is near" or "God is talking to me" or "God created this flower," and so on. These are properly basic and justified.

JOHN: But how does this help us with the Jim Jones case?

MALCOLM: Well, I don't think it does help us very much. But Plantinga thinks it is obvious that some beliefs are not justified; he gives examples of beliefs about the Great Pumpkin or about Voodoo. Jim Jones's beliefs would be included here. Plantinga would say that these beliefs are not called forth in the right conditions. We would discover, for example, when investigating the beliefs of

Jim Jones that he was not quite rational and that his beliefs were not connected to his experiences. Or that he was taking drugs or something like that. So the right conditions for Jim Jones to hold the basic beliefs that he claims to hold do not obtain.

PATRICIA: I don't think I can buy that. I mean couldn't one argue that ordinary religious believers may not be quite rational either, if they claim they are directly experiencing God? If they claim that their belief in God is inferred in some way, then of course you can debate with them about the inference.

MARY: I do not think we can simply say that religious believers who claim to have had religious experiences are simply irrational, Patricia. Because many of them are not irrational people! And religious experiences have changed many lives—surely a pretty good test that they are credible?

BRIAN: I agree, Mary. But the problem with Plantinga's view is that he appears to be saying that we have a way of life going on—for example, the religious way of life—and *within that way of life* certain beliefs are standard or accepted and so on. Yet I do not see what, in Plantinga's view, gives the way of life, or form of life to use Wittgenstein's phrase, rational respectability—except for the fact that it is well established in a culture and accepted by many people. Isn't he only getting rid of the Jim Jones problem by saying that Jones's followers are a kind of fringe group that no one takes seriously? And isn't he implying that religion is legitimate because it is not a fringe view?

RENEE: So your point is that if we had a society where Jim Jones's beliefs were widely accepted by many people, then on Plantinga's view, they would have to be regarded as basic and justified?

MALCOLM: That seems to be where he is headed. Because then one couldn't give his reply that Jim Jones's beliefs are not called forth in the right conditions. For many people *would* regard the conditions as right.

FRANK: But on a standard of objective rationality, though, Jim Jones's beliefs would still be wrong.

MALCOLM: Yes, that is true. Remember that Plantinga is saying that some people—many people—have some kind of direct experience of God (which he does not describe fully), an experience that makes their belief in God basic, rational, and justified. He is also saying that nobody has the kind of direct experience of God that Jim Jones claimed to have had, or if they do, then it could not be regarded as a basic belief and would end up being open to question.

JOHN: My problem is that I do not see how he can rule out the rationality of Jim Jones's beliefs if all he has to go on is the fact that the criterion for judging beliefs comes from inductive examples taken in the right conditions. Because, as Brian mentioned, if we had a well-established Jim Jones community—in which many claimed to have these experiences—then they could all say the conditions are right and the examples good.

JEAN: Plantinga would probably insist that we would never have a huge community like this of widely irrational people.

JOHN: I'm not sure about that. There are all kinds of crazy people out there.

MALCOLM: I don't think he can consistently make that claim, Jean, because then he would be saying that their *experiences* are not justified, but he will *not* allow the atheist to say this about the experiences of the ordinary religious believers or the religious experiences of the ordinary religious community. It is not clear that he has the philosophical resources to criticize Jim Jones's experiences and *still* claim that standard religious experiences are basic and justified.

BRIAN: As I recall, Malcolm, John Hick develops a view that is very similar to Plantinga's. Can his ideas throw any light on these issues?

MALCOLM: Actually, yes Hick's view is similar in a number of respects, but he does introduce several new points that can help us with our discussion. Hick believes that in general the universe is "religiously ambiguous," by which he means that there isn't really enough evidence to decide one way or the other on the question of the existence of God. The evidence is pretty much fifty-fifty; there is some evidence in favor of belief in God, but then there are other features of the universe that seem to indicate that there is no God.

RENEE: So Hick believes you cannot prove the existence of God, but he still thinks you can offer some kind of evidence in favor of the existence of God by means of religious experiences? He can't be talking about the traditional argument based on religious experience, can he, since this was offered as a proof for the existence of God?

MALCOLM: That's right. But we must be careful here to state Hick's position correctly. He is not arguing that if a person has a religious experience then he can directly infer that God exists on the basis of the experience or that philosophers in general can conclude on the basis of the number of reports of such experiences that God exists. He says that this is the traditional argument and that he is not offering another version of this argument. He is leaving open the question of whether or not *God* actually is the cause of the experience. Instead, he wants to ask what it would be rational for a person to believe about the existence of God on the basis of having a religious experience.

JEAN: That seems very subtle; could you go over it again? You're making this very complicated. Remember, you are the one with the doctorate in philosophy!

MALCOLM: I'm trying to make it as simply as possible! It is a quite subtle point, and the role the inference plays in his argument should be clarified at the outset. Hick will acknowledge that—looking at the issue from the side of the objective question of whether God exists or not—we do not know if God actually is the cause of the religious experiences. But looking at the issue from the side of the person who has the religious experience, he is asking: Is it rational for that person to believe in God on the basis of his experience? And, secondly, would it be rational for me to believe in God on the basis of A's report of his experience?

JOHN: This sounds very like our distinction made in one of our previous conversations between a belief being rational and a belief being true. Hick is saying that if a person has a religious experience, it may well be *rational* for that person to believe in God on the basis of it, even though we cannot know whether his belief in God is *true* or not. He is not concerned with this latter question.

MARY: Yes, I see what he is saying. So his view is similar to Plantinga's? However, it looks like Hick believes there is an inference involved generally in religious experiences, unlike Plantinga, who says there is not. But Hick wants to focus on whether the religious believer is *rational* or justified in making the inference, not on whether the inference is actually true. So there is not much of a difference between Hick's view and the traditional view?

MALCOLM: No, very little; some people would probably say that there is no difference at all.

PATRICIA: How does Hick handle the objection then that a religious believer might be mistaken about God being the cause of their experience? He must handle this objection because, unlike Plantinga, Hick is not saying that the experience of God is *carried directly* in the experience. The believer is making an *inference*—which Hick claims is justified—*to* the existence of God.

MALCOLM: On that particular objection, Hick is, I think, quite insightful and gives us more to go on than Plantinga does. He holds that religious beliefs often arise out of *a natural response of the human mind to its experiences.* And then he adds that we should trust these experiences if two conditions are satisfied. First, we should trust them if there are no countervailing considerations that would count against our experiences. This is what Richard Swinburne calls the "principle of credulity." Second, we should trust our experiences if the experience is *consistent* with the rest of our experiences and knowledge and does not go against our existing body of belief.

MARY: Yes, that seems fairly sensible. But could you illustrate what he has in mind by working through an example, Malcolm?

JEAN: Yes, I think I follow what he means, but an example would really help to clarify the matter further.

MALCOLM: Okay, take this example. Suppose you had the experience of living in God's presence. It is important initially to emphasize that Hick believes this kind of experience arises from a natural response of the human mind to reality.

FRANK: I like the way he puts that. He is saying that these experiences are common, almost part of what it means to be human, resulting from an expression of our spiritual side. He would not be happy with somebody who says that they do not understand what he means when he says this. He would probably say they were resisting the experience of something greater than themselves. Would that be fair?

MALCOLM: I think so.

JOHN: As a critic of the view that religious experiences are indications or might count as evidence that there is a God, Frank, I wouldn't wish to say that the experience that there is something greater than ourselves is uncommon. I think Hick might well be right that the human mind does predispose us toward *that* type of experience. But I think it is a far cry from that somewhat vague and ambiguous feeling to come to believe either that God exists, or, Hick's weaker claim, that it is rational to believe in God *on the basis of* these kinds of experiences.

RENEE: I'm not sure I agree with you, John. After all, I do not think those kinds of experiences are as vague as you say they are. I think people do have more specific experiences—that someone is watching over them, say, or that God created the universe. And it seems to me to be reasonable to say that if you have such an experience, it is at least rational to believe in God on the basis of it.

FRANK: It would still be a bit vague, though, in terms of what kind of God we are talking about, or in terms of what God wanted us to do, and so on. So you would still need Scripture to fill out the details.

PATRICIA: Yes, that's all well and good, but suppose it is a Muslim who is having the experience?

MALCOLM: These points are all first-rate. But let's not get ahead of ourselves. Let's all relax! We said that one has the experience first, right? Now, Hick says it is rational to believe in God on the basis of the experience if the two conditions are met. The first condition would not be met, for example, if we had just been drinking heavily! Because the experience might be alcohol induced rather than God induced! And the second condition would not be met if the experience is not consistent with the rest of our experience or knowledge. For example, if we thought we saw a flying saucer, we would doubt that it really was a flying saucer. If the two conditions *are* met, then Hick believes that normally we would and do trust our experiences. He says, for example, that Jesus's belief that he lived in God's presence *evokes a confirming echo in our own experience* (which is a very good way to put it, I believe), but he says that Jesus's belief in demons does not. So while it was rational for Jesus to hold these two beliefs it is rational for us to believe only the first— that is, that Jesus lived in God's presence—because the second is not now consistent with our knowledge.

FRANK: Wait a minute! So, according to Hick, Jesus was not divine? I do not see how he can avoid this conclusion if he thinks Jesus held irrational beliefs and also did not recognize they were irrational. And why is a belief in demons not now consistent with our knowledge?

MALCOLM: You're right, Frank. Hick does not believe in the divinity of Jesus.

FRANK: Well, that directly contradicts Scripture. He sounds like another liberal theologian trying to have his cake and eat it.

JOHN: So he believes that when one has a religious experience in normal circumstances, one should trust the experience? But how does he guard against the fact that the religious believer might be simply interpreting certain more vague types of experiences in a more specifically religious way? For example, he might be interpreting a feeling that there is something greater than the universe or a feeling that the universe had to come from somewhere and so must have been caused, in such a way as to believe that the God of Christianity exists, and is worthy of worship, and has a plan for us, and so on.

MALCOLM: I think that is a fair point. Hick makes a distinction between general and specific religious convictions (not experiences) to handle this issue. He thinks, first, that religious awareness or experience does not always constitute cognition of the divine. He argues that this range of experience, while constituting our human consciousness of a transcendent divine reality, takes a great variety of concrete forms developed within the different historical traditions. It is neither a pure undistorted consciousness of the divine nor merely a human projection, but rather the range of differing ways in which the infinite divine reality has in fact been apprehended by finite and imperfect human beings.

PATRICIA: I must come back to the vagueness of this view again. He seems to be saying that the divine reality manifests itself in different ways to people in the different religions. But remember, our question is: Is it rational to move from a vague kind of experience to the existence of God, or to the existence of Buddha, or Brahma, or whoever? Without a close description of a few cases, I do not think Hick is persuasive.

JEAN: What would the description add that is now missing?

PATRICIA: Well, I think John and I agree that the move from the experience that there is something greater out there to belief in God, and behavior appropriate to that belief, is not rationally justified, or is at least quite controversial. Now Hick thinks it is rationally justified, but he does not give us a description of the experience to show *how* this move is justified. Even if he claims that the experiences are more specifically religious in character right from the beginning, he still owes us a description of them, and without it his view is somewhat empty. Also, if he claims that the Christian, say, experiences the Christian God in some way directly in his experience, then this seems to be incompatible with saying that the Muslim's experiences are also veridical.

MARY: But aren't you leaving something out? Could he not insist that we are influenced in formulating our full, mature interpretations or readings of our religious experiences by our respective religious traditions, but that at a more basic, general level, our experiences are still *religious* in character?

JOHN: He could make that point, but then I do not see how he gets from that to the claim that these general experiences justify one's belief in *God*. That seems to be a recurring problem in his work.

MALCOLM: He could say that the experience of a divine reality is religious in the sense that it is a genuine experience of a being greater than the universe. However, he believes we cannot get much more specific than that, and it is left to the different religious traditions to articulate more fully a vision for their respective religious communities. This way the experience of the transcendent reality is justified, but we must stop short of claiming that any particular world religion has the truth. And that is Hick's position.

JEAN: And Jim Jones?

MALCOLM: He rules Jim Jones's beliefs out by saying that they are not consistent with our knowledge. Jones's belief that nine hundred people should commit suicide seems totally contrary to our understanding of the value and purpose of human life, for example.

BRIAN: I am afraid I see in the work of both Plantinga and Hick a move away from rationality in religion to an emphasis on human experience. This seems to be because they do not think it is possible to give a general justification of religious belief taking the natural theology route. So they retreat, as it were, to saying something like: "Well, my experiences justify my beliefs; and one cannot criticize them from some outside, or independent, standpoint." I am suspicious of this approach, because it seems to make an unnecessary concession to scientific naturalism.

RENEE: Before we finish our discussion, let's move on to D.Z. Phillips's fideistic view. Following up on your remarks, Brian, Phillips goes further and argues that traditionally in philosophy we have approached the whole question of justifying belief in God in a wrongheaded way. He was influenced by Ludwig Wittgenstein's (1889–1951) brief, and often cryptic, remarks on religious belief. In fact, one could argue that the flight from reason evident in both Hick and Plantinga, and in much of contemporary theology, began with Wittgenstein and Phillips and others.

MALCOLM: An interesting insight, Renee.

JEAN: What is a fideist?

RENEE: In theology, it generally refers to a religious believer who believes on faith alone or who places more emphasis on faith in religion than on reason. In philosophy of religion, it is used nowadays to describe philosophers like Phillips and Kierkegaard who believe that the quest for evidence in religion is a mistake. These philosophers have very little time for natural theology.

MALCOLM: Yes, let us bring our discussion to a conclusion by showing how Phillips's view of "Wittgensteinian Fideism" fits into what we have been saying. Phillips claims, like Wittgenstein, that life consists of language-games, which make up forms of life. A language-game is a set of cultural meanings, practices, and rules that emerge out of and that are specific to particular groups within society. The key point is that *each language-game has its own internal criteria of meaning and rationality.* The function of philosophy is to describe, not to evaluate, language-games. Science is a language-game in which the question of evidence and emphasis on experiment, observation, measurement, and verification are important criteria for evaluating a scientific claim or theory. However, the religious language-game is completely different. Its internal criteria of meaning and justification are not the same as in science, and it is a mistake to judge one language-game by the criteria of another. Religion should not be judged according to the criteria of justification in science.

BRIAN: I have to confess to feeling a certain excitement when I first read the work of Wittgenstein and Phillips on religion. Phillips means that if I claim that God exists, it is not appropriate to ask me for evidence for this belief in the way that it would be appropriate to ask me for evidence if I said that an electron exists.

RENEE: Yes, that is the fideist view. Religion and science are in two totally different categories. Phillips holds that this is so because, as he puts it, *coming to believe that God exists is not like coming to believe that an additional being, or a new object, exists.* This is different from the case, say, of coming to believe that an electron exists, where you do come to believe that a new object exists.

PATRICIA: Hold on a minute! That seems wrong to me. When a religious believer comes to believe in God, doesn't he believe that an additional being exists? That there is another being outside the world—who created the world according to a plan? A being that the atheist does not think exists? That is why it is not just acceptable, but necessary, to ask for evidence for the existence of such a being.

MALCOLM: That objection poses a difficulty for Phillips. For he is quite up front in saying that he does not think that God is a being outside the universe. God is not an additional consciousness beyond our consciousnesses. Nor does Phillips believe in immortality.

JOHN: So he is an atheist like me!

PATRICIA: Renee, you hold that view; what do you believe?

RENEE: I would not go as far as Phillips. I do believe that we cannot know anything much about what kind of being God is. We must use our very inadequate human concepts to try to capture religious realities and must recognize that we inevitably distort them. I also think that it is perfectly respectable—and here I agree with Hick and Plantinga—to believe in the divine reality on the basis of one's experiences. The religious world-picture is a perfectly respectable philosophy, though I would not say that it is any better than an atheist world-picture. Here I disagree with Malcolm, who agrees with Willard and Craig, that the religious world-picture is more rational than the atheist world-picture.

JOHN: But does this not bring us back to the old question of why we should adopt this world-picture in the first place, which is partly to ask: Why should we believe in God? Now if you are saying that this is not an appropriate question to ask or that evidence is not relevant to the answer, then your view seems to have *no justification*. Justification seems to be in short supply this morning!

MARY: It would help if you could explain what coming to believe in God actually means, if it does not include coming to believe that an additional being exists. Because when I say I believe in God, I believe that God really exists over and above the universe, that he created the universe, and has a plan for humanity, and so on. I agree that we may not know all the details and that our concepts are inadequate, but when I pray to God, for example, I believe he really exists and hears my prayers. How does Phillips explain prayer?

MALCOLM: I do not think it is unfair to say that Phillips offers a kind of metaphorical view of God and prayer, and that is why I think John is not far wide of the mark in saying that Phillips appears to be a kind of atheist. He does not believe that there is a

God outside the world, so obviously no being hears our prayers, since he is not there to hear them. So prayer must be understood in a metaphorical, or in what is sometimes called an *expressive*, way. According to Phillips, we must appeal to the religious community to see what religious believers are actually doing when they talk to God. In Phillips's terminology, we must make explicit the *grammar* of religious language and worship, that is, we must examine what religious believers say and mean when they use religious language.

JEAN: But aren't religious believers talking *to* God?

MALCOLM: To give you a taste of how Phillips argues these points, he says that talking to God is not like talking to another person. So we should not judge our talking to God in the same way we might judge our talking to another human being. For example, it makes no sense to say we are having a conversation with God or that we must get God to understand. In prayer, for Phillips, we reach a better understanding of *ourselves*.

JOHN: Oh, puh-leeeeze! That does sound metaphorical. Prayer is a form of contemplation, but with the added, key difference from the traditional understanding that the one to whom you pray does not exist.

FRANK: And I think he has misdescribed the nature of prayer for most religious believers. Praying to God, for many, is a conversation—an unusual one, yes, but a conversation, nevertheless. And talking to God *is* like talking to another person in the one crucial sense that the other person must exist in order to talk to him or her, just as God must exist in order to talk to him.

MALCOLM: Here is how Phillips describes some of our prayers: A prayer of thanksgiving is closely connected with seeing life as a sacrifice for God. Petitionary prayers—where we ask God for things—are best understood not as an attempt to influence God's will, but as asking for strength to go on living whatever happens.

FRANK: I find that very problematic; it seems like he is saying God does not exist so there is no point in asking him for things; so we need either to reinterpret petitionary prayers or give them up altogether. He reinterprets them. He is odd in that sense. He is giving up most of what we mean by religious belief, in my view, and yet trying to retain religious *language*, such as the language of prayer. Yet he has to interpret it in a metaphorical way. I think I am right in saying that religious believers understand prayer in a literal way.

MARY: Yes, surely people are really asking God for things, such as health, success, and things like that, in petitionary prayers and not just asking in a roundabout way for strength? That seems far-fetched.

RENEE: But Phillips is surely right in rejecting the view that God is some kind of additional being, because he does make the point that for the religious believer it makes no sense to say that God might not exist, in a way that it does make sense for the atheist to say this.

BRIAN: I am a religious believer, and it does make sense to me to say that God might not exist. However, I believe that this particular claim is false. I don't think Phillips is adequately distinguishing here between the *meaning* of a claim and the *truth* of the claim.

MALCOLM: Phillips claims that coming to believe in God is not like coming to believe that an additional being exists. It is rather *to come to die to the world's way of regarding things*. He calls this eternal love; it is other than the world because it is not dependent on how things go. He says that the Old Testament figure Job is an example of a person who exhibits this kind of love. Job adopted an entirely selfless attitude toward life and was therefore in the reality of God.

PATRICIA: Yes, I think Brian's point is correct. One could plausibly give that interpretation of Job's beliefs and actions after he came to accept God's will. Yet Job undoubtedly believed too that God existed over and above the world. Phillips does seem to be abandoning the factual or truth claims of religion and then offering novel interpretations or metaphorical readings of other religious experiences.

MALCOLM: His view does not appear to be a particularly satisfactory way to justify the rationality of religious belief. It is less convincing than either Plantinga's or Hick's view, I think. Phillips is offering a radical reinterpretation of religious belief that seems to distort what most people mean by religious belief and that seems to invite serious philosophical questions. It is interesting to wonder whether you could actually live this kind of religious life and still claim to be a religious believer. Even Renee—who describes herself as a fideist—would not claim that God does not exist, but prefers to emphasize the point that faith and reason are in two different categories.

JOHN: I do not think Phillips has even established the claim that faith and reason are in two completely separate categories because he has given up religious belief completely and adopted a theory of religious metaphor to preclude the question of evidence in religious belief. Once you do that, I think that you are stuck with more problems than you began with. Of these three approaches, Malcolm, I think that Brian's earlier remark is accurate. They do seem to me to be motivated at least in part by the evidentialist critique of religion. They are all seeking alternative ways of trying to establish the rationality of theism. That would seem to indicate to me that they have conceded the moral high ground as far as the evidence is concerned to the naturalists and the atheists.

MALCOLM: I think you could make that case. But as I have argued in some of our conversations in the last few days, I do not think that we need to do that, for natural theology is still a very promising route. And don't forget that one of the natural theology arguments is the *traditional* argument from religious experience, not the more modern view that we have been discussing. I believe religious experiences have great value and that there is a key role for religious experiences in justifying the existence of God within a natural-theology framework. Anyway, let's leave it at that for today and go over to the playing field and get the softball game going!

PATRICIA: Now, that's more like it!

BRIAN: But softball is not a sport!

Key Terms and Distinctions

Religious experience
Traditional argument from
    religious experience
Contemporary argument from
    religious experience
Reformed epistemology
Classical foundationalism
Basic belief
Inferred belief
Evidentialism

Religious experiences vs.
    perceptual experiences
The principle of credulity
General and specific religious
    convictions (Hick)
Fideism
Wittgensteinian fideism
Language-game
Meaning vs. truth in religion

Questions on Chapter 6

1. Explore the question of whether or not religious experiences involve inferences by attempting a fairly detailed *description* of what you think a religious experience might involve.

2. Select one of the saints mentioned in Chapter 6—for example, St. Teresa, St. John of the Cross—and read their report of their religious experiences. Write out a very careful description of the experiences paying attention to some of the issues raised in the discussion in Chapter 6.

3. Is it a fair criticism of Plantinga's position that his description of the nature of a religious experience is vague? Explain why or why not.

4. Do you think that Plantinga captures something important in his view that belief in God is properly basic? Explain your answer.

5. Compare and contrast the approach of Plantinga or Hick with that of the approach of natural theology discussed in Chapter 1.

6. The various contemporary arguments from religious experience make much of the similarities between our ordinary everyday perceptual beliefs and religious beliefs. Compare and contrast the relationship between these two kinds of belief.

7. What do you think of John Hick's view, as expressed by Malcolm, that "the experience of a divine reality is religious in the sense that it is a genuine experience of a being greater than the universe . . . [But] we cannot get much more specific than that, and it is left to the different religious traditions to more fully articulate a vision for their respective religious communities. This way the experience of the transcendent reality is justified, but we must stop short of claiming that any particular world religion has the truth."?

8. Are human experiences like the experience that there is something greater than the universe or the experience of the majesty and mystery of the universe *religious* in character, or do they fall short of being *religious* experiences? Discuss the role of interpretation in these experiences also.

9. Assess the fideist view of D.Z. Phillips that religion and science are different language-games, each with its own internal criteria of meaning and rationality, and that it is a mistake to criticize one language-game using the criteria of another.

10. Do you think that Phillips has correctly described the way religious believers actually do use religious language, for example, the language of prayer, as he claimed to be doing? Compare his view with your own experience of these religious phenomena.

Bibliography

Alston, William, *Perceiving God: The Epistemology of Religious Experience* (Ithaca, NY: Cornell University Press, 1991).

Goetz, Stewart C., "Belief in God is not Properly Basic," in *Contemporary Perspectives on Religious Epistemology,* ed. R. Douglas Geivett and Brendan Sweetman (New York: Oxford University Press, 1992), pp. 168–177.

Hick, John, *An Interpretation of Religion* (New Haven, CT: Yale University Press, 1989).

John of the Cross, St., *Dark Night of the Soul,* trans. and ed. E. Allison Peers (Garden City, NY: Doubleday, 1959).

Kierkegaard, Soren, *Concluding Unscientific Postscript* (original edition 1846), trans. David F. Swenson; introduction, notes and completion of the translation by Walter Lowrie (Princeton, NJ: Princeton University Press, 1941).

Phillips, D.Z., *The Concept of Prayer* (London: Routledge and Kegan Paul, 1965).

———, *Faith After Foundationalism* (London: Routledge and Kegan Paul, 1988).

Plantinga, Alvin, "Is Belief in God Properly Basic?" in *Contemporary Perspectives on Religious Epistemology*, ed. R. Douglas Geivett and Brendan Sweetman (New York: Oxford University Press, 1992), pp. 133–141.

Plantinga, Alvin, and Wolterstorff, Nicholas, eds., *Faith and Rationality: Reason and Belief in God* (Notre Dame, IN: University of Notre Dame Press, 1983).

Swinburne, Richard, *The Existence of God* (Oxford: Oxford University Press, 1991, second edition).

Teresa of Avila, St., *The Life of Teresa of Jesus*, trans. and ed. E. Allison Peers (Garden City, NY: Doubleday, 1960).

Wittgenstein, Ludwig, *Lectures and Conversations on Aesthetics, Psychology and Religious Belief* (Oxford: Blackwell, 1966).

Chapter Seven

Religious Pluralism

Sophia, a friend of Jean, joins the company to talk about the problem of religious pluralism. She advocates John Hick's position that all religions are diverse efforts to express the same divine reality. Patricia and John defend Joseph Campbell's view that religious doctrines are myths, which express the collective psychologies of cultural groups. There also occurs a discussion of the relationship of religion to science. Malcolm and Brian challenge Sophia's pluralism and Patricia's and John's defense of Campbell.

JEAN: I'd like you all to meet my friend, Sophia. Sophia is a Unitarian minister. She can add a lot to our conversations. She studied at the university after we all left. I got to know her during some retreats that she sponsored up high in the mountains. It was a wonderful experience for me. Sophia is very wise about all things spiritual.

SOPHIA: Please, Jean. You make me sound like some "New Age" guru. Jean has been known to exaggerate.

MARY: Speaking for all of us, we're happy, Sophia, that you're able to join us.

RENEE: I wish you had been involved in our earlier conversations. I'm sure you would have had a lot to say.

FRANK: Yeah, as it is, there's a break in the action. I'm not sure what new theme we're ready to discuss next.

BRIAN: Maybe we should go back over some of our former territory. Maybe we could revisit some issues. There are some details I would still like to see worked out on arguments for God's existence and on immortality.

181

JOHN: No, no, there's no need to backtrack, Brian. I can think of a very important issue. It has been at the back of my mind throughout our preceding discussions. And I dare say, it's an issue that will make many of you very uncomfortable.

MARY: Go ahead, John. You've got us all curious.

JOHN: Perhaps I could put it this way: Speaking with my philosophical hat on, I don't see how anyone could ever think that he or she had sufficient grounds to believe in a particular religion. I mean it is one thing to take up certain problems like the existence of God or life after death, examine them, ruminate about them, and conclude in certain cases that reason supports a religious claim. But that's not so much religion as it is philosophy. To look at religion from the philosophical point of view is to suspend the whole question of revelation. All the stories and myths about how this or that religion rests on an authoritative communication from God, that is to say, a revelation, are ignored. Philosophy of religion can in this or that isolated case reach a positive conclusion: One might think that one can prove the soul is immaterial, for example, or can establish that God exists. But that doesn't touch on the validity of the overall religion in which that particular issue or belief, now philosophically examined and justified, occurs. An isolated philosophical conclusion about the merits of this or that religious belief do nothing to contribute to the validity of the religion in general. Religions in general are accepted by a leap of faith, not by philosophical examination, even though I would grant that particular creeds within the religion might be philosophically supported, although my suspicion is that even that occurs rarely, if at all. People accept religions as true not for philosophical reasons. People believe in their religion because of less persuasive and often just arbitrary influences, such as tradition, family upbringing, cultural demands for acceptance, self-interest, even laziness. Commitment to a particular religion, then, is just a leap, a jump that no rational, truly philosophical person should make. In other words, it is never justifiable philosophically to believe that any general religious outlook or creed is true.

FRANK: It's not really as difficult as you make it, John. Religion is not like working through a philosophical problem. You're talking apples and oranges here. Religious commitment is a matter of accepting revelation. Our faith, the Christian faith, has been revealed to us by God. So belief is pretty easy when you look at it that way. We believe on God's authority. Having revealed divine truths to us, he himself has called us to believe. Some people substitute their own "truth" for God. They reject God's authority. But that is a mistake.

JOHN: God hasn't spoken to me directly, so I don't really have faith on his authority, do I? If I had it, it would be based on reports and testimonies from people like you, Frank—you and everybody else who constitute Christian culture, both now and in the past. That's how most people come to have faith. But you see that creates quite a problem.

FRANK: Help me out. I don't see a problem.

JOHN: Frank, you believe as a Christian because you grew up in a Christian culture and became intimate with the so-called Christian revelation. But you surely are not so naive as to believe that you would be a Christian if you had been brought up in a non-Christian country.

RENEE: I've always suspected you'd make a great Druid, Frank.

JOHN: Had you been born in such a land, you would have been indoctrinated with another "revelation." You probably wouldn't be a Christian but something else. Besides there are diverse and conflicting claims even within Christianity. Christians are often fighting about how the Gospels should be interpreted or about whether the Catholic Church is the decisive voice in matters Christian.

PATRICIA: John's right. If you had been born in Saudi Arabia, you'd be a Moslem; in Cambodia, a Buddhist; in India, probably a Hindu. This makes it look like religion is more a cultural phenomenon than a revelation of God.

JEAN: Wow, Patricia has been brushing up on her geography again!

FRANK: No, Patricia. Some cultures have faith-systems that are false because they contradict Christian revelation. I'm not saying that those religions don't have something of value. They provide many benefits for the people who believe in them. For instance, these faiths give to their people codes of morality to live by. But ultimately Christianity must judge these creeds as mistaken, at least to the extent that they conflict with Christian doctrine. In some cases, one may have to go so far as to judge those opposing religions as being more like superstitions or mythologies than actual revelations. I guess I'm saying that Christianity is *the* revealed religion.

PATRICIA: But who are you, Frank, to dismiss these other religions as mere superstitions. Many of these creeds—certainly those that are theistic—claim to be based on revelation just as Christianity does. Unless you're prepared to say that your religion is right just because it is yours or just because your culture is somehow better, there is no way to justify your revelation over any others.

FRANK: But we have the evidence of miracles. Christianity is founded on the miracles of Jesus. Many people saw Jesus raise Lazarus from the dead. He miraculously healed lepers, the lame, and the blind. There were hundreds who witnessed Jesus' resurrection and ascension. And, by the way, I'm not saying that other religions are "mere superstitions."

BRIAN: Don't forget that miracle at the wedding, where he turned water into wine. That reminds me I need to return this zinfandel to the bartender. I could have sworn I ordered club soda.

RENEE: Also there were the miracles of the Jewish prophets even before the time of Jesus. For examples, Moses parting the Red Sea and Joshua bringing the sun to a standstill.

FRANK: And let's not forget the miracles of the saints who lived after Christ. Miracles witness to the legitimacy of our Christian revelation.

PATRICIA: Yes, I'm sure they do. Just the way that miracles in India witness to Hinduism; miracles in Egypt witness to Islam; miracles in China witness to Buddhism. Each culture appeals to its own miracles to provide a foundation for its own religion. So which miracles count? Why are Christian miracles any more decisive?

MALCOLM: So, are you saying, John and Patricia, that all religions are true?

JOHN: Oh, no you don't, Malcolm. I'm wise to your tricky Socratic ways. I'm not going to answer your question affirmatively. I'm smart enough to know that I can't.

RENEE: Why not?

JOHN: Clearly, not all the revelations can be true, because some of them are in conflict with each other.

FRANK: In conflict?

PATRICIA: John is not saying that there are religious wars going on out there, but he is saying that not all the religions can be true because in some cases they contradict each other. They conflict in that sense.

MALCOLM: Exactly. The fact that religious beliefs are often in conflict with each other about what they declare as true poses quite a hurdle for someone who wants to say that all religions are equally valid, equally acceptable.

FRANK: Well, it would certainly be the case in my way of thinking that if a revelation does not accept Jesus Christ as the incarnate God, it is mistaken.

MALCOLM: That exemplifies the point exactly, Frank. Additionally, there are many other ways in which revelations contradict each other. For example, some creeds hold that the divine is personal, but others hold that it is impersonal. Some believe in reincarnation; others do not. Some believe that God became incarnate; others believe that God is purely transcendent. Some believe in personal immortality—That our souls survive death with our *selves*, our personalities, intact, destined to enjoy the eternal company of God; others believe that, if there is life after death, it involves the dissolution of our personal identities and the absorption of our souls into some kind of divine or cosmic soul. Some believe that the *Bible* is the word of God; others the *Bhagavad Gita* or the *Koran*. Clearly, if one of these views is true, its opposite must be false.

PATRICIA: But there is the possibility, don't forget, that given a pair of opposites in religion *neither* of them is true. In other words, they could be thought of not so much as "contradictories" but as "contraries," to pay homage to Aristotle's usage. Remember he said that contradictories cannot simultaneously be both true or both false, but contraries, on the other hand, while they can never be both true, can be both false. If we think of religious differences as contraries, we could minimize religious conflicts by dismissing a lot of them as just plain false. For example, if monotheism is true, polytheism must be false, and vice versa. However, it could be that there is nothing divine, whether one or many, in which case both views are false. They both can't be true, but they can both be false.

MALCOLM: Yes, it's important to remember that, Patricia. And I think that is one of the reasons people become skeptical about religion altogether. They're uncomfortable with the thought that some religions would be false if others are true. They're more comfortable with the step that no religions are true. David Hume observed long ago that "in matters of religion whatever is different is contrary." He explained that since every religion is presumably founded on certain miracles, the miracles that establish one creed serve to overthrow contrary religions. Reflecting on this point, Hume drew the following inference: Every reason for supporting the truth of one religion is a case against every other religion. But this means that for every religion there are far more grounds for believing it to be false than for believing it to be true. So, you see, John has brought up a very important issue for discussion. Philosophers of religion refer to this as the problem of religious pluralism or the problem of the plurality of the world's religions.

JOHN: Well, it may be a problem for you, Malcolm, but it's not for me. I'm with Hume. I think all these claims about revelation and the like are just hokum. In a modern scientific age I think one has to look for natural and cultural explanations for religion rather than medieval talk about revelation.

PATRICIA: Yes, Malcolm, you can't really expect people in this day and age to accept as literally true beliefs like the virgin birth, the promised land, the incarnation, the resurrection, and so on. In a prescientific age, like medieval Europe, you might see why people could accept such beliefs. They did not have the education to explain them otherwise. But today we do. You religious types act as though you've never heard of the social sciences, fields such as psychology, sociology, and anthropology. It seems to me that if a person is intellectually responsible today, he or she should first try to explain religion in light of what these fields have contributed to the understanding of humankind.

MALCOLM: And what is their explanation?

PATRICIA: Well, I don't want to oversimplify things, but some people in these fields explain religion in terms of group psychology and of the development of social habits for survival. Our collective psychology produces myths, like "the chosen people" and "the burning bush," to give our society a special sense of place and cohesion. These myths define how a people are special, even in the eyes of God. These myths also help to give society a social and moral order. Over time these myths are reinforced by expected behaviors among the members of the tribe; for example, how to marry, how to honor your parents, how to respect the elderly, how to treat children, how to honor the dead, and so on. Religion codifies and formalizes these behaviors. All this goes together to form powerful customs and traditions in a society. Religion, in the last analysis, becomes a device to preserve the status quo.

FRANK: So in steps the anthropologists explain away thousands of years of religion as the results of social and psychological drives and projections. Come on, John. Remember these various psychological theories are mere hypotheses, which seem to have little evidence to support them. Secondly, many psychologists themselves are very reluctant to explain religion in the way you've suggested because it commits them to a Freudian or Jungian analysis of culture. Psychologists who are not sympathetic with Freud or Jung are unlikely to accept your explanation.

BRIAN: Such disagreement among the psychologists casts doubt on whether psychology is a science, doesn't it?

MALCOLM: It seems to be a problem for the discipline, yes.

FRANK: Furthermore, John, I think that you are identifying science with naturalism. This is a common mistake. Theologians do it all the time. Opponents of theology do likewise. It is important not to confuse them. Science is simply knowledge obtained by scientific methods. Naturalism, however, is a philosophical worldview that uses science to support its interpretations of the universe, as we saw in our earlier discussions. Naturalism holds that there is no God and that matter in motion alone explains everything that exists. Of course, one can be a scientist and not subscribe to naturalism, but the distinction is often overlooked. Many apologists for naturalism assume that science presupposes the naturalists' atheism and materialism. Of course, science need not.

BRIAN: People like Stephen Jay Gould and Carl Sagan come to mind.

FRANK: Yes, they've been so successful that they've created the idea in education and popular media about science that science and naturalism are the same. One must be on guard against granting them this point, however.

MALCOLM: Right, Frank. You can see naturalism lurking behind what John is saying. He seems to think that a naturalistic explanation must always be preferred to a religious one. Since you assume that naturalism is science, you've made up your mind that science and religion are in conflict, so that you can't have religious truth if you have scientific truth, and vice versa.

FRANK: You seem to think that religion is a threat to scientific understanding. Hence, you let science trump religion, and in this way you think you're done with the problem. But isn't that a big mistake? Isn't it wrong to assume that science and religion are in conflict at all? Science and religion are about different things. The truths of the one subject belong to a different sphere of human inquiry. They don't conflict; they're just different. Why are you so afraid of religion, Patricia?

PATRICIA: I'll tell you. Beyond the fact that religion has been the source of unspeakable strife in human history—a strife that has resulted from people making the mistake of thinking that they alone have the privileged revelation—religion is antiscientific for just the reason you've suggested: It claims to be separate from science and thus unanswerable to the standards for scientific truth and inquiry.

JOHN: Your position, Frank, that religion is "different" from science is a way of trying to excuse religion from being open to criticism by other forms of human research. You see, your view is really a cop-out. It's a ruse to get religion off the hook, to make it immune to criticism.

PATRICIA: Yeah, believers are desperate to make it immune, because they know that if religion has to answer the challenges of science, it has much to lose. In short, it will be exposed as incredible, as something no self-respecting, modern, educated mind should believe.

FRANK: I'll reverse the tables and insist that your view is really the cop-out. In your desperation to debunk religion, you gloss over the key difference between science and religion. The former is concerned with this world; the latter with the spiritual world. That is why scientific examination is pointless where religion is concerned. They're two altogether separate realms of human knowledge. You can't use the one to criticize the other. You're talking apples and oranges.

PATRICIA: Really original, Frank.

RENEE: Frank's right. You guys don't want to admit it because you've already got an animus toward religion, and you're looking for any excuse to criticize it.

FRANK: Come on in, Malcolm. Help me out. Things are starting to get a little *ad hominem*. Isn't this business about science evaluating religion really a red herring? Aren't science and religion responding to two different realms of life? How can one tell the other what to do or think?

MALCOLM: It may surprise you, Frank, but I'd have to disagree with you on that score. I'm not at all comfortable with the view that consigns religion and science to separate compartments, so that the one can never communicate with or judge the other. That view seems to me to do violence to the unity of truth and human understanding.

FRANK: But isn't that to do violence to the nature of each discipline? I mean, how can religion be subjected to scientific method? Religion is not like scientific hypotheses, nor can it be examined by laboratory techniques. What are we going to do, send a chemist to Mecca to test it for holiness? They're different, radically different, and never the twain shall meet.

MALCOLM: I believe you're thinking with rigid dichotomies. I'm fully aware that science and religion differ. Nonetheless, they are alike in one very important respect: They each seek the truth.

FRANK: Yes, but they each seek the truth in a unique way.

MALCOLM: That's all well and good, but you've got to be very careful. You can't be so casual and flippant about the difference that you disregard the logic of truth. The uniqueness of each discipline can't allow one to say that what is true for science need not be true for religion. Logic requires that if something is true, it is true for all disciplines. Otherwise you're left with the intolerable relativistic position that something is at the same time both true and false.

FRANK: But that's acceptable since it's from two different perspectives: religion or science.

MALCOLM: But can't you see where that is contradictory? It amounts to saying that human understanding judges that one and the same thing is both true and false. How can something that is true suddenly be false just because we put off our scientific hat and don our religious one?

FRANK: But there is no worry about contradiction, because science and religion are separate. They deal with two separate realms of knowledge.

MALCOLM: Don't you see the problem, Frank? If one takes your view, then it becomes impossible for religion and science ever to disagree or agree. But that doesn't make sense, as is evident in the fact that in some cases they judge common objects. This is where it becomes obvious that the two disciplines can really contradict each other, showing that their agreement or disagreement is obviously logical and relevant. For example, according to the Christian religion God created the world, the universe, out of nothing. This is usually interpreted to mean that the world began. It had a first moment in time. Thus, revelation has spoken to the issue. Now, reason and science have spoken to this issue as well, holding that this view that the world was created is more plausible than the alternative, which is of course that the universe has existed from eternity. The Big Bang, the second law of thermodynamics, the debunking of the steady state theory of the universe, all lead modern physics to concur with Christian doctrine about the temporality and formation of the world, as we mentioned in our discussion about the evidence for God's existence. Clearly, it is only reasonable to say that science in this case coheres with religion. Its truth coincides with religious truth. This shows that science and religion should not be consigned to separate realms. They can communicate with each other; they can support each other. Both can express the same truth.

FRANK: Okay, perhaps sometimes they happen to agree. But what about when they disagree?

MALCOLM: This has important consequences for the debate about religion, because it provides a way of supporting some religions and challenging others. Science, coupled with philosophical reflections on science, becomes not so much a proof of religion but a kind of disproof. For this reason, I must insist that science is very relevant to religion. It's just a matter of logic. Unless one is willing to suffer intellectual schizophrenia, one must hold that if something in science is true, it cannot be false for religion, and vice versa. For example, if science shows that the universe is not eternal, then those religions that hold otherwise are false on that particular point.

JOHN: Well, I suppose that by sheer coincidence, sometimes scientific conclusions and religious doctrines agree, although we have to remember that science evolves and changes, and scientific agreement for religion now might turn into scientific disagreement in a hundred years. But I won't be small about it. I won't begrudge religion a little support from science. As long as science tells the tale, that's fine with me.

PATRICIA: Yes, but notice the asymmetry here. Science supports religion, but religion doesn't support science.

MALCOLM: I hate to be contentious, folks, but I would say that religion's support of science is more profound than science's support of religion. Did you ever stop to think that science itself wouldn't even exist had it not been for the Judeo-Christian religion?

PATRICIA: You're asking a lot, if you expect me to swallow that one, Malcolm. History records that Christianity has all too often been a sworn enemy of science.

MALCOLM: It's true that Christianity has not always been the most sympathetic parent, but it is the case that science is its offspring.

PATRICIA: What in blazes are you talking about, Malcolm?

MALCOLM: Perhaps if you would expand your reading, Patricia, you would know. If you were familiar with the work of Stanley Jaki, you would be already familiar with my point.

PATRICIA: Go on.

MALCOLM: Well, Father Jaki argues in some of his excellent books, such as *The Savior of Science* and *God and the Cosmologists,* that in the Western world we've become so habituated to scientific ways of thinking that we take science for granted. However, when one investigates the origins of science one is struck by how dependent on religion science really is. Science, like every other cultural phenomenon requires a culture, a social milieu, in which it can find a home, take root, and thrive. Did you ever stop to wonder why it is that science developed in the Western countries and not in Eastern ones? Science struggled and failed to find a foothold in other cultures because the religious climates elsewhere resisted it. Science has to be acquitted at the tribunal of the theologians, as it were. Jewish and Christian theologians were willing to give science a fair hearing, in spite of PR you hear to the contrary.

JOHN: Tell that to Hypatia, Galileo, and victims of the Inquisition.

MALCOLM: Unfortunate cases, one and all. Nonetheless, it is the West that appropriated and supported the teachings of a Galileo. Such appreciation of science was possible only in the West.

FRANK: And why is that?

MALCOLM: As Father Jaki explains, the Judeo-Christian worldview was congenial to scientific method. You see, according to Christianity, the world was created. This means that the world is contingent, just one of a plurality of worlds God could conceivably create. For the Christian, nature is not just a brute necessity. Instead it is a contingent existent conceived by God and conserved in existence by divine will. The radical contingency of the universe—the hallmark of Christian theology—could also find expression in scientific method, specifically through its use of hypotheses. Hypothetical method is a way of experimenting with contingencies. The universe is itself, according to Christianity, shot through with possibilities. Science is invited to test and explore those possibilities through hypothetical method.

BRIAN: Other cultures—such as those in Asia and in ancient Pagan times—had a harder time accommodating scientific inquiry and developing hypothetical method because their theology holds that the universe is necessary, not created and contingent.

MALCOLM: Once Western theologians realized that hypothetical method was compatible with Christian teaching about creation, they could befriend science, even if the friendship has been uneasy at times. At any rate, Christianity should have every confidence that science, to the extent it may have some objects in common with Christian dogma, will accord with Christian teachings.

PATRICIA: And, of course, if it does not, then science is wrong. So sayeth the Church.

MALCOLM: But the Church holds that its doctrines are in harmony with science, so there doesn't have to be a problem, even if the Church says that science may have to rethink a particular position, for example, the theory that the universe has an eternal past, the so-called "steady state" theory in cosmology.

PATRICIA: But you have to admit that the unity of truth is not a one-way street. If religion can question science, then science can challenge religion. If you don't grant that, you're not being consistent with your demand that disciplines unite in the truth.

MALCOLM: That's a good point, Patricia. One has to be open to the falsification of either science or religion on my point of view. Religion sometimes has to reassess its interpretations of dogma in light of scientific evidence. The dogmas, being true are perennial, of course; that is to say, they accommodate truth wherever and whenever it may be discovered. But various, competing interpretations of dogma have been overturned by science, and that shows the openness to science that is obligatory of religion. For example, there have been theologians who thought that the Copernican theory and evolution undermine Christian doctrine, when in fact Christianity appropriated both quite comfortably once these scientific claims were properly understood.

BRIAN: We saw that in our discussion of "Creationism I" during our first conversation.

JOHN: But religion insists that all positions are to be understood in the light of dogma, not of truth. You see, this is where you and I differ. I agree religion has to answer to science, because science deals with the truth. But I don't think religion is about the truth at all. I don't mean to belittle religion; I just think it differs from science. Religion is not about getting to the truth; it is about expressing the world in a mythopoetic way.

PATRICIA: John is right. Science is about truth. After all, science comes from *scientia*, meaning knowledge. But religion is about something else. Religion comes from *religio*, meaning to tie back or connect with something. Religion ties us back to ancient myths. This is why you don't have to worry about religions contradicting each other. They no more conflict than, say, my story about the tooth fairy conflicts with yours. They don't contradict each other because these stories don't consist of assertions, that is, statements that are true or false. They are mythic narrations, not statements of fact.

JOHN: I'm afraid, Malcolm, that in your vast reading you've neglected to study writers such as Carl Jung, James Frazer, Mircea Eliade, and Joseph Campbell, who explain how myth is significant, as it gives expression to the collective psychology of a people. But they caution us against the error of interpreting myths as if they were factual.

PATRICIA: Yes, Malcolm, you've committed that error. You've mistaken religious utterances for truth claims. But religious utterances have a different function: They express symbols and emotions, not literal truth. For this reason, religious utterances do not contradict each other. They are not evaluated by the standards of logic or truth, but by the standards of poetic narrations.

JOHN: Joseph Campbell says that this is the error and the tragedy of modern religions: Religious believers have become transformed from followers of myth into ideologues who subscribe to their myths as facts. Campbell says that this is what defines religion as superstition: the naive belief that the mythopoetic narratives of a people are intended to be assertions, factual utterances. That is an egregious error that puts one in the position of having to believe and defend obvious nonsense such as Joshua stopping the sun, the virgin birth, the incarnation, the resurrection, so on and so forth. Again, it goes back to what I said earlier. You religious believers ignore the existence of the social sciences.

PATRICIA: Yes. In light of what Campbell says, it's the social sciences that answer the problem of religious pluralism. Different religious beliefs reflect differences in myths developed over time in distinct cultures. None of these myths should be taken as literally true. The problem of religious differences is a cultural and psychological problem. We should not ask "which religion is true?" or "which religion is false?" Instead, we should ask "for what historical and psychological reasons did this set of cultural beliefs and myths, none of which are literally true, arise?" To understand religion properly, then, is to engage mainly in the sociology of religion and in comparative religion.

MALCOLM: I admit, John, that your interpretation is interesting and has the weight of authorities like Jung and Campbell behind it. But in the last analysis, it's just an interpretation and one that rests on its own set of assumptions. I'm not sure I want to accept those assumptions at face value. Of course, one must go your route if one accepts the naturalistic and secularist assumptions of Joseph Campbell. But I'm not sure I want to accept those assumptions unless he makes a case for them. As I read his books, I don't see him making that case.

JOHN: Aren't you risking being unscientific in a scientific age, Malcolm?

MALCOLM: No, it's nothing like that. I pride myself on my high regard of science. But I don't see why science requires the nullification of revelation, which you and Campbell seem to think it does. Yours is a very simple hypothesis that explains away religious disagreement with one broad stroke, but I very much doubt that traditional religious believers are just going to roll over and replace their interpretation of religion as made up of assertions with your view of religion as made up of nonfactual utterances.

JOHN: Malcolm, I never knew you were such a fundamentalist!

MALCOLM: Now, now. Let's not turn my position into a straw man. There is certainly mythic content to religion. There are narrative elements in religion that should not be taken literally. But revelation ultimately depends on a non-negotiable core of utterances that aim to be factual. To deny that is to grant assumptions of a purely naturalistic and secularist kind that want to reinterpret religion in such a way as to nullify it. I'm not saying that your view is necessarily wrong, although I certainly believe it is. I'm just saying that it's an extreme position that altogether dissolves religion as we've traditionally understood it. It defines religion out of existence by saying that only naturalistic interpretations of cultural phenomena count. There are other ways to interpret religion. We've already explained that natural theology interprets the evidence so as to support the judgment that God exists. One can defend interpretations that justify other claims endorsed by religion as well. For example, consider the immortality of the soul or the possibility of miracles. One has to be open to multiple points of view and ask which is the most plausible. It's not enough for me to accept a position just because it has the weight of authorities like Jung and Campbell behind it.

SOPHIA: May I add to our conversation?

MALCOLM: Of course, Sophia. It was understood that you could step in at any time. Please shed some light on our confusion here. I'm sure you have a lot to teach us on this.

SOPHIA: I don't want to assume that role, please. But I have thought about this problem of the diversity of the world's religions. In fact, my reflections on the problem of the world's different religions is one of the reasons that I became a Unitarian.

MARY: Please, elaborate. I find this very interesting. I've always wondered just what a Unitarian is exactly.

SOPHIA: By answering that question, Mary, I think I can propose a solution to our debate. I'm not sure unitarianism is the kind of thing one can define exactly. I'm sure there are people who call themselves Unitarians who might protest my definition. But in my way of thinking a Unitarian is someone who insists that on some fundamental level all religions are true. I know this runs contrary to what John and Patricia have been saying. They seem to prefer the interpretation that because religions differ, they're all false, at least if religious claims are taken literally. But I think another option is possible. That option is to embrace all religions as efforts, using the finite, inadequate human mind and its tools of language, to express divine reality. As human intellects situated in time and space, we're unable to do this in a way that transcends our own distinctive cultures and histories. In short, Frank, that's the unitarian creed as I understand it: Different religions are really all trying to revere the divine; they just do it in different ways. Religions differ, sometimes dramatically, in their cultural expressions and interpretations of the divine. This accounts for the apparent conflicts in doctrine. But these doctrines are so many concepts, metaphors, images, and myths endeavoring to understand divine reality. In that sense, religions are all true—each *truly* reflects its perspective on reality. That is to say, each religion truly describes how God appears to it. But no religion is true exclusively. We're all bound by our individual and cultural perspectives and, thus, we're unable to find some asocial and timeless perspective by which we could judge that one religion is absolutely right and the others are absolutely wrong. Religions are all partly incorrect, but—and this is the good news—they're also partly correct. Unitarianism asks us to appreciate the latter point.

MALCOLM: I see. So your distinction between appearance and reality enables you to say that religions need not contradict each other.

SOPHIA: Exactly. There are no contradictions if each religion is merely expressing its perspective. Analogously, the claims that something appears to me to be ugly and to you beautiful are not contradictory. They would be contradictory only if we both claimed that the object itself was what each of us perceived it to be. Since religious believers can describe the divine only from their historical and cultural perspectives, not from some transcendent, detached, impersonal point of view, their descriptions do not contradict one another.

BRIAN: So, yours is a compromise position—an attempt to blend both John's and Malcolm's views?

SOPHIA: Something like that. That religion involves truth is a point of agreement I have with Malcolm. And yet, you're right that my view does accommodate John's attention to religious differences. The differences should not be understood as conflicting truth claims in some literal sense. They are expressions of myth, custom, and practice that do not constitute the substance of religion itself. They are merely signs, symbols pointing to something else. In a sense, while they are interesting in their own right, they are beside the point. They are limited, and tragically so. They are meaningful, but as failures—as failures to achieve what religious belief pursues, the existence of an infinite, ineffable God. The human mind is bound to fail in its conceptualization of God. How can the finite mind comprehend in conceptual categories the infinite reality?

BRIAN: I see. That's why Unitarians are so insistent on ecumenism.

FRANK: In fact, they're ecumaniacs!

SOPHIA: As a Unitarian, I believe that Western religions have made the mistake of turning the different cultures into ideologically competitive religious communities. A lot of that is the fault of philosophers who let their zeal for apologetics get the best of them. All this results from mistaking the form for the content; the way of speaking for what is really meant. Ecumenism is a way of trying to reverse the tendency we Westerners have of putting everybody into ideological pigeon holes. We've done this for so long that it has become an habitual way in which we think about issues, especially religious ones. Unitarianism challenges us to think with a fresh perspective, to try to reverse our bad habits.

MARY: Are you saying that religions are all equal?

SOPHIA: They're certainly all equal in that they try to express a common object of worship. This sameness is important. In this age of universal communication, it's time we rose above our outdated ways of emphasizing our differences and recognized that we live in one world, that we make up one humanity, and that we all are trying to know the infinite God, a divinity that we can only know and express in terms of finite categories—hence, the myths, customs, and doctrinal interpretations of the various religious communities. We Unitarians are calling for a "Copernican Revolution" in religion comparable to the one we've had in astronomy. Christians must resign themselves to the fact that they no longer are the center of the theological solar system. Christians must accept that their "planet" is only one among many circling around the "sun" of ultimate reality.

BRIAN: But aren't some planets more habitable than others?

SOPHIA: Good point. I might grant that there are ways to evaluate religions pragmatically, perhaps judging how one religion might be superior in the way it transforms people's lives morally and spiritually or perhaps in the way it leads to political and social cohesiveness, freedom, compassion, knowledge, appreciation of beauty, and other benefits. Religious beliefs are metaphors, but the influence of these metaphors might make an evaluative difference in the lives of religious believers.

JOHN: Surely, you're satisfied with Sophia's compromise, aren't you, Malcolm?

MALCOLM: It's an ingenious attempt to deal with the problem of the plurality of religions. I'm familiar with her position. It is spelled out in detail in John Hick's interesting book, *God and the Universe of Faiths.* As ingenious as it is, I'm afraid I have some problems with it.

JEAN: I knew it.

MALCOLM: Before I address Sophia's view, I would like to say something in general that especially addresses some remarks made by John and Patricia. Patricia suggested earlier that *exclusivism,* the view that one religion has the primary truth about salvation, fosters religious strife, even violence. It is important to address this point. It seems to me to rest on a very basic confusion. I refer to the confusion between the intellectual status of religious belief and its moral implications. It is often assumed that if religious members hold committed beliefs, this will inevitably require that they mistreat others of different faiths. This is a fallacy of course, a failure to distinguish between the epistemological claims and moral practices of a religion. One may disagree with others and still respect them as God's children.

JOHN: Fallacy or not, Malcolm, history is checkered with episodes where religious differences were the pretext for persecutions.

BRIAN: John thinks that it's only the officially atheistic states, like Mao's China and Stalin's Soviet Union, that are benevolent to one and all.

MALCOLM: We'll reserve a debate about the history of persecutions to another time. As a philosopher I just wanted to alert us to the fallacy of confusing epistemological religious claims with claims about religious practices. Now I would like to say a few words about Sophia's *pluralist* solution to the problem of diverse religions. I must admit there is something very attractive about a position that holds that religions are diverse perspectives on one divine reality and that holds that these different viewpoints become ever more adequate as they are correlated with one another and added up. Unfortunately, these different views in many cases are not just *different;* they're *contradictory,* at least some of them are.

BRIAN: Exactly. Pluralists liken religions to pieces of a jigsaw puzzle, assuming that each piece offers something to the big picture when they are all, at last, put together. This analogy unfortunately will not do. Some of the pieces of the puzzle belong altogether to *different* pictures. When it becomes clear that my piece belongs to a picture of, say, the Battle of Trafalgar, while the other's piece belongs in a picture of dancers at a school of ballet, it would make no sense to try and put these pieces together as part of one grand puzzle. This seems to me to be a serious problem with pluralism. It glosses over *contradictions,* pretending that they are merely reconcilable *differences.*

MALCOLM: Well said, Brian. Let me add some further remarks about Sophia's position. First, I'm not sure your position, Sophia, is consistent. On the one hand, you want to posit a transcendent reality, a divine Ultimate; on the other, you say that we can only know it as it appears to us in cultural and historical descriptions. But I'm not sure you can have it both ways. Doesn't your view—that we're all bound inescapably by our cultural perspective—commit you to an epistemological skepticism that ultimately prevents you from positing that transcendent reality, the common ground of religions? By what epistemological rights can you say it exists, if you cannot escape your limited cultural perspectives and cannot know anything transcendent or objective? Second, and I suppose this is just a corollary of my first objection, how is your position really different from atheism? If any expression of ultimate reality is compatible with any other, all expressions are ultimately nondescriptive of divine reality. How can we believe that they say anything at all? If we cannot employ definite predicates about God so as to distinguish our account from those who deny those predicates and their subject, God, how can our view be any different from atheism? Third, it is the nature of a theistic religion to refer to an object of worship. This means that prayer, devotion, and other forms of worship are intentional behaviors, which is a fancy way of saying that they relate to an object in thought and speech.

But it is impossible to refer to an object unless thought or language contains some truthful ideas about the nature of that object. Accuracy of intention is a necessary condition for thinking about an object. If two religious utterances are not similar in intention and reference, then it is unreasonable to say they are thinking about the same thing. Accordingly, it is possible that someone's conception of God is simply erroneous. If this is not possible, it seems again that the religious claim is just empty and no different from atheism.

BRIAN: Good point, showing that Sophia's view seems to trivialize religion. Because if religion is salvific, as, say, Christianity claims, it must have truthful historical content.

MALCOLM: Last, Sophia's view seems to strip religion of content in a way that runs contrary to how the ordinary believer looks at religion. Most believers would say that Sophia's view simply deforms the nature of religion so as to solve a problem that disturbs intellectuals who are uncomfortable with exclusivism. Pluralism solves the problem by destroying the content of religious belief. This is a "solution" that will not be satisfying to many.

SOPHIA: But if you don't go with my view, you're left with exclusivism. And *that's* the position that will not be satisfying to many.

MALCOLM: If I were an exclusivist I would agree. But, as it turns out, one can reject pluralism without being an exclusivist. There is another position: *inclusivism.* That is the view I would champion.

PATRICIA: But what do you mean by inclusivism? Does your view not condemn you to inconsistency? You earlier said that you thought religions made truth claims that contradicted each other in some cases. But that means that religions are poles apart. To contradict a position is to be as distinct from it as possible. So you're trying the impossible. You can't hold your view about conflicting religious claims and be an inclusivist.

MALCOLM: Well, maybe I can't be. I don't have the wit for it. But there have been philosophers greater than I, like Karl Rahner and Jacques Maritain, who have found a way to maintain an inclusivist view: that is, that Christianity alone brings salvation and yet that salvation may come to those who formally belong outside the Christian religion.

PATRICIA: How can that be? How can salvation be limited to one religion and yet be available to people who have never heard of that religion?

MALCOLM: It can happen because of things specified in that religion. It is certainly God's will, Christianity teaches, that everyone be saved. This is true even of those in non-Christian cultures, even if they have never heard of Jesus Christ. God's grace is given to one and all, even if ideally he desires it to appear in Christian culture and to foster a Christian community. God is not limited to space and time; he isn't bound by formal religious differences or by geographical and cultural borders. God can extend his grace to one and all.

JOHN: Isn't this just an *ad hoc* effort to escape the problematic character of inclusivism?

MALCOLM: No, it's not *ad hoc,* because it has an explicit basis in the Christian faith. Karl Rahner points to the fact that Scripture speaks about the salvation of those righteous Jews and non-Jews who antedated Christ, persons who longed to know the God who would send the Messiah. Analogously, those who live now in non-Christian cultures can enjoy salvation because they thirst after the true God.

PATRICIA: But how could they yearn for the God of Christianity when they've never heard of Christ?

MALCOLM: I don't see any reason why God couldn't take that into account. Their desire for God could be unconscious and unclear, but because of their purity of heart God knows they intend ultimately to love and worship him only. Such a person aims to know the God of Jesus Christ, the Triune God of Christianity, as much as do formal Christians. By rights, they too, Rahner concludes, are Christians. He calls them "anonymous Christians."

SOPHIA: In this way, a Christian may achieve a kind of inclusivism, but it seems to me that it doesn't go far enough.

MALCOLM: What do you mean?

SOPHIA: You're willing to acknowledge an exceptional person here and there who happens to overcome the limits of his own formal religious affiliation and become a "closet" or "secret" Christian. But this is still not really to *include* those other non-Christian religions themselves, and that's what is required for a true inclusivism.

MALCOLM: As I said before, my view is committed to Christianity as the decisive, unique way to salvation, but to the extent other religions are in concert with Christian teachings and to the extent that they see in weaker and dimmer ways Christian truths, they are to be acknowledged and appreciated. So, I'm not just taking into my inclusivism "anonymous Christians." I'm also including elements of different faiths themselves. I agree with Aristotle, if you will allow me to draw on the wisdom of a pagan philosopher in this context, that one should always try to save as much of his opponent's position as possible. It is in that spirit that inclusivism offers its solution to the problem of religious pluralism.

BRIAN: Good, Malcolm. I remember a quotation from Jacques Maritain. It is from his *Degrees of Knowledge*. He sums up well how inclusivism is indeed a part of Christian faith. I've recited the passage so often in homilies and lectures that I can reproduce it word for word: "[W]e know that unbaptized persons, even though they are not stamped with the seal of unity so as to participate through the virtue of the Church in the proper work of the Church (which is the redemption continued), can nevertheless (inasmuch as they receive without knowing it the supernatural life of the self-same divine blood which circulates within the Church and of the same spirit which rests upon it) belong invisibly to

Christ's Church. Thus they can have sanctifying grace and, as a result, theological faith and the infused gifts."

MARY: We'll let you and Maritain have the last word, Brian.

Key Terms and Distinctions

Revelation	Science and religion
Truth	Unity of truth
Miracles	Logic of truth
Myth	Appearance and reality
Superstition	Pluralism
Faith	Exclusivism
Religion	Inclusivism
Science	

Questions on Chapter 7

1. Does Malcolm succeed in showing that the statement "all religions ultimately believe the same things" is incoherent?
2. Do you accept Joseph Campbell's judgment that a superstitious person is someone who believes that religious dogmas are factual?
3. What is myth? How does myth relate to religion?
4. Is it the case, as Frank argues, that science and religion can never conflict because truth claims in the one discipline have no bearing on truth claims in the other? In other words, is compartmentalizing science from religion illogical? How does Malcolm argue against Frank's position? Which view do you find more convincing, Frank's or Malcolm's?
5. In the end, is Sophia's position indistinguishable from atheism, as Malcolm charges?
6. Do you agree that Sophia's position makes impossible prayer and worship?
7. Which alternative do you find more defensible: exclusivism, pluralism, or inclusivism?

Bibliography

Adler, Mortimer, *Truth in Religion* (New York: Macmillan, 1990).
Bultmann, Rudolf, et al., *Kerygma and Myth: A Theological Debate* (New York: Harper & Row, 1961).

Campbell, Joseph, *The Inner Reaches of Outer Space: Metaphor as Myth and as Religion* (New York: Harper & Row, 1986).

————, *The Power of Myth* (New York: Doubleday, 1988).

Cox, Harvey, *Many Mansions: A Christian's Encounter with Other Faiths* (Boston: Beacon Press, 1988).

Gilson, Etienne, *Reason and Revelation in the Middle Ages* (New York: Charles Scribner's Sons, 1946).

Hick, John, *God Has Many Names* (Philadelphia: Westminster Press, 1982).

————, *God and the Universe of Faiths* (New York: St. Martin's Press, 1973).

————, *Philosophy of Religion* (Englewood Cliffs, NJ: Prentice-Hall, 1983, third edition).

Jaki, Stanley L, *God and the Cosmologists* (Edinburgh: Scottish Academic Press, 1989).

————, *The Origin of Science and the Science of Its Origin.* The Fremantle Lectures (Edinburgh: Scottish Academic Press, 1978).

————, *The Road of Science and the Ways to God.* The Gifford Lectures (Chicago: University of Chicago Press, 1978).

————, *The Savior of Science* (Edinburgh: Scottish Academic Press, 1990).

James, William, *The Varieties of Religious Experience* (New York: Modern Library, 1902).

Maritain, Jacques, *The Degrees of Knowledge,* trans. G. Phelan (New York: Charles Scribner's Sons, 1959).

O'Flaherty, Wendy Doniger, *Other Peoples' Myths* (New York: Macmillan, 1988).

Rahner, Karl, "Christian and the Non-Christian Religions," in *Christianity and Other Religions,* ed. John Hick and Brian Hebblethwaite (Glasgow: Collins, 1980), pp. 70–85.

Smart, Ninian, *The Religious Experience of Mankind* (New York: Charles Scribner's Sons, 1979).

Chapter Eight
The Meaning of Life

The friends gather for one last conversation. Renee asks whether atheists, such as John and Patricia, can find meaning in life. John and Patricia insist that they can. Renee is skeptical. Malcolm and Brian concur with Renee, arguing that belief in God contributes a depth and enthusiasm to life that is not likely to be supplied by atheism. The discussion also treats morality, human nature, and the nature of happiness and shows how such issues illuminate the question of the meaning of life.

MARY: This is our last conversation I'm afraid.

BRIAN: Yes. It's been a great reunion. But we'll all be saying goodbye again shortly.

FRANK: I hope we do a better job of staying in touch in the future.

MALCOLM: I agree. It's shameless to let old friends drift apart the way we have.

JEAN: Let's try to stay in contact. I know it's hard with the full and meaningful lives we all lead!

FRANK: Mine's very meaningful, if you call boredom meaningful.

RENEE: Speaking of meaningful lives, I've been wanting to ask something, if I dare. Excuse me, John and Patricia, but I've been hoping to pose a question to you both. I've sat here and listened to your interesting and brilliant views for these several days now. And yet, I wonder about something. How do you guys find a reason to live? I'm not being mean or flippant, really. I'm just curious. You see, I can't imagine living without my faith. I don't see how I could have any zest for life. Oh, I guess I'd trundle through each day. I'd survive. But I don't see how life would have much meaning for me. Please tell me how you do it. How do you find meaning in life in spite of your atheism? Forgive me, if this question is blunt or impolite. I don't mean it to be. In a way, I admire you both. You seem to be able to do something I don't think I could do.

FRANK: I must say I've always felt sorry for those who don't give religion first place in their lives.

MALCOLM: Perhaps John and Patricia have changed their minds because of the overpowering and persuasive nature of our dialectics. What do you say, guys?

JOHN: Sorry to disappoint you, Malcolm. I'm afraid I'm still a skeptic. But I must say, you've all provoked me and stimulated me to rethink some of my positions. I'll give you credit for that much.

PATRICIA: Yes, I must salute you all. I must say that I thought theists and religious believers were pretty much air-heads who believed what they did to fill some psychological void in their lives or to compensate for the fact that they can't face reality. But I've got to admit, there are some strong and respectable philosophical foundations to many of the views I've heard you express. Believe me, these conversations have had an impact, just as John said. I'll be going over these conversations in my mind for some time to come.

MALCOLM: Let us know what revisions you make.

PATRICIA: I've got your e-mail address. You can bet you'll hear from me.

FRANK: But anyway, let's get back to Renee's excellent question.

JOHN: I think I'll respond this way, Renee. My view about the meaning of life is pretty much shaped by Bertrand Russell's famous essay, *A Free Man's Worship*. He says that the universe we live in, which consists mostly of empty space, is impersonal and cold. But precisely because we live in an indifferent, Godless universe, where death speaks the final word for each one of us and where the solar system itself will eventually pass away, our lives, concentrated against this stark background, can have meaning nonetheless. I have only this brief span on this earth to live well. Let me make the most of it!

PATRICIA: Good point, John. Don't you see, Renee? From John's point of view, life is actually richer and more meaningful when one does not depend on God or an afterlife to give it meaning. The immediacy of life, the significance of the here-and-now, is decisive.

JOHN: Yes. As the existentialists say: "You are who you choose to be." You are ultimately responsible for what you become. Life has profound meaning when you consider it as the result of your radical freedom. Life's meaning is entirely up to you.

RENEE: Malcolm, what do you make of all of this?

MALCOLM: I have to say I've read Albert Camus, Jean-Paul Sartre, and Bertrand Russell. I've been impressed by their genius as writers and by their courageous handling of this question on the meaning of life. But I've never been convinced that their solutions are satisfying. For one thing, I find the existentialists' constant lament about how the universe is "absurd" tiresome. If you say the universe is absurd, then you've already begged the question in favor of the existentialists' position: that there is no God and man alone creates meaning. I simply reject their worldview. I don't find it persuasive. They simply *assume* that there is no God, but I think we've seen that one simply should not do that.

JOHN: But surely they're not begging the question any more than you are. Thinkers like the existentialists are simply responding to one perspective on the universe that seems reasonable. For one thing, it's a perspective that takes into account modern science. If science has proven anything, it is that we don't have to posit Providence or Purpose to describe how the universe works. There doesn't appear to be a God; and if there is, he doesn't seem to care. At least, he doesn't seem to interfere in human affairs. It seems that the existentialists have as much right to say the world is Godless and pointless as you religious types have to say it's created and sustained by God.

MALCOLM: Well, I'm not going to bring up the whole debate about theism again. But I think we've seen that science cannot explain everything and that religion and science are very compatible. Let me say further that science is possible only if the universe makes sense, that is, if it's intelligible. But if it's intelligible, I'm not going to allow that we should call it "absurd."

BRIAN: Yeah. There's no point in ignoring the obvious. Without an intelligible universe we couldn't even be having this conversation right now. You couldn't know that the vibrations that I'm causing in the air with my vocal chords signify meanings or thoughts that I'm trying to convey from my mind to yours and vice versa.

MALCOLM: Not only does the universe make sense, there is strong evidence, as we discussed earlier, that its intelligible nature is a sign that God exists. Both the lament of the existentialists that the universe is absurd and their exhortation that we must invent our own meaning in life are exaggerations that follow from the particular worldview they espouse—that the universe and the human condition are in and of themselves meaningless.

BRIAN: Right, Malcolm. While it is true that the universe is often an untidy, messy, apparently cold, impersonal, indifferent, and even painful place, it does not follow that it is absurd, as we pointed out when we discussed the problem of evil. The universe may be *ambiguous*, but it is not absurd; that is to say, rational minds might disagree about how they interpret the evidence, but at least there is evidence to interpret. Further, while John and Patricia may find some comfort and excitement by promoting their lonely, solitary quest for meaning, I find a deeper and richer quest in

God cares vs make most out of life
          since it's all we have

believing that in addition to my personal choices, there is a God who cares about my choices and their consequences.

PATRICIA: But you need to characterize our position fairly. We are saying that even *if* the universe and human life are empty, which many philosophers believe, human life can still be meaningful. Human beings can create greatness for themselves. They can have grand, meaningful lives through their own choices. So *metaphysically* the world and life may be absurd, but *personally* the world and human life can be meaningful. Meaning is brought about through the drama of human choice.

JOHN: Yes. Since some of us don't believe there is a God to ensure that the cosmos and human history arrive at some happy conclusion, it's left to each of us to decide for herself what life will mean. So *de facto* life can have meaning. We can change its metaphysical absurdity into personal meaning. That's the genius, mystery, and excitement of the human condition.

RENEE: That might be great for you. But if there is no God or an afterlife, I find the whole scenario unspeakably tragic and depressing. To think that all we are and accomplish in the end will be dust; that each of us will die and that we will never know one another again; that our loved ones will never meet us again in eternity, a place where God ensures there is no sorrow—to think that death and obliteration is all there is is ultimately to rob life of its joy, its zest, its meaning. The way you guys, John and Patricia, are trying to get meaning is a trick. Given your worldview, that's all you have. Isn't it a big game, a deception, a delusion? Aren't you deceiving yourself into thinking life has meaning when it doesn't?

MARY: Wow, Renee! You're taking the gloves off now.

RENEE: I'm just being frank. This is the kind of thing we can't sugarcoat.

JOHN: I don't mind your being blunt, Renee. But let's examine your claim for a minute. It seems to me you're saying several things here. First, you're saying that life can have no meaning without God; second, that life can have no meaning without immortality; and third, that life can have no meaning without love—this seems to follow from your remark about how we need to enjoy an eternal afterlife with both God and our loved ones. Have I accurately summarized your view?

RENEE: Yes. Thanks. It's even clearer to my mind now.

JOHN: Now, I agree with you about your last claim. Life will be impoverished without love. But I don't see why love depends on God or immortality. Love is still a reality in human experience, even if there is no God. And the fact that we're all going to die makes love all the more intense and significant, doesn't it? Yes, it's unspeakably tragic that our loved ones will die and we will never meet again, but that puts all the more a demand on us to love one another fully and intensely at every moment we are together. This is a point made very persuasively by Kai Nielsen in *Ethics Without God,* a book that we referred to during our discussion of religion and morality.

BRIAN: I remember it. And I'll say now what I thought then: Sure, that's why all those people who share Nielsen's godless worldview are always so benevolent. Stalin and Pol Pot come to mind.

PATRICIA: The religious wars of the godly match those atrocities victim for victim, and you know it, Brian.

BRIAN: Only if you're into revisionist history. The Spanish Inquisition, and this is not to excuse it, was unjust to relatively small numbers of people compared to the ravages of twentieth-century atheistic politics. Millions have been left in its wake. Besides, the Inquisition was very much a product of its time. That's just how political business was done back then. It's not fair to judge the fifteenth century by modern-day social standards and expectations. But even by those standards, what excuse do modern-day tyrants have?

MALCOLM: Well, I don't want us to get back into the question of religion and morality, but I do think there is one reply to what

John has said. One of the things a religious view of life supplies is
a depth of regard for human life and moral experience. I think
that such depth is missing and unlikely to be found in your position, John and Patricia.

JOHN: But I just explained how, if you leave God and immortality out of the picture, love is deepened and enhanced.

MALCOLM: That may be true in the exceptional case, but I think
most people will respond to the pointlessness of the cosmos and
human destiny in the way Renee says they will. Most will find it
tragic and depressing. In the face of that realization, most people
will probably retreat into selfishness and their own interests. Most
people's respect and love for their fellow humans will actually be
diminished.

JEAN: We see much more selfishness today, and it seems to
correspond with the decline in religion, as you mentioned, Frank,
in one of our previous discussions.

JOHN: But there doesn't have to be so much selfishness. Weren't
you listening to what I said about love?

MALCOLM: Very closely, and you expressed your point very well.
But I'm trying to be practical here; I'm trying to listen to the
lessons of history and common sense. Don't you think that there is
a difference between someone who appreciates his fellow human
beings as special creations of God, as creatures fitting into God's
overall plan for the universe, and someone who sees life and the
universe as just an accident?

JOHN: As I explained, our time together is made all the more
significant because it's brief and entirely up to us.

MALCOLM: But remember, it's not only brief on your view, it's
ultimately pointless. If most people were to accept your worldview—
that the universe is a pointless accident—the consequence is likely
to be that the majority of them will lack motivation to regard their

It's not pointless if you make it meaningful

fellow human beings as special and their vocations as anything but ultimately a waste of time, if they're honest about it.

BRIAN: Even worse, I think the view that says the universe is aimless and godless plays into the hands of bloody, ruthless people and tyrants. I mean a person is bound to care less about the morality of his actions and his respect for his fellow human beings if he believes, first, that they are just accidental, evolutionary products, originally emerging from the primordial slime, and, second, that there is no God to judge the moral quality of our lives. Disrespect and moral abandon would be likely to be the products of your account of things, John, if it became popular. As I said, the Joseph Stalins of the world are there to take advantage in an instant of the nihilism implicit in your philosophy.

JOHN: I think that you and Malcolm are just so accustomed to explaining human behavior and reality in religious terms that you don't have the imagination to see that life could be intelligently interpreted otherwise. True, it might take time and it might require that we reeducate humanity out of its stubborn religious ways of thinking—which aren't as benign as you guys think—but I think it can be done. Human happiness and love are compatible with a philosophy that denies God and immortality.

JEAN: Oh no, you're not going to sing John Lennon's *Imagine* for us again, are you John?

JOHN: Only if you'll accompany me on the harmonica!

MALCOLM: But consider for a moment, John, the different kinds of love we're talking about here. Yours is a desperate and perhaps naive love, a love that denies anything transcendent and eternal. Many people are not going to commit to love in the absence of belief in the transcendent and the eternal. Most people are going to retreat into their own narcissism and thus be indifferent to engineering this "heaven on earth" that you think is possible if we just get rid of religion. Bringing about utopia is going to require sacrifice. I'm not sure your way is going to inspire people to put others' interests ahead of their own. We already mentioned that your position has problems with moral obligation in our earlier discussion of religion and morality.

BRIAN: Oh, make no mistake about it, Malcolm. People *won't* retreat into narcissism if they go John's way, because the Joseph Stalins of the world will be right there forcing them to "love" their fellow humans. If they don't, then, "to the Gulag with them!"

PATRICIA: If the world would just try it John's way, we'd all be surprised how better off we would be; how we would discover our true potential for happiness on this earth, once we are no longer weighed down by the guilt trips and the terror tactics of religion. The world would at least do as well as it has. I don't see that religion has been much of a help to human betterment.

MALCOLM: I grant we might limp along, but I think that without religion the individual's heart is likely to be left an empty shell. I doubt that in our hearts we are going to be especially motivated to love others as we might if we see them as "children of God." The atheist regimes of the twentieth century may be sad testimony to the hardening of the human heart when God is "officially" removed from human life.

FRANK: I read somewhere recently that ours is the first generation that is trying to live as if there is no God. And you can clearly see that we are not doing very well and are in a mess because of it.

BRIAN: Good point. The contemporary theologian, Paul Tillich, once distinguished between a "moralism" and a "morality" to make that point. He admits that in a godless ethic, human beings could work out regulations for themselves. In other words, they could set up what he calls a moralism, an itemization of culturally accepted commands and prohibitions. He concedes that such a *moralism* might indeed enable people to establish and keep social order, but he suspects that these regulations would be sterile and lifeless, devoid of the motivation that comes with the conviction

[handwritten margin notes: "yes good point exactly" next to Patricia's paragraph; "are you kidding me? there has been so much damn mess in the south in 1800's... there's always been brutality WTF" and "give an example" near Frank's paragraph]

that God is the Creator of our lives and the judge of our moral destinies. On the other hand, a *morality* exists when these regulations do not stand by themselves, but are seen as ways in which human beings relate to each other as "Children of God." It is naive, Tillich argues, to think indifference to God provides the same depth of conscience and moral outlook as commitment to divine expectations. He likens a godless ethic to "a whited sepulcher," an analogy Jesus used when condemning the Pharisees. They appear righteous on the outside; they do everything as the "regulations" require; but they hide rottenness and decay on the inside; their "regulations" are lifeless legalisms, lacking motivation and depth. Moralism is a lifeless legalism. That's all that the naturalist gives us. But morality is inspired and energetic, because it sees God in other people. Thus, there's a world of difference between a moralism and a morality, and a religious perspective, Tillich argues, is required to accomplish the latter.

FRANK: As Scripture says, "the letter kills; the Spirit gives life."

PATRICIA: It seems to me that there is still a lot of evidence that many people who don't give a hoot about God and religion lead loving, meaningful lives. It's up to the individual. That's all John and I are saying. Yes. shitty people will be shitty, good people will be good.

RENEE: As long as their lives are going well, and as long as there are no serious distresses in their lives, I'm sure that these atheists and agnostics get along fine. But the question I ask is how do they do when they're faced with a personal crisis. I want to see how they get along when they're faced with the death of their own child or their spouse. I want to see what strength they can draw from their atheism when they have to cope with grief, pain, and oppression. Believe me, those are the laboratories of life where the differences would be vividly evident.

BRIAN: Good point. I recall a remark by the philosopher, William James. I remember it because I've often used it in homilies. "Probably to almost every one of us here the most adverse life would seem well worth living, if we only could be certain that our bravery and patience with it were terminating and eventuating and bearing fruit somewhere in an unseen spiritual world."

FRANK: Someone once said that "one can endure any *how* so long as he has a *why*."

RENEE: That's the remark that Viktor Frankl likes to quote in his book *Man's Search for Meaning*.

PATRICIA: Yes, but he borrowed it from Nietzsche, who was an atheist! Nietzsche is saying that one's life can have meaning and purpose without God. You don't have to posit a spiritual world, God, or immortality to give yourself a "why." Your life can have meaning right here with both feet on the ground.

RENEE: Don't you think it's harder, though?

JOHN: Perhaps so. But in any case, we must be brave.

PATRICIA: Bertrand Russell says in his *Autobiography* that he has found his life very meaningful on account of three things: the longing for love, the search for knowledge, and compassion for the suffering of his fellow human beings. That's enough for me. You will notice that he does not include God among the three reasons.

MALCOLM: Certainly, no one is denying the agnostic and the atheist their *right* to try and find a way through life without God. But in light of what we've said, it seems that theism provides resources for finding meaning in life that atheism lacks.

JOHN: What if I conceded this much, Malcolm: perhaps you're right in some *ultimate* sense. The atheist must live, love, and behave as if there is no God, and that must affect his outlook. But it doesn't prevent him or her from investing this life with meaning. Perhaps, as Kai Nielsen put it, although there is no meaning *to* life, there can be meaning *in* life.

FRANK: What do you mean by that?

JOHN: Well, there may be no ultimate point to human life or the universe—hence no meaning *to* life—but there may still be an opportunity for each of us to create meaning in her or his own life—hence, meaning *in* life. yes this good

RENEE: But as you've been saying throughout our discussions, Malcolm, it's a matter of which view is more plausible. It seems to me that human nature being what it is, it is naive to think that strength and meaning can be supplied in life if one is an agnostic or an atheist. It just seems to me that there is an underlying hopelessness and helplessness to that "choice." I don't see how such a life can really be satisfying. I can't see how there can be meaning *in* life if there is no meaning *to* life.

[margin: but saying theses better a way life after this one makes it seem less important]

PATRICIA: Maybe that's your problem. You don't see it because your imagination is constrained by belief in God. You just now mentioned another belief that I would question. You referred to "human nature." It turns out, Renee, that there is no human nature. No philosopher has believed in such a thing since Darwin. Since there's no human nature and since there's no God—at least, we can ask "what has he done for us lately?"—our lives can be shaped by our own choices. We must choose what we want to become.

JOHN: I'm reminded of that essay by the Spanish philosopher, José Ortega y Gasset, in which he argues that there is no human nature.

PATRICIA: I recall the French philosopher, Merleau-Ponty, saying that "it is man's nature not to have a nature."

BRIAN: Oh, yeah. I remember that Ortega y Gasset article. That's that essay that only human beings read! I read it to my two cats, Bosworth and Clovis, and they were utterly indifferent.

MALCOLM: You see, Renee, people like John and Patricia have to run away from human nature as fast as they have to run away from God. Both impose limits on their choices. Because of those limits *yes you can make it whatever you want it to be* ✓

the existentialists can't make up "meaning" out of the blue. God's will and human nature impose standards on our choices, reminding us that some choices are right and some are wrong. That throws a serious obstacle in the way of their existentialism, their "free to be you and me" philosophy.

BRIAN: Yes. You remember our discussion on religion and morality. We had the occasion to point out that atheism seems to have a problem restricting choices. It has a problem decisively saying this action is right and that wrong. Where are clear moral standards in a purposeless universe, in a cosmos brought about by random events? It seems to me that as naturalistic atheism has taken hold so has moral relativism. The sordid social experiments of the twentieth century, which have led to the deaths of millions of people, may bear witness to what happens to morality when people rest it on atheism.

MALCOLM: Theism, a philosophy that maintains that God has created the world and has created human beings as purposeful creatures to work out their moral destinies, is a surer way than atheism to supply justification and motivation to moral life.

JOHN: Just how are people "to work out their moral destinies," as you put it?

MALCOLM: I'm saying that in order for people to lead moral and purposeful lives, they must know what it is to be a human being in the first place. In other words, a correct understanding of the meaning of life depends on a sound philosophy of human nature.

JOHN: And you're going to provide such a sound philosophy? You're going to make the case that there is such a thing as human nature?

MALCOLM: It looks like somebody's got to! It's obviously relevant. If there is such a thing as human nature, it's important to the question of the meaning of life. There's no point in trying to create meaning for oneself that is antagonistic to human nature. That would be counterproductive.

JEAN: What do you mean by human nature?

MALCOLM: I certainly don't mean that there is human nature in some Platonic sense. I just mean that there are common potentialities among human beings, regardless of their cultural and historical circumstances, which if left unfulfilled prevent them from living satisfactory human lives.

JOHN: If you're denying that human beings are cultural and historical creatures, you're getting about as Platonic as you can be.

MALCOLM: No, I'm not saying that. To be cultural is itself one of the potentialities that human beings have in common. It's one of our distinctive traits. I'm just saying that, if we look at the inductive evidence, that is, if we examine how human beings live, both in the past and today, we can identify very basic capacities that make us what we are. Some of these capacities we have in common with other animals; some of them are distinctly our own.

MARY: What are these potentialities exactly?

MALCOLM: Nutrition, health, love, and knowledge are obvious examples. We may call these potentialities "needs," since it's difficult to imagine how one could live a satisfactory human life without fulfilling these potentialities. Obviously, human beings have other needs as well: shelter, physical pleasure, freedom, aesthetic experience, self-respect, play, meaningful work. You could probably add to the list.

MARY: You mean that these needs are rooted in our biology, our nature as human organisms?

MALCOLM: Human beings are more than just biological organisms. Remember as we argued in our discussion about immortality, there are in human nature certain powers that transcend mere biology. To be a human creature is to be more than an animal. The complex creature we are is multidimensional. We have biological needs like the other animals, but we have needs that surpass them as well.

JOHN: You realize, of course, that what you say runs contrary to what social scientists such as psychologists, sociologists, and anthropologists maintain today. They hold that culture is the determining factor in human life. "Biology," "nature," or whatever you want to call it, plays a part, but even our nature can be overridden by cultural conditioning.

JEAN: This sounds like the old "nature versus nurture" debate.

MALCOLM: Exactly, Jean. And I would be the last to deny that the social scientists have a strong argument. There is certainly a decisive part in human development that culture plays. But I deny that it is the whole story. As I said, there wouldn't even be human culture if there weren't human nature.

BRIAN: Yes. It's a matter of striking a balance. One must combine the nature-nurture position. Each component in the debate must be given its due.

FRANK: Why is this relevant?

MALCOLM: For the simple reason that if there is a human nature, our conception of the meaning of life must be in concert with it; otherwise our lives will be reckless and on a risky, if not self-destructive, course. Without human nature as a standard for how we ought to behave, ethics is reduced to either empty formalisms, lists of "do's" and "don'ts," or to a state of affairs in which each person is free to invent morality for herself.

BRIAN: Another way to put it is that our happiness, the attainment of the human good, both individually and socially, depends on the actualization of human nature, that is to say, on the realization of all those potentialities that make us human. We need to develop good habits or "virtues"—such as courage, honesty, patience—to assist us in satisfying our potentialities. Since obviously the character of human happiness is part of the question of the meaning of life, the question of human nature and of the development of virtues is an important issue.

MARY: So that's all there is to happiness? We just work up some good habits, some virtues, and we get what we need? Isn't that too simple? Isn't life a lot harder and riskier than my own efforts to get what I need?

BRIAN: That's a very good point, Mary. There is a certain amount of luck involved in living well. But to the extent we have control over our destinies, we should try to satisfy those capacities and desires that make us most human. We can maximize success and minimize risk in attaining our happiness if we cultivate good habits, virtues, and avoid bad habits, vices. Vices—such as cowardice, mendacity, and impatience—are bad habits undermining intelligent choices in the management of our lives. Virtues pull us toward happiness; vices push us away.

JOHN: I don't know. I've known some pretty vicious people who seem perfectly content. We all know about gangsters, murderers, and psychopaths who sleep like babies every night.

BRIAN: Well, that is something of a puzzle. Maybe that's the job for the psychologists—to explain those kinds of exceptions. But I don't think such cases undermine our account, for we're talking about the requirements of human happiness as a general rule. There will always be some people, who, through twists of fate or through lack of conscience, are indifferent to the moral quality of their lives. Such people, of course, are dangerous.

RENEE: Sometimes they walk among us and pass themselves off as moral people.

JEAN: Yeah, remember Ted Bundy and John Wayne Gacy. They were the pillars of the community, or so people thought.

BRIAN: Still, isn't it remarkable that there are so few of them. Most people do care about morality and generally try to be decent. I think it's safe to say that normal people want to be able to regard themselves as moral beings.

MARY: Yes, that's probably one of the reasons we get so good at rationalizing some of the things we do. Sometimes we do things we suspect may not be altogether wholesome. But because we're moral beings, we still want to be able to look at ourselves in the mirror. So we feel driven to put a spin on what we did to make it look good to ourselves and others.

BRIAN: Our need to feel moral also says something about human nature. Human beings are specifically those creatures who alone are concerned with the moral character of their lives. Normal human beings generally see that there is more than coincidence between being moral and living well.

MALCOLM: Living well is another way of expressing happiness. Once one recognizes that there are rooted in human nature certain basic potentialities, then one has arrived at a working definition of happiness. In light of what Mary said, perhaps we could define happiness as the realization of all those capacities or needs in a human life, *plus* luck. If "happiness" is another word for expressing the good life, the attainment of the good for human beings, then these potentialities or needs, are also real goods, the *truly* desirable aims of human life.

JOHN: I'm very uncomfortable with this. Your view is a subtle way to demand that people all act alike. Your view requires that happiness is all the same for everybody. But that's not true. What makes me happy doesn't necessarily make you happy.

MALCOLM: My view doesn't rule out individual differences, but it does insist that human beings have to attend to basically the same things in order to be happy. But there is plenty of room to move about in spite of those basic requirements. For example, in order to be happy one must be free. But that doesn't mean that you must exercise your freedom in exactly the way I do. You can choose to be an athlete or a businessman; I can choose to be a writer or an explorer. But still each of us is fulfilling freedom, without which we cannot live truly human lives.

BRIAN: The nature of happiness is important, because people today are confused about it. I think one of the reasons people suffer anxiety in the modern world is that they have a mistaken conception of happiness. Today we tend to think of happiness as just feeling good. Modern people think of happiness as a purely *psychological* state. The view of happiness that Malcolm is expressing, however, is that human well-being is more of a *normative*, rather than a psychological, condition. Happiness is more than just feeling good, although that is surely *part* of happiness. More basic to happiness, however, is the actualization of all those potentialities, those real goods, that make us fully human. The pursuit of that actualization is compatible with periods in one's life, perhaps even sizable periods, in which one does not feel good. This makes sense, however, if happiness is a norm or standard of well-being. But because people today think of happiness as feeling good at every possible moment, they fret about their "unhappiness" when they don't attain the desired psychological state. That's one reason that we're an anxiety-ridden culture.

MALCOLM: And that's why we keep the psychologists in business.

FRANK: At least here in America.

MALCOLM: We have a shallow conception of happiness. Happiness should mean a norm or standard of excellence for a human life; instead modern people have distorted it so that it means feeling good, having a "buzz on" as often as possible. This is not happiness but its perversion.

RENEE: Of course, such a shallow view of happiness is bound to happen when God is left out of the picture. If happiness becomes just a matter of the here and now, it is bound to become hedonism.

FRANK: In fact, is anything really satisfying short of God?

MALCOLM: That's a good question, Frank. I remember Tolstoy's powerful piece, *My Confession,* in which he argues that the things esteemed by human beings are ultimately unfulfilling. It is only God that brings final, permanent happiness.

BRIAN: That was certainly St. Thomas Aquinas's position. He believed that no finite good, like wealth or fame, nor any accumulation of finite goods, would ever ultimately satisfy human desire. Even our natural happiness—which is all we can attain under our power—is not enough. The human will has a thirst for ultimate satisfaction, or *supernatural* happiness. Only a perfect, infinitely good object can satisfy our will. That object is God, the *Summum Bonum*. According to Aquinas, then, the human person has a thirst for God, a desire for God that is ultimately only satisfied in beatific vision. He puts it paradoxically: God is our ultimate happiness because he is greater, more desirable, than even our happiness.

JOHN: And if there is no God?

BRIAN: Then human life must be tragically limited, forever incomplete. *← only if you view it to be*
← these people don't give humans enough credit

MALCOLM: Hence, the lament of the existentialists, like Camus and Unamuno. They grant that human life needs and hopes for God. But since they say there is no God, then human life is ultimately tragic and pointless.

BRIAN: But we Christians find meaning because we have hope that there is a God and that life is not tragic and pointless.

FRANK: And that hope, being one of the theological virtues, is given and nurtured by God himself.

RENEE: Your use of that word "virtue," Frank, brings up another question. In order to find meaning in life, does a person have to be moral?

PATRICIA: Certainly, a person must be moral to find *authentic* meaning in life.

MALCOLM: But aren't you on thin ice here, Patricia?

PATRICIA: How so?

MALCOLM: You've already called into question God and human nature. Without those standards for conduct, I'm not sure you can distinguish between *authentic* and *inauthentic* choices in life.

PATRICIA: One can be true to herself. One can live as one decides. That's authenticity.

MALCOLM: But it's not just a matter of choice, as you yourself admitted earlier. The choice must be moral for it to be authentic.

PATRICIA: Well, I don't want to get us back into the debate on morality and religion, but it seems to me that we agreed then that one can have standards for judging the merits of choices without appealing to God or human nature. For example, choices that help oneself and humankind are authentic.

JEAN: I think we did appeal to human nature. In order to explain what *really* helps a person or a community one has to distinguish between what is really good for people and what is really bad for them. Doesn't that require suppositions about human nature, about what it is to be a human being?

FRANK: Touché, Jean.

BRIAN: Yes. That's why human nature is a boomerang principle. You may think you throw it away, but it comes right back on you. It is always implicit in one's theory of how a human being should live, because human beings are distinct kinds of creatures.

JOHN: It seems to me all you have to suppose in order to have a moral outlook on life and to have moral standards is the consensus of the community about how human beings should live.

MALCOLM: Surely you can guess how I would respond to that. You've just presupposed cultural relativism, a view we mentioned in a previous discussion. Right and wrong are not a matter of consensus. History records countless communities that have enthusiastically and unanimously practiced atrocious things: for examples, bigotry, ethnic hatred, infanticide, slavery, genocide, subjugation of women, neglect of the infirm and the elderly. What happens when you have communities that disagree about these practices. Surely, you have to decide on some criterion beyond mere consensus.

BRIAN: Good point. You see, my position can explain readily why it is that a moral life contributes to a meaningful life. Because morality, on my view, is a matter of realizing our potentialities. The capacities we have as human beings, if fulfilled, make our lives fully human. That provides a standard for what human beings should do. We should live so as to actualize, complete, and integrate our potentialities. That's what human life is about. That's how we attain meaning and happiness. At least that's how we attain it in this life. As we said earlier, it's ultimately attained through Beatific Vision.

MALCOLM: That's why it is no coincidence that those people who live the most meaningful and self-satisfying lives seem to be those people who live moral lives. They are simply trying to be as human as possible. They enjoy the satisfaction that comes from being an excellent human being. That's *true* authenticity.

BRIAN: It's an authenticity grounded in nature and nature's God. Also because God alone ultimately satisfies human nature, God is both the Alpha and the Omega of our destinies. Therein lies the meaning of life. God is the Alpha because he creates us; God is the Omega because we are designed so as to know him. That's why I said earlier that without God life ultimately is diminished and tragically unfulfilled.

FRANK: Let us hope then that we will be fulfilled, as Christianity promises.

MALCOLM: Well, I suppose "hope" is the operative word here, Frank.

BRIAN: Speaking of hope, I am hopeful that we can all meet again and continue these discussions.

MARY: Yes, let's make a point of it.

PATRICIA: You can be sure, I'll have brushed up on my reading list. I'll be ready for you next time, Malcolm.

MALCOLM: I can't wait. See you all at the next reunion!

Key Terms and Distinctions

Existentialism	Virtues
Motivation to be moral	Vices
Love	Happiness
Narcissism	Rationalization
Morality vs. moralism	Character
Meaning to life vs. meaning in life	Luck
Human nature	Psychological vs. normative
Potentialities	happiness
Needs	Supernatural happiness
"Nature versus nurture"	Natural happiness

Questions on Chapter 8

1. Do you agree with Brian, Renee, and Malcolm that people without belief in God would probably lack motivation for being moral?
2. Is the Existentialist's view correct? Is it morally reasonable that people make up their own morality and meaning in life?
3. Is Malcolm's case for human nature convincing?
4. Is happiness basically the same for all of us because of our common human nature? Or is happiness purely an individual matter?
5. What do Aquinas and Malcolm mean when they say that we desire God more than our own natural happiness? Is there a supernatural happiness?
6. Is Paul Tillich's distinction between a moralism and a morality reasonable?
7. In order to be happy, must one be moral?
8. Why be moral?

9. Can one be happy and not believe in God?
10. Can one be happy and not believe in life after death?
11. Is Kai Nielsen's statement that there may be no meaning *to* life but there may be meaning *in* life reasonable?

Bibliography

Aquinas, St. Thomas, *Summa Theologiae,* First Part of Second Part, Question 5, article 5, Blackfriars Translation (New York: Benziger Brothers, 1947).
Camus, Albert, *The Myth of Sisyphus and Other Essays,* trans. Justin O'Brien (New York: Alfred A. Knopf, 1955).
Frankl, Viktor, *Man's Search for Meaning* (Boston: Beacon Press, 1992).
James, William, *The Will to Believe and Other Essays* (New York: Dover, 1956).
Nielsen, Kai, *Ethics Without God* (New York: Prometheus Books, 1990, revised edition).
Nietzsche, Friedrich, *Beyond Good and Evil,* trans. Walter Kaufmann (New York: Vintage Books, 1965).
Russell, Bertrand, *Mysticism and Logic* (London: Home Library, 1918).
Sartre, Jean Paul, *Existentialism,* trans. Bernard Frechtman (New York: Philosophical Library, 1947).
Tillich, Paul, "Moralisms and Morality: Theonomous Ethics," in *Philosophy of Religion,* ed. David Stewart (Englewood Cliffs, NJ: Prentice Hall, 1992, third edition), pp. 374–378.
Tolstoy, Leo, "My Confession," in *Vice and Virtue in Everyday Life,* ed. Christina Hoff Sommers and Fred Sommers (New York: Harcourt, Brace, Jovanovich, 1993, third edition), pp.946–958.
Unamuno, Miguel de, *Tragic Sense of Life,* trans. J.E. Crawford Flitch (New York: Dover, 1954).

Index

About the Authors

Curtis L. Hancock, Ph.D., Loyola University of Chicago, 1985. Professor of Philosophy, Rockhurst College. He is coauthor of *How Should I Live?* (Paragon), a book on ethics, and coeditor of *Freedom, Virtue and the Common Good* (AMA/University of Notre Dame, 1995). He is president of the American Maritain Association. He has published articles and reviews on ancient and medieval philosophy, on Jacques Maritain, and on topics pertaining to political philosophy and ethics. He is coeditor of the series, "Contemporary Perspectives on Philosophy of Religion," for M.E. Sharpe.

Brendan Sweetman, Ph.D., University of Southern California, 1992. Associate Professor of Philosophy, Rockhurst College. A native of Ireland, he is coeditor, with R.D. Geivett, of *Contemporary Perspectives on Religious Epistemology* (Oxford University Press, 1992). He has published several articles and reviews on Continental philosophy and philosophy of religion, the most recent being "The Deconstruction of Western Metaphysics: Derrida and Maritain on Identity," in R. Ciapalo (ed.), *Postmodernism and Christian Philosophy* (Catholic University of America, 1996). He is coeditor of the series, "Contemporary Perspectives on Philosophy of Religion," for M.E. Sharpe. He was a member of the executive committee of the Gabriel Marcel Society from 1993 to 1996.